Political Persuasion
in
Presidential Campaigns

Political Persuasion
in
Presidential Campaigns

Edited by

L. PATRICK DEVLIN

Transaction Books
New Brunswick (U.S.A.) and Oxford (U.K.)

Library of Congress Catalog Number: 86–7055
ISBN: 0-88738-078-6
Printed in the United States of America

Library of Congress Cataloguing in Publication Data
Political persuasion in presidential campaigns.

Includes bibliographies.
1. Presidents—United States—Election.   2. Campaign management—United States.   3. Electioneering—United States.   I. Devlin, L. Patrick (Lawrence Patrick)
JK528.P58   1968   324.7′0973   86–7055
ISBN 0-88738-078-6

Contents

To the politicians, consultants and staff professionals, journalist, academics, students and audiences who participated in the University of Rhode Island Honors Colloquim Lecture Series, "Political Persuasion in Campaign '84."

Acknowledgments

All chapters were first presented as lectures during the Honors Collo-quim Lecture Series titled "Political Persuasion in Campaign '84" at The University of Rhode Island during the fall, 1983 and spring, 1984.

Subsequently, all lectures were edited and revised for publication by the editor and participants. Some of the chapters were published in periodicals prior to their publication in this book. The following were published pre-viously:

L. Patrick Devlin, "Campaign Commercials," *Society* 22(May/June, 1985), 45–50

Doris A. Graber, "Magical Words and Plain Campaigns," *Society* 22(May/June), 1985, 38–44.

Bruce E. Gronbeck, "Functional and Dramaturgical Themes of Presidential Campaigning," *Presidential Studies Quarterly* 14(Fall, 1984), 486–511

Dan Nimmo, "Elections as Ritual Drama," *Society* 22(May/June, 1985), 31–38.

Thomas E. Patterson, "Voters' Control of Information," *Society* 22(May/June, 1985), 51–56.

Larry Sabato, "PACs, Parties and Presidents," *Society* 22(May/June, 1985), 56–59.

Introduction

L. Patrick Devlin

This book focuses on how politicians run for president and how the media cover a presidential campaign. There has been no greater change in American politics in recent years than the manner in which candidates run for the presidency. We have entered an era of perpetual campaigning: candidates announcing two years before an election; increasing importance of early caucuses and primaries; continuous polling both by candidates and the media; use of political consultants and campaign specialists; federal financing coupled with political action committees; emphasis on expensive TV advertising and deemphasis on other forms of advertising; campaign coverage by hundreds of TV, newspaper, and magazine correspondents; stress on a candidate's personal style. In short, campaigning for the presidency is going through historic metamorphosis.

The book focuses on the interrelated components of a campaign—the candidate, the professional staff, the media, and the electorate. Prominent and experienced professionals—a pollster, media producer, mass mailer, and the press secretary—will share their insights on what it takes to run campaigns and win elections. Noted journalists both from print and television examine how a presidential campaign is reported. Academic experts in various aspects of campaign communication will analyze how these key components affect campaigns.

Campaign Management

In his book *The Rise of Political Consultants,*[1] Larry J. Sabato chronicles that there has been no more significant change in the conduct of campaigns than the consultants' rise to prominence, if not preeminence. These consultants—pollsters, mass mailers, campaign managers, media producers—are businessmen, not ideologues, and work in campaigns in a dozen states simultaneously. According to Sabato they eat, breathe, and live politics.

These political professionals have helped homogenize American electoral politics, added significantly to campaign costs, lengthened campaigns, and often have given an extra boost to candidates who are more skilled at electioneering than governing.

1

Consultants are sellers of advanced campaign technology and techniques. They can sell a one-shot service like advice, a poll, or a fundraising campaign, or they can become the grand strategists who design and supervise the game plan for an entire campaign and hire associates who do polls, create media, and handle fund raising. Matt Reese, one of the best managers with well over 200 campaigns to his credit, stated: "There are three things in this business that are important. Winning, or the reputation of winning. . . ; working for people whose names are known; and winning when you're not supposed to."[2] Reese and other consultants mix and match their clients to better ensure a healthy percentage of victories. They enjoy citing their win/loss records of successful campaigns. But it is a rare consultant who takes on too many long shots in any year. The largest number of clients are usually incumbents or candidates with a reasonable chance at an open seat. Most consultants work for candidates of one party, not both, and for candidates of one ideological stance. So liberal Democrats use different consultants than conservative or moderate Republicans.

Matt Reese has learned two things from his numerous campaigns. First, "you can't do everything everywhere," and second, "you've got to use your strengths to counter your weaknesses."[3] The purpose of a political campaign according to Reese is getting a voter to avow to vote for his client, and Reese emphasizes the technique of repetitive persuasive contact through the four channels of communication available: mass media—electronic and print, free and paid; mail; phone; and in-person repetitive persuasive contact. Repetition is necessary according to Reese because the voter is not listening and does not care very much. Reese also uses exaggeration, but he must also be careful that his appeals be truthful because voters will not tolerate candidates' lying to them: "The bottom line between a politician and a voter is 'Trust me.' if we break that we lose them."[4] Reese repeats a convincing message over and over until it makes an impression and "gets a spark."[5]

Campaign Finances

Herbert Alexander, an expert on campaign finance, estimated that $345 million was spent by candidates and their political parties in campaigning for the presidency of the United States in 1984. Alexander holds that money serves as a tracer element in the study of political power.

There are a number of reasons why campaigns have become more costly in recent times: a larger electorate, inflation, changing technology, national travel, the competition of more candidates, party reform leading to more primaries and caucuses, the decline of parties, and the availability of money through $1,000 donors, political action committees, and individual mass solicitation through the mails with donations averaging $50 per contribution.

In 1984 each candidate could raise and spend approximately $20 million on primary campaigning, and for the general election the Democratic and Republican standard-bearer received approximately $40 million from the Federal Election Commission funded by tax checkoff dollars designated by taxpayers. Alexander holds that while the $239-million cost of electing a president in 1980 was enormous, the nation's leading commercial advertiser, Proctor and Gamble, spent $649 million simply in promoting its products in 1980.

Less than 30 percent of all taxpayers contribute to presidential campaigns through the checkoff system as part of their tax return. Less than 10 percent of the electrorate contribute any additional campaign funds through individualized solicitation. So involvement in campaigns by giving money is not a pattern for the majority of the electorate.

There are ceiling limits on presidential campaigns spending in the primary and general election campaigns. Candidates could spend around $400,000 in the New Hampshire primary in 1984. This compared favorably with limits in other early primary campaigns such as $660,000 in Iowa, $1,400,000 in Massachusetts, or $2,500,000 in Florida. While most candidates spend the limit in New Hampshire, costing candidates such as McGovern in 1972, Udall in 1976, and Kennedy in 1980 around $11 per vote, few candidates raise or spend the limit allowed in more expensive contests in Florida, Illinois, New York, or California.

In 1980, while candidate Reagan received almost $30 million in federal matching funds, his campaign also was aided by $13 million spent by independent committees, the $4.5 million spent by the Republican Party, and the $9 million spent by state Republican Party accounts. Thus a total of approximately $65 million was spent on behalf of the Reagan campaign in 1980. In contrast, President Carter was able to generate only $14 million in funds in addition to the $30 million received directly from the federal government. So in 1980 an incumbent president was outspent by a challenger $44 to $65 million. In 1984 candidate Mondale could not reverse the historical trend of Republicans' being able to outraise and outspend Democratic presidential candidates.

In 1984, Robert Smith's firm, Targeted Communication, handled the mass mailing money solicitation for Walter Mondale. Almost $7 million was raised by the Mondale campaign through the techniques of computerized mailing lists using long substantive letters, personalized and colloquial language, and emotional appeals to immediate need to counter well-financed opponents.

Randy Huwa, director of the Campaign Finance Monitoring Project for the watchdog group Common Cause, chronicles how in the old days before the campaign spending reform laws of 1974, a candidate like Richard Nixon raised over $60 million, with $2 million coming in from one contributor and 100 other contributors giving $14 million more. Currently a candidate, because of $1,000 limits on giving, must raise large amounts of money from relatively small contributions (averaging around $50) from a large number of contributors.

Polling

Vincent Breglio, a pollster, was once a senior partner of Decision Making Information (DMI). In addition to working as the polling firm for candidate Ronald Reagan in 1980, DMI simultaneously polled for over twenty statewide gubernatorial or senatorial campaigns and over fifty congressional campaigns. Pollsters sign on the greatest number of clients—unlike media production consultants who normally take on no more than a dozen or fewer candidates per election.

The political pollsters and their sophisticated and costly surveys have become omnipresent in current campaigns. Pollsters are more than data collectors or statisticians. They are analytic interpreters and grand strategists. Peter Hart, pollster for Mondale in 1984 and Kennedy in 1980, compares himself and his colleagues to highly trained X-ray technicians: "We learn to get the best angle to get the best profile and the best shot."[6] Pollsters measure voter mood, interpret trends, and reveal the shape of politics in the past, present, and future.

Now almost all polling is done by telephone. Personal visits are simply too costly. A 20- to 30-minute telephone survey costs about $35 per household and approximately 400 to 600 households are used in a statewide survey. It costs currently $15,000 to $20,000 for a comprehensive quality survey of voters. National surveys typically use 1,500 to 1,600 voters and costs increase proportionally.

Polls have been criticized for creating public opinion and not simply reflecting it. This may be truer of public polls (Harris, Gallup) than of private polls (Breglio, Hart). Public polls often are published on a regular basis in newspapers or magazines. Often polls are taken and questions are asked for the sole purpose of filling these columns. So newsworthiness is often a criterion of public polls. By listing certain candidates and omitting others or by asking a particular question and not wording it another way, polls often are criticized as manufacturing opinion.

Private pollsters—those who work directly for candidates and with no publication or TV distribution outlets—make a reputation on the accuracy and objectivity of their polls. Private polling data helps determine resource allocation, media issue emphasis, media time buying, scheduling of candidate appearances, and groups to be reached for optimal effect. Private pollsters will selectively leak poll results when it is in the candidate's best interest as a morale boost for workers or as a money motivator for needed campaign funds.

Recently, pollsters have had to deal with the increasing volatility of voters. In the past, knowing a person's party would be the single best predictor of his/her vote. Now with the decrease of party affiliation, the increase in number of independent voters, and the presence of ticket splitters, it is harder for pollsters to predict election outcomes. This is especially true of primary elections, because only a small percentage of the electorate votes in primaries and trying to reach these voters and not simply potential voters is increasingly difficult.

In 1980, Vincent Breglio traced how the Reagan campaign polled over 35,000 registered voters in more than twenty-four major surveys and tracking polls. They collected data on a national basis and also from seventeen targeted states. Breglio was involved in collecting survey research during the presidential campaign on an average of once every two weeks, and during the last twenty days of the campaign he was involved in tracking polls on a daily basis.

One of the prime uses of survey research in presidential politics, according to Breglio, is to guide the media strategy of the campaign: what ad themes need to be stressed and what ads should air and where.

Advertising

In the 1980 campaign Ronald Reagan received almost $30 million in federal funds. He spent $18 million (60 percent) of it on advertising. He spent approximately $13 million of that $18 million on TV ads. Therefore, 70 percent of the money Reagan spent on advertising in the 1980 campaign was spent on TV advertising. In 1976 Jimmy Carter spent 74 percent of his advertising money on television. In 1984 Reagan and Mondale spent approximately $25 million each on advertising.

Well-financed presidential candidates spend vast sums and a major portion of their budgets on TV advertising. Few corporations, aside from Proctor and Gamble, McDonalds, or Miller Brewing, advertise for a full year at the volume of political advertising during the months of September, October, and the first week of November. During a presidential campaign commercials flood the airwaves.

Political commercials come in various time frames: They come in half-hour speeches or biographies, in mini programs, or in four-minute-and-

20-second segments sandwiched-in before Johnny Carson or before the evening news. But more commonly they come in 60-second or especially 30-second segments. Political commercials can also be categorized as to type or format: documentary, talking head, man-in-the-street, cinéma vérité, production idea spot. There are several purposes or functions of political ads.

The principal advantage of political advertising is that it can be controlled. Candidates may not be able to control what the opposition says or does, or what the media televises or prints. But candidates, if they are properly financed, can control the message and image conveyed through paid TV advertising. There are other advantages of political advertising.

One purpose of ads is to help make an unknown candidate better know. Examples of unknowns using television in presidential races to become known is less frequent than in gubernatorial or senatorial campaigns. However, McGovern in 1972, Carter in 1976, Bush in 1980, and Hart in 1984 used television extensively to become better known during the primary campaigns.

Ads are often aimed at late-deciding or disinterested voters. Ads are unobtrusive and unavoidable invaders of peoples' living rooms. They reach thousands, or in large media markets or across the nation, even millions. Many of these uninvolved voters see little else of the campaign except possibly on the evening news or what they see in these ads. Professor Lynda Kaid in one of her many studies on political advertising concluded that "political advertising is more effective when the level of voter involvement is low."[7] These late-deciding or uninvolved voters are that crucial 10 to 20 percent of the electorate and normally they are reached only through television in the last stages of the campaign.

In 1972 scholars Patterson and McClure researched the effectiveness of ads and found that only 18 percent of voters were late deciders. In 1972 many people had made up their minds. The ads of the 1972 campaign were found to have influenced "roughly three percent of the total electorate."[8] In 1972 there was a 23-percent spread between Nixon and McGovern in the final tally. Therefore, a 3-percent impact with a 23-percent spread was not much of an impact. Yet in the 1976 campaign there was only a 2-percent disparity between Ford and Carter in the final tally. If the 1976 ads affected 3 percent of the electorate, and there was a 2-percent spread, the effectiveness or ineffectiveness of ads might become crucial.

Ads are also used to reinforce supporters and partisans. When partisans saw pictures of Ronald Reagan by the Statute of Liberty or Jimmy Carter standing in front of a gigantic American flag at town meetings, these reinforced partisan feelings toward them. For example, partisans watch half-hour programs but few others do. Only one in twenty people watch half-hour programs and these are primarily partisans. But their partisan feelings are reinforced and they may end up giving more money to the campaign through these commercials.

Ads can be used to attack the opposition. As Reagan's 1980 pollster, Vincent Breglio, maintained: "It has become vital in campaigns today that you not only present all of the reasons why people ought to vote for you but you also have an obligation to present the reasons why they should not vote for the opponent. Hence, the negative campaign, or the attack strategy becomes an essential part of any campaign operation." Therefore, a mix of positive and negative ads is increasingly used to convince voters they should vote for a candidate and not for the opposition.

Ads develop and explain issues. Research by McClure and Patterson[9] has demonstrated that there is more substance and more issue information in presidential ads than in TV news. A 60-second ad has, on average, five times as much issue information about the candidate than a 60-second snippet on the evening news. Voters can find out better where a candidate stands by watching his ads than by watching the evening news. And ads have a cumulative effect. In presidential campaigns a multiplicity of ads are used and often repeated. Using 30-second time frames voters can see 10 or 12 ads during the course of a campaign, with 5 or 6 of them repeated. So the idea comes across not simply in thirty seconds, but multiplied by the number of times voters see the 30-second ad and are attentive to it.

Ads can soften or redefine an image. If a candidate has a reputation for not caring about unemployment or is weak on defense issues, ads can be created to emphasize the candidate's commitment to these areas. In 1968 candidate Nixon was redefined through TV. In 1976 Jimmy Carter was accused of not taking strong stands on issues, so his advertising man created strong issue-oriented spots to redefine this hazy image through a series of ads in which Carter took strong stands.

Ads are used to target particular demographic groups. This is how ads go hand in hand with polling. Polling tells you where your potential voters are and ad demographics tells you how to reach them. For example, women, Blacks, males, single mothers, or union members might be targeted voters. Careful time buying before, during, or after key programs such as a hockey game to reach more male voters or the Donahue show to reach more female voters during the daytime is used. Polling and time buying helps to maximize the potential to reach a particular category of voter.

Ads cost money, but they can also be used to raise it. Money appeals at the end of half-hour ads or five-minute ads are often used. McGovern in

1972 and Anderson in 1980 paid for their TV commercials mainly through these appeals coming at the end of their ads. In 1984 Mondale used a special five-minute commercial and beamed it into house parties to raise money. People did send in money so that future ads went on the air.

Ads are adaptable. They can be made, revised, discarded as the necessities of the campaign change. Multiple generations of spot commercials are extremely common during the presidential campaign, and often several hours of ads using six or seven distinct generations are made.

Finally, ads are used because the competition uses them. Few candidates, aside from Jesse Jackson in 1984, can afford the luxury of foregoing the opportunity to have commercials. There is an adage in campaigns which states that half of all advertising money is wasted. The only problem is nobody in a campaign knows which half, so all advertising continues.

Tony Schwartz, maker of ads for hundreds of campaigns and creator of the famous 1964 "Daisy Girl" Johnson ad, holds that politics is a fight where presidential candidates spend millions of dollars to defeat the other candidate. Schwartz stresses people can vote four ways—for or against either candidate. Thus Schwartz, who has created many negative ads, maintains that a candidate like McGovern would be better served by ads attacking Nixon rather than showing McGovern's good points, because he would have a better chance of getting more votes through using Nixon's weaknesses than from his own positive aspects. Schwartz uses ads like Rorschach patterns. Ads function best when they elicit feelings that people already have within them.

Richard O'Reilly, the operating director of the 1980 Reagan advertising campaign, thinks that ads should inform and persuade. How much of it is information and how much persuasion varies depending on the political situation. How much of the advertising campaign is rational and how much is emotional depends on what people know or don't know and feel or don't feel about a candidate.

Media Coverage

Most Americans say they get their news from television. A 1981 Roper study found that 39 percent specified they got their news only from television, 20 percent said from both television and newspapers, and 22 percent said newspapers only. From this study most people think they get most of their news from television. But according to Lawrence Lichty, television is far from the dominant source of news.[10] According to Lichty there are two types of Americans who view television. One sees a lot of TV news because he happens to watch a lot of television, but TV news is only a small part of the daily fare. For this type of viewer TV news is just another show. They are fickle watchers, missing days of TV news, often interrupting news with meals and family, and watching passively with little remembered. The second type of news viewer is younger, better educated, and is also a heavy reader of news. This viewer watches a lot of news and information shows like "60 Minutes," but not much else on television.

Lichty cites data from the Simmons Market Research Bureau that holds that (1) more than two-thirds of U.S. adults (68 percent) read at least part of some newspaper every day—12 percent of adults read two or more newspapers a day; (2) fewer than one-third of U.S. adults watch local or national TV news on a given day; (3) about 31 percent of adults read *Time, Newsweek,* or *U.S. News and World Report;* (4) only 1 percent of the 78.3 million American TV households watch the highly rated CBS news with Dan Rather as often as four or five nights a week. The average for households that watch his program at all is five broadcasts per month. Newspapers and magazines are higher-effort media as compared to television and radio.

Lichty maintains that Americans get news from many sources, but judging from exposure data, most of what they get every day still comes from newspapers. This is because newspapers are easy and efficient news source: Items can be scanned, selected, put aside, retrieved, poured over, even reread at the reader's convenience. Also, newspapers take less time than the 60 to 90 minutes it takes to sit through the 22 minutes of news per TV half hour with its format of 17 to 18 brief stories.

Patterson[11] supports Lichty's myth-shattering conclusion that newspapers reach more people than TV news. Patterson in his research during the 1976 presidential campaign found that newspapers, not television, had a larger regular news audience. Patterson polled in Erie, Pennsylvania, and Los Angeles. In Erie 48 percent of those polled said they regularly read a daily paper's news section, while 34 percent said they regularly watched the evening newscasts of ABC, CBS, and NBC. In Los Angeles 33 percent claimed to be regular readers and 24 percent were regular viewers. Moreover, the frequency of use is higher among newspaper regulars. Regular newspaper readers said they read their paper's news pages 6 days a week, while regular viewers said they watched the evening news 3 or 4 times a week.

There is an overlap of viewers and readers, but Patterson found it instructive to look at where people get most of their news. He found the newspaper was the preferred source among people who used at least one news source regularly, and the less closely people followed the news, the greater the chance that television provided most of their news.

Patterson also examined how much attention readers or viewers give to the news. Evidence suggests that people often are not closely attentive to the news they see or read, but that newspaper coverage leaves a more lasting impression than TV news. Patterson found that over 55 percent of newspaper readers could accurately recall a news story within twenty-four hours, while only 45 percent of viewers could do so.

Politics is an activity dominated by words, and Patterson and McClure in 1972 found that people were more attentive to the pictures than to the words of TV news.[12] They concluded that what is read is more apt to be retained than what is heard or seen.

Thomas R. Marshall[13] argues that TV networks and major nationally oriented newspapers and news magazines play a critical role in presidential politics. His analysis of news coverage of the 1980 elections led him to four major conclusions. First, the networks and newspapers provide the public with a remarkably similar picture of the race. Second, the media has a major impact on the nominations race by choosing which primaries or caucuses to cover, focusing on the competitive horse-race aspects of the race and evaluating winners and losers. Third, the media's impact is greatest when the field of contenders is crowded and when many of the would-be nominees have slight resources and low name recognition. Fourth, the media's impact has increased as an unintended by-product of recent party reforms: party rules changes, new fund-raising and spending regulations, and the increasing numbers of contested primaries and caucuses.

Patterson[14] argues that today's presidential campaign is essentially a mass media campaign, and that for the vast majority of the electorate the campaign has little reality apart from what the media covers.

Paul Weaver[15] has characterized campaign coverage as a melodrama. The media reports it as a narrative combat between candidates; an intensified struggle filled with peril: the game is covered, not the substance. Television stresses action pictures at the expense of informative or analytic reporting. Television news is not primarily informational but narrative (drama) and judgmental (contest combat). According to Weaver, it filters a distorted picture of the campaign.

David Nyhan, a political report for the *Boston Globe*, emphasizes that only fifty to 100 journalists make their living by writing about politics year round. A relative handful of the 1,700 daily newspapers covers politics with a commitment of money and personnel. The *New York Times, Washington Post, Wall Street Journal, Los Angeles Times,* and regional papers like the *Boston Globe* are in the forefront of papers covering politics. The *Globe* put seven reporters on the road for the 1984 race.

Nyhan holds that reporters police the action of the campaign: where the money is coming from and what it is spent on, telling what's fair and foul, who is messing up and who is not, and what the issues are. Nyhan admits that the print press is often treated like a poor relative of the TV press, yet print reporters write the stories first that television ultimately picks up.

John Mashek from *U.S. News and World Report,* stresses that news magazines are scene setters and analyzers of the political scene. They do primarily "before" and "after" pieces. He thinks they can probe the issues or focus on the candidates more deeply than television or even newspapers because they can do a four- to six-page spread on these aspects of the campaign.

David Broder, thought by many to be the most respected and influential political columnist currently, takes a self-deprecating view of himself and his influence and on the impact of political columns in general. While David Nyhan thought that Broder's article in the *Washington Post* on Ed Muskie's crying in New Hampshire "was probably the single most influential thing that knocked Muskie out of the race," Broder himself holds that columnists are "about as influential as a snowflake falling on the broad bosom of the Potomac River." While others hold that a complimentary or damning column by Broder can be pivotal, Broder believes that his pieces are often like "spitting into the wind on a windy day."

Columnists, Broder holds, help build momentum for a candidate or keep an issue going that already has captured the attention of the electorate, but they cannot get people interested in a candidate who does not have a reasonable chance of victory or interest people in a topic that is not a matter of real concern to them. Broder views his news reporting as primary and his twice-weekly columns as secondary.

TV Coverage

Local TV news is an important communication vehicle for candidates. Often campaign days are planned around stops in Iowa's eight television markets or appearances in Boston are planned so they can be beamed into both New Hampshire and Massachusetts homes during their primary campaigns.

Local news ratings are important to the economic vitality of the station. The local news is usually more highly rated than the evening network news which follows it. Good local ratings deliver a larger audience for network news. As Edwin Diamond concludes in his analysis of local news,[16] the latter is watched because viewers care about their weather, sports, roads, strikes, or candidates coming to their town.

Laureen White, who was the news assignment editor for the CBS affiliate WLNE in Providence, knows that when a presidential candidate holds an airport news conference the local stations will come running. And if a candidate's visit is on a weekend when competing news is light, they can expect a lot of TV time on all three network affiliates: "That's expensive and useful TV time they could not otherwise buy. It's free publicity."

Kirby Perkins, a political correspondent for WCVB in Boston, maintains that in major markets like Boston there is much competition among stations in their political coverage and "there is as much interest in their competitive coverage as in the campaign itself." Each of the Boston stations has an anchor desk in New Hampshire for its primary and devotes ten to twelve minutes a night to its political coverage. Perkins holds that early in a campaign the networks are not as important to a candidacy as the local stations because more people watch local news than network news.

In the general election campaign local coverage is still important and candidates often plan stops in three to four different states in different media markets each day. However, network coverage also becomes important during a general election because of the nationwide campaign.

Richard Gregg[17] has analyzed network TV news as it covers a campaign and reached some interesting conclusions. First he found that television focuses attention on the anchor person or correspondent. Often the newscaster gets more time on camera—or certainly in voiceover time—than the candidate. It is the reporter who is zoomed in on with the candidate often in the background. Second, TV campaign coverage is hurried. The pace and style of the newscast take priority. All networks emphasize 13 to 18 stories in their 22 minutes of news chopped into 60- and 90-second segments. Third, campaign coverage is like sports. There is attention to strategies and tactics more than issues. The present score or momentum is stressed with poll results receiving more attention that personal or political qualities of governing. TV news presents one or two key plays of the day for instant replay. A speech that took forty-five minutes to deliver is capsulized in the replay of a 13-second segment. Key moments like candidate Reagan saying, "I paid for this microphone" in 1980 in Nashua, New Hampshire, or Mondale asking in 1984, "Where's the beef?" are the stuff of TV news because they highlight the competition and drama of the campaign in a short, clear, and simple way. Fourth, TV coverage emphasizes the visual with pictures of crowds, motorcades, and candidates speaking, which provide the visual backdrop for the story. Action pictures are stressed at the expense of informative or analytic reporting.

TV news has been characterized as analogous to the front page of a newspaper—headlines and pictures. The average recall of people watching is 1 story of the 19 broadcast, according to Edwin Diamond,[18] and 51 percent of the viewers could not recall anything after watching 30 minutes of the evening news. Diamond breaks down viewer time this way: one-third watch all of the newscast, one-third watch all but are distracted, and one-third watch only part of the newscast. So 50 million may be watching all or part of CBS, NBC, and ABC network news on a given night but recall is neglible for the average viewer. Diamond sees little difference in the three network news shows except that the anchor person tells the viewer which channel they are watching.

Roger Mudd, who has had experience both as an anchorman for CBS and NBC news in addition to many years of experience as a political reporter for both networks, stresses that in a campaign year one out of every six minutes of TV network news is political. The 3 network news departments spent about $125 million in 1984 to cover the campaigners. Mudd, as Perkins did in describing local news, holds that the competition between the networks and the anchor people becomes almost more important than the political story itself. Something is wrong if the network's coverage becomes the story, according to Mudd. Cameras should not try to force too much excitement out of politics. Exit polls should not be used to project results before portions of the country have had a chance to finish voting. Networks should not cover front-runners only or focus on primaries as two-man races. Networks should not insist on presenting fifteen stories superficially rather than six stories well in their half-hour of news. All of these are steps Mudd thinks networks need to, but are unlikely to, take.

Press Conferences

A press conference serves three groups: politicians, the press, and the public. A politician gains exposure to the press and public through press conferences. According to McMillan and Ragan[19] politicians control press conferences by (1) determining when, where, and how frequently press conferences are held; (2) preparing extensively for anticipated questions; (3) controlling questions asked by limiting the press conference to specific topics, calling on reporters whose questions can be answered easily and/or managed, overlooking hostile reporters and controlling the sequence of questions; (4) issuing a policy statement prior to answering questions, thus setting the tone for "appropriate" questions; and (5) terminating the press conference at their discretion.

For the press, according to Orr,[20] the conference is a question and answer session in which reporters quiz the politician. The press conference is a news-gathering or news-making event. A presidential press conference is accompanied by a sense of deference and decorum—the chief of state is treated with respect. However, the press confirms by their questions that the press conference is a press event wherein they have the right to confront the president with criticism. For reporters the press conference is a test of their competitiveness to ask the pertinent, tough, or needed question to help make news.

For the public the press conference is a chance to see the politician and press in action. People watch, listen to, or read about press conferences to obtain information and to make or sustain judgments. This information sharing symbolizes that democracy is alive and well—the politician is open and the press is probing, questioning, challenging.

Jerry terHorst, who was a reporter and columnist for many years and was President Ford's press secretary, posits that press conferences are held by candidates often in hope that their story gets out and gets wide distribution. When not a single reporter from the *New York Times* wrote a story about George Bush calling Reagan's economics "voodoo economics," a press conference was held. Bush used the term again and the wire services, networks, and national press picked up on the term a single reporter had not picked up. In this way a press conference plays an important role in political campaigns but only if the news media are there and agree that what transpires is important for the public to know. The decision to hold a news conference may be up to the candidate, according to terHorst, but the judgment of whether holding it was useful or newsworthy is totally up to the media.

Use of Campaigns

For politicians and reporters campaigns are work and provide their livelihood. So campaigning has an economic and ego-satisfying function for people involved in campaigns full-time. But most of us become involved in campaigns only peripherally. Campaigns may get us to think about what issues or topics are important, and as we think about things campaigns can be a self-reinforcing or self-adjusting activity. Campaigns also give us a sense of involvement with the electoral process. We read about campaigns, we watch campaign events like conventions and debates on television, we talk with family and friends about candidates, and we may go to hear a candidate speak or we may be contacted on the phone by a campaign worker.

Ultimately, campaigns are supposed to function to get us to vote, but this behavioral effect is achieved with only slightly over half of us. There is a democratic function to campaigns. Elections confer legitimacy to our governmental process and after the struggle for power during an election the consensual power conferred on the chosen leader normally creates a consensus to govern.

One scholar, Bruce Gronbeck, focuses on the functions of campaigns. He stresses that people subject themselves to campaigns because certain needs can be satisfied and certain gratifications can be gained from their exposure to campaign communication. He identifies fifteen functions or uses to which campaign communications could be put by different people at different times during a campaign. He groups these fifteen into two categories—instrumental and consummatory functions. Instrumental functions serve as a means to some other secondary end. For example, a candidate shaking hands in the hope that a voter will vote for him. Consummatory functions are ends in themselves, that is, psychological states which are in and of themselves gratifying. For example, a viewer may watch a debate as a competition between two rivals, but the viewer watches and roots for his favorite to win. Thus he watches to root and see how his candidate and opposing candidate do in the debate.

Another scholar, Dan Nimmo, holds that because campaigns are a continuous exercise of mobilizing the electorate by the transmission of verbal and non-verbal symbols, campaigns can best be analyzed as ritualistic dramas. For Nimmo, politicians are actors and like a play with heroes, villains, or fools, the candidates become characters in an ongoing drama. Our elections become a recurring series of acts—announcement speeches, primary campaigns, conventions, debates, speeches, television coverage— which occur in a patterned way that can best be analyzed like a drama with characters, plot, scene, and audience.

Another scholar, Thomas Patterson, holds that elections for most of us are interesting or surprising but not important. If 10 percent of the electorate cannot make a decision until the last day of a presidential election, that is a revealing commentary on our current uncommitted and uninvolved electorate, according to Patterson. And because there is less partisanship, longer campaigns, less involvement through media, and the electorate does not have or want direct experience with politics, Patterson holds that elections are controlled by an increasingly indifferent electorate.

Communication and Language

There are two elements to speaking: what politicians are saying and how they are saying it. Reagan's eloquence comes from his delivery and not from his substance. Reagan is gifted, however, on some substantive techniques. He can make things concrete and he personifies well. Walter Mondale's strength is his sense of conviction and compassion, but his rhetoric is bland because he, unlike Jesse Jackson, has no deep-seated rhetorical tradition. Jackson, with his use of metaphor, alliteration, rhyming, and powerful delivery in cadence, is the product of the Black preachers who specialized in exciting their church audiences. Communicative style is a combination of what politicians are saying and how they are saying it.

One scholar, Doris Graber, emphasizes how language functions in politics as condensation symbols to economically create meanings—e.g. "rainbow coalition" and "where's the beef." Graber focuses on five uses of language: (1) How politicians use it to define their reality; (2) how it is used to reconstruct the past and to promise for the future; (3) how linkages are used in language between politicians and groups; (4) how language functions as agenda setting; and (5) how language becomes a surrogate for action. There are dangers in the language barrage during a campaign. Graber notes how verbal demolition takes place and leads to a communicative cynicism by the electorate.

Notes

1. Larry J. Sabato, *The Rise of Political Consultants* (New York: Basic Books, 1981).
2. Sabato, p. 18.
3. Matt Reese, speech at the University of Rhode Island, Kingston, September 28, 1983 (audio taped transcript).
4. Ibid.
5. Ibid.
6. Sabato, p. 73.
7. Lynda Lee Kaid, "Political Advertising," in *The Handbook of Political Communication,* ed. Dan D. Nimmo and Keith R. Sanders (Beverly Hills: Sage, 1981), p. 265.
8. Thomas E. Patterson and Robert D. McClure, *The Unseeing Eye* (New York: Putnam's 1976), p. 135.
9. Patterson and McClure, *The Unseeing Eye.*
10. Lawrence W. Lichty, "Video versus Print," *Wilson Quarterly,* Special Issue (1982): 49–57.
11. Thomas E. Patterson, *The Mass Media Election* (New York: Praeger, 1980).
12. Patterson and McClure, p. 87.
13. Thomas R. Marshall, "The News Verdict and Public Opinion during the Primaries, in *Television Coverage of the 1980 Presidential Campaign,* ed. William C. Adams (Norwood, N.J.: Ablex, 1983), pp. 49–67.
14. Patterson, *The Mass Media Election.*
15. Paul H. Weaver, "Captives of Melodrama," *New York Times Magazine* (August 27, 1976): 6+.
16. Edwin Diamond, "News Forms: The Local News," in *The Tin Kazoo* (Cambridge: MIT Press, 1975), pp. 87–110.
17. Richard B. Gregg, "The Rhetoric of Political Newscasting," *Central States Speech Journal* 28 (Winter 1977); 221–37.
18. Edwin Diamond.
19. Jill McMillan and Sandra Ragan, "The Presidential Press Conference: A Study in Escalating Institutionalization," *Presidential Studies Quarterly* 8 (Spring 1983): 231–41.
20. C. Jack Orr, "Reporters Confront the President," *Quarterly Journal of Speech* 66 (February 1980): 17–32.

1

New Technologies in Campaigns

Robert Smith

I will examine what I do as a consultant and a provider of services in political campaigns. But I would like to do it in a context of the future. One of the things that outrages me the most in my business is how little thinking is done about the future. Hopefully, this will be a thoughtful reflection on what we do, why we do it, how it affects political campaigns, and what is changing. I want to put my work in the context of a few trends occurring in society which will affect political campaigns. These trends will also affect virtually anything any of us do in the future.

There are two major trends. First, the public is becoming far more knowledgeable and aware of current events. They want to know more about why we were in Lebanon or about what is happening in Central America. We are in an intense information age. If you are not aware of that, I do not think you can be a successful computer salesperson or candidate for public office. This intense information age will dominate much of the reality in the years ahead. People are getting to be far more knowledgeable about what is going on and they will want to know more.

The second major trend which affects us is the merging of two great technologies—data processing and telecommunications technology. This merger will dramatically affect the future. This trend represents the second major revolution in communication in the twentieth century. The first revolution was television in the 1950s, revolutionizing the notion of communication. A visual image changed what you could do with advertising and with a political message. The notion of a picture being worth a thousand words is true. And the fact that you could put a picture on a TV screen and bring it into every home brought a new dynamic. Now we are entering the second major technological revolution. It is a revolution where communication will be highly personal to an alert audience and it will be interactive. This development will create a communications medium that will permit people to react to what they see.

This is especially important considering that people are becoming far more independent-minded. They want to make personal judgments. People today are far less likely to accept conventional leaders and to accept their employer's opinion about politics. This independence and the opportunity to provide individual treatment is changing everything we do.

If you follow elections, you will recall some recent election where a particular candidate was believed to be way ahead only to fool the pollsters on election day. Take the presidential election of 1980 as an example. The November 1st issue of *Newsweek* magazine had a cover with a picture of Ronald Reagan, Jimmy Carter, and John Anderson all jumping over a hurdle stating in big letters, "Too Close to Call." One week later, Ronald Reagan won one of the greatest landslides in the history of American presidential campaigns.

In 1982, Adlai Stevenson ran for the Senate in Illinois. Seven days before election day, the pollsters said he was going to lose by thirty points. Thirty points in electoral politics, particularly in such a highly visible race, is enormous. Yet he lost by only half a percentage point. I like to kid my pollster friends and say the reason for that is that pollsters are getting worse. That is not true. The reality is that the electorate is becoming volatile. Long-standing Democrats, people who have been Democrats for forty years now say, "I don't care what my local union president says, I am going to vote the way I want. For the first time in my life, I am going to vote Republican."

The electorate is becoming far more volatile because people know more about what is going on. They hear more about a candidate and they want to make their own judgment. That volatility is significantly affecting elections. We are seeing this emerging independence in voter attitudes and in other places, too. When labor unions say they can deliver the votes or they can get their people to write Congress on a certain piece of legislation, they cannot deliver.

One of the things that corporations who are my clients are dealing with is they are finding that employees do not want to do what the president or chairman of the company has been guiding them to do for years and they had accepted without question. They are finding that stockholders who traditionally voted with management now are saying, "Wait a minute. I don't like the fact that you are selling computers to South Africa." People are beginning to break away and make their own judgments. This dissolution of group behavior and bloc voting is pervasive.

Legislation is moving through Congress that used to be decided by four or five people. Three weeks ago, I testified in front of a Senate committee along with four of the most powerful lobbyists in Washington. One of them, who has lobbied for thirty years said, "It is getting a lot harder to lobby in Congress. Back in the 1950s, there were four people to lobby. Three of them were in Congress and one was in the White House. These four made all the decisions on 99 percent of the issues. If you had them on your side, you were in business. Well, today it is crazy. Everybody is voting in different directions. Tens of thousands of people are writing Congress. It is a different world."

We can see this trend in advertising, too. For example, Mobil Oil decided they wanted to improve their image so they spent about $20 million in newspaper ads in the editorial sections of newspapers on public policy questions. Mobil thought they would improve their image because what they were saying was, "We are about America. We are investing."

After months of those expenditures, the American Petroleum Institute conducted a few polls to determine which oil companies had the best image and why. They found that Shell had the best image. The reason it did was the Shell Answer Man. It represented somebody who was there at the local gas station saying, "Well, hello, Mrs. Johnson. Good to see you. I will treat you personally. Come on in. What's your problem?"

General Motors has its Mr. Goodwrench. He is a clean-cut guy who is waiting at the service station for you to drive in and personally deal with your problem. Madison Avenue is figuring out that people are saying, "I don't want to be treated like a number. I don't want to be treated like a labor union member. I want to be treated as an individual who has these concerns." How that emerging attitude affects every industry is dramatic. If you lose sight of that fact, you will be at a distinct disadvantage. The personal touch is the reason Shell is out ahead of its image.

If the first trend is the volatility of attitudes and new individuality, the second trend, technology, is accelerating the former. Data processing technology is now more manageable, less expensive, and its application is more sophisticated. Data processing takes a lot of information and moves it around so you can come out with different looks, segmentations, or views of information. As people's attitudes become more volatile, new computer technology can handle the permeations to meet their needs. A computer can address all those people individually and you can capitalize on those attitudinal variations and individual trends. Data processing technology is also becoming more accessible, more widely used, less expensive, and easier to use and understand.

The next explosion is telecommunications. If anyone graduating from college today does not understand the significance of merging data processing technology and telecommunications development, they are going to be handicapped. In telecommunications, you can communicate in different ways quickly. Examples of telecommunications developments are satellite TV communications, remote telephone communications, and the linking of your telephone with your computer.

In elections, these data-processing improvements significantly assist in delivering the "right message" to the "right people" more often. We can take all those permeations, all those variables factored in the individuality of voters to track it, watch it, and analyze it. Telecommunications technology merged with data processing allows you to communicate with people very effectively in a very personal way.

The new telecommunications technology can be interactive, meaning you can respond. We know people want to have a role in what is going on. They want to respond. When they see something on television, they want to be able to call in and make themselves heard. You have probably seen local or national network TV shows, particularly ones on controversial issues, that increasingly encourage calling. Computers allow the analysis of even the busy signals. Five hundred thousand people can call in on *Nightline,* and they all call in an hour. Although all the calls cannot come through, new technology permits you to count the number of people who call.

Another interesting thing about *Nightline* is, who would ever have thought that millions of Americans would stay up until 12:30 A.M. watching an in-depth program on politics or on issues? They are doing it. On some issues, half a million people are calling to register their opinion. Five years ago, if you had gone to a network president and said, "Look, I want to put on a late night show to discuss things like Lebanese immigration into Southern California and I want to do telephone polls. I want to have computer banks set up because I think hundreds of thousands of people will call in on a given subject," the network president would have thrown you out of the room. But we see it happening today, and it is happening because people want to be involved. They want to be interactive.

Let me given you some examples of how increased individually along with computer and communications innovations are affecting elections and how we have tried to capitalize on it in direct mail. Evidence of these trends can be seen in the 1980 elections, both in the major congressional races and in the presidential race. I will cite my clients as examples of candidates who did not heed these changes, which is part of the reason they lost. They were Birch Bayh, John Culver, and George McGovern. Each was a strongly supported national liberal Democrat who tried to pull together the old coalition in their campaigns. They said, "Well, if I get my labor union members together, we're going to talk about economics. If I get the minorities in my state together, we will talk about civil rights. And, if I can get the Catholic and the Italian vote, people who have been Democrats for two or three generations, I will win the election because there are three times as many Democrats in this country as there are Republicans."

Meanwhile, the Republicans were unleashing more advanced technology than the Democrats. The GOP strategist said, "We only have 20 percent of the voters who consider themselves Republicans, and we need 51 percent if we are going to win, so we have to do something else. We will have to get some of the Democrats." Using the new technologies at hand, they decided to deliver a message to these people—who were now beginning to break away from the original party coalitions and think individually. What the Republicans did was mail that Italian Catholic union household that had voted for Democrats for these generations a letter that said, "Did you know that Birch Bayh voted for abortion five times in the last Congress? Can you believe it?" They focused on one issue and capitalized on a vulnerability they discovered in survey research that had specifically broken down voter demographics.

Similarly, they wrote gun owners and said, "Did you know Birch Bayh voted for gun control, Mr. Gun Owner?" Then they took ten other individual issues they knew other people cared about and reminded these people of how Birch Bayh had voted on their concerns.

The GOP did it largely through the mail and telephone. They knew they could segment the smaller and more homogeneous audiences. With mail, they could find the people who opposed abortion rights or people opposed to the Equal Rights Amendment. A week before these voters were going into the booths, the Republican challengers reminded them of their opponent's stand on that particular issue. They isolated the voters with specific concerns and addressed them in a personal fashion. If you reach a prolife voter and say directly to him, "Birch Bayh is probably responsible for the loss of more lives than. . . ," and you go on to explain it in graphic terms, when they walk into the voting booth, they will remember that very strong personal message and will vote against Birch Bayh.

The Republicans managed to defeat a lot of Democrats in 1980, even though the registration and polls showed the support to be very much the other way. Reagan also did this in 1980. Jimmy Carter was defeated because many solid Democrats crossed over to vote for Ronald Reagan. They voted for him because a few specific issues angered them. There were people who voted for Ronald Reagan whose opinions on tax, economics, and social welfare issues went straight against their own interests. Yet they voted for Ronald Reagan, and when you look at some of the groups that voted for him, they were groups where Reagan should have been viewed clearly as an adversary. Reagan put aside those issues and went after the one or two issues he knew could pull the voter to his side.

Future political campaigns will have to understand this desire for individual attention and they are going to have to track voters' volatility in attitudes and behavior. Tracking polls show a day-by-day assessment of how that volatility shifts. What is the electorate doing now? How are they moving daily? There is going to have to be more of that kind of tracking.

The second thing that political campaigns will have to do is target their audience far better. If you wanted to run for Congress you would have roughly 500,000 people in your district. Of these, 200,000 would vote and

40,000 would be persuadable voters. With the rest there is very little you could do. Only with 40,000 voters could you hope to change their decision. So you need to find out everything you can about those 40,000 people. Knowing their demographic description, income, age, race, or religion can be a great advantage. You also want to know what they are thinking about and what issues concern them the most—in other words, their psychographic description. Which one or two issues can ultimately make them change their mind and make them think independently?

Next, you have to speak to them very personally. They must hear you speaking to them directly. It is that direct person-to-person communication that will make the difference. You are treating them specially. You are going to be the Shell Answer Person of that campaign.

The last thing you want to do is permit them to interact. You want to allow them to say something, do something, get involved, write back and say, "I don't like your position on this," "What about that?" "When are you going to be in my neighborhood?" "Have you ever thought about this?" You want to permit them to interact.

Now I will give some examples from my business where we have capitalized on those changes. First, I would like to explode some myths. One of them is that people do not read direct mail letters, do not read substantive material, do not want a lot of information, that poor people do not read and will throw away six-page letters. In 1980, we worked for Jay Rockefeller who was running for governor of West Virginia. Coal miners in West Virginia represent a very substantial part of the electorate. Obviously, for Democrats, it is important to reach coal miners. Jay Rockefeller was viewed as an outsider not knowing much about West Virginia. So the myth went that he was not a great supporter of coal miners. The notion was that he just could not identify with them.

We wrote to every coal miner in the State of West Virginia, many of whom did not even have street addresses. They had rural routes way out in the hollows. We sent them a long letter saying, "Jay Rockefeller is starting an organization called *Coal Today. Coal Today* is an organization that is going to work in Washington with as much political clout as possible to pass the coal conversion bill so that it will bring more jobs to West Virginia. We want you to join *Coal Today* and be part of this effort."

In writing to 80,000 coal miners in West Virginia, we got a 35 percent response. That meant one out of every three coal miners wrote back and responded, "Count me in. What can I do?" Most political pros would tell you that people who are down low on the economic ladder and who are not high on the educational scale are not interested in mail. Well, we showed that a third of these people would not only read their mail but also respond favorably.

In addition, we developed an ongoing relationship with the coal miners. It was an interactive personal relationship where the people would write in, "How is the conversion bill going? What can I do?" We would send them back things like bumper stickers or a little sticker for their helmets which glowed in the dark while in the caves. We gave them a little map they could put up on their wall to show where the new jobs would be. We got them involved in a personal way.

Another example is from the Anderson presidential campaign in 1980. Anderson was a speck on the wall of political history in January of 1980. He had less than a 1-percent recognition in all the polls. Then suddenly in the Iowa Republican presidential debate everybody looked at the other Republicans and thought they were pretty dull. Anderson looked good in comparison. Anderson was a "hot character," as they say in the media world. He was seen as angry and full of energy. Suddenly Anderson's appeal took off and he became very popular.

One of the things we said of the Anderson campaign was "If the people really want to be involved and they really want to know, let's try this on them and that on them." The theme in the campaign was "you don't count." Everyone said that Anderson did not have a chance. What everybody was saying—the press, Reagan, and Carter—was that you do not count, no matter what you do, no matter how you vote, and no matter what you care about. You just do not count. We based that on the notion that people wanted to be more involved, they wanted to be treated more personally, and that message would ignite our supporters. It did.

About a month before election day, the Anderson campaign was nearly broke. We had raised about as much money as we thought we could from donors. Yet we needed to raise far more than we normally could with one letter to the 250,000 donors we had acquired. We decided to try a loan. We were sitting around one day trying to figure out how we could raise $2 million for media in the last month and how could we do it in two or three days. We asked, "What people have given seven or eight times this year? How are they going to give more?"

I said, "Well, let's ask them all to loan the campaign four times what they ever gave before." Everybody laughed at the idea yet said, "Well, let's give it a whirl." So we sent out an appeal to anyone who had ever given money to John Anderson. It said: "We know you have given $25 in the past. If we get 5 percent or more of the vote, and we are sure to get that, the federal government will give us $5 million to match what we have been able to raise recently. All you have to do is loan us the money and we will repay you after election day." We gave them a loan number to make it official. We were able to raise $2 million in five days. We did that by raising money from people who had given $20 before and who now gave $80. People sent money because of the intensity of their commitment and the novelty of our request.

People really want to count. They really want to matter. Here is another example that people have become more interactive, far more involved and concerned than they were before. We ran the fund-raising for Mayor Marian Barry's 1982 reelection. Washington, D.C., demographically, has one of the poorest constituencies for a campaign. A large percentage of Democratic voters from Washington, D.C., have incomes below the poverty level. Conventional wisdom said that these people would not respond to direct mail. Many thought it would be the last thing they would do because they were far more interested in feeding their kids, dealing with crime, and with other issues in their day-to-day world. We argued that was not true. We held that people were far more involved, interactive, and aware, regardless of social class. We also understood that if you get people to interact, if you get people to do something, they become more committed.

You will notice on direct mail promotions from magazines or a publishing house there is often a sticker that you peel off and put on something. The reason they use these little gimmicks is that these things are what get people involved. They get people to participate, and interact, because this helps build commitment. They combine this understanding with an option of easy action when they tell you to "send in this card and we will start sending you the magazine. We will bill you later." They know that as soon as you fill out the reply card and ask for the magazine, you are partly committed. And after you receive it, you will be even more committed.

So with Mayor Barry we sent a letter to all the senior citizens in Washington, D.C. In it we talked about the issues that concern senior citizens, like crime and housing. We warned them that the federal government and the Reagan administration would cut back on their benefits. They were going to hurt them. Well, Mayor Barry said he was going to resist that if they would pledge to help him fight these threats. We gave them a two-part form. The top part had the picture of the mayor and a quotation of his commitment suitable for framing. The bottom part was a statement of commitment for the voter to send back to the candidate.

We mailed this sixty days before election day. Conventional wisdom in elections says that sixty days before election day is too early. At best, you have 10 percent of the electorate really focusing on the race and really committed. Nevertheless, 25 percent of the senior citizens sent back their pledge. In this business a 1-percent response might be expected. Yet their response defied conventional wisdom and was dramatic. And responses are dramatic in terms of what is happening in elections today.

My final point concerns direct mail letters. If you look at any of the direct mail letters in your mailbox, the ones we have written for Walter Mondale or those written for any cause or organization, there are a number of similarities. The first thing to notice is that even if the letter was "cheap" enough to address you as "Dear Friend," it was still personal in tone, often colloquial. Lines such as "I hope you" and "together we can" are included. It was very personal. The pronouns "I" and "you" make use of one-to-one communication opportunities. The increased use of direct mail sprang from the strength of its highly personal style of communication. One to one is the strength of direct mail whether it is fundraising, voter persuasion, or consumer sales. Direct mail can convey the same impression as the Shell Answer Man speaking to you.

The second thing to notice about the letters that are most successful, particularly the fundraising letters, is that they are long. They are substantive. We know that people are becoming more knowledgable and are proud of it. One of the clichés in the advertising business is that you cannot overestimate the intelligence of the public. I think that is baloney; it is the reverse. Far more times political campaigners make the mistake of assuming that the public is stupid, uneducated, ignorant, or unconcerned. The reason a letter is five to seven pages long is because you are saying to these people: "Even if you don't have the time to read this letter, I wanted you to know that I understand that you are intelligent and thoughtful and that you really would require all of that material before you would make up your mind about my campaign." Long letters compliment people who are aware and knowledgeable and impress people who are not. Fund-raising letters are particularly long because you are asking people to make a commitment by asking them to send $25. You are indirectly saying to them, "I know you don't take your commitments lightly. You make them with great seriousness. That is why we have included all this information."

A third thing to notice about the letters is that they are written sometimes in sentence fragments. There is a lot of indenting, short paragraphs, underlining. This writing style is not what you would find in good literature, but it permits the individual to skim the seven pages. So even if they do not read it word for word, you give them the opportunity to get the gist of your message. One way to test a good direct mail letter is to pick the letter up and try to get through it in thirty seconds. Skim it, and then write down the key points. Then read the letter through, and if the major elements were different or unclear, the letter is probably not well written or structured correctly. People need to be able either to skim it or to read it thoroughly and get the same points.

Now for the most important characteristic of all—substance sells. People want to know details. The thing I find most frustrating with political campaigners is their inclination to want to say things as thinly as possible. That is wrong. Most people want to know who you are, what you are suggesting for them to do, why you want to do it, why you are asking that they get involved, and what is it specifically they must do. They want answers to all these concerns.

Over a year ago when I was preparing to write the first Mondale letter, I spent a couple of hours with Mondale on a plane ride to Florida. We were kicking around a few ideas and he asked, "Don't you think it would be great if I had a letter from well-known signers from all areas of life, like a great pianist, a scientist, or an astronaut? It would show the presidential style of my campaign." I replied, "Everyone assumes that the former vice-president of the United States can call upon all these types of people to sign a letter. Rather, people want to know who you are." He still has not done that successfully.

Voters have great instincts and they really want information. They say, "I am about to vote for president of the United States and I want to know who you are." So I told Mondale, "Tell them who you are. What are your values? What shaped your values? How did you live your childhood? Why is your nose funny?" (The reason Walter Mondale's nose is a curious shape is that he broke it playing football.) There are a lot of men in this world who do not want to vote for Walter Mondale because they think he is a liberal and that liberals are "wimps." They do not want to vote for wimps. Polls show this. I thought he should show them he played football, that he was a tough kind of guy. He should tell them how he broke his nose. It would help. It does.

They also want to know where Walter Mondale's views about humanity, people, caring, and children come from. He has deep personal feelings about children, education, and the future. He really cares. We told him, "You should talk about your concerns personally. People will understand that. They want to know who you are."

Unfortunately, he is of Norwegian stock, and they do not like to talk about themselves. Norwegians keep all this stuff inside. So it has been a hard process for him. One of the sad parts about this campaign was the negative press portraying him as a political hack who went around the country trying to enlist different special interest groups. The truth is that Walter Mondale spoke to the AFL-CIO because deep in his heart he had seen what happened to unemployed families. When his father lost his farm, the man had to wander with his family around southeastern Minnesota. They were very poor. He understood poverty because he had seen it. Mondale needed to reveal this better because people want to know who you are.

The other thing they want to know is what you are going to do when you are president of the United States. They want it to be believable and they want to know specifics. Yet getting a politician to talk in specifics is like pulling teeth. They learn in the political world that specifics are not what gets them elected, it is what messes them up. It is errors they make, not great touchdowns they score, that seem to matter. So politicians have learned that what they say gets them in trouble, not what they forget to say. They learn to be very cautious. Trying to tell a politician that he must speak substantively and that the public is willing to hear it, is difficult for him to understand.

The first half of the John Anderson campaign was based on going around to groups in the country and telling them the opposite of what they wanted to hear. Because he was way back in the pack, it was not a risky strategy. There was not much to lose. What are you going to do with 3 percent in the polls? So he went to gun owners and told them, "We ought to have gun control." And he went to Southerners and told them they ought to support busing. One thing we know about people is that if you tell them precisely what you are going to do and how, you are a notch up. Ultimately they want to hear that you are going to do what they want, but you can score points initially the other way.

Much of what I have discussed runs counter to conventional wisdom. Conventional wisdom says you have to be slick and deceptive. I believe that is wrong, and in the future that approach will be increasingly detrimental. It will not work.

2

Polling in Campaigns

Vincent Breglio

I am a Republican pollster and I think it is unethical for a pollster to work both sides of the street. Therefore, what I discuss is biased in the sense that it comes from a Republican perspective. If Pat Caddell, Peter Hart, or any number of good Democratic pollsters were explaining their techniques, they might interpret the same events and circumstances somewhat differently.

I would like to examine the role of polling in a presidential campaign. There are two points I want to make at the outset. First, you cannot understand the role of polling in a presidential campaign unless you understand the role of strategy. Polling and strategy go together hand in glove. The pollster for the president must also be a strategist for the president. You cannot separate polling and strategy.

The second point focuses on history. I believe it was the philosopher Santayana who said that those who fail to learn from history are bound to relive it. That is very true in politics. Since Ronald Reagan will run as an incumbent president in 1984, he must recapture 80 percent of the coalition he had in 1980. So by going back and looking at some history in the campaign of 1980 we can begin to understand the tasks for polling and strategy for the presidential campaign of 1984.

To begin our historical review we must go back to the Friday before the election—October 31, 1980—to the Reagan-Bush headquarters in Arlington, Virginia, where we held our last campaign strategy meeting. Because it was the last meeting, the essential question at that meeting was what would happen on election day. This particular strategy meeting dealt with the end-game strategy of both major candidates. We tried to answer the question—Was Ronald Reagan in a position to win on Tuesday?

The data made available from the research we had been doing showed the following: Ronald Reagan had 44 percent, Jimmy Carter 37 percent, Anderson 10 percent, and 9 percent were undecided. When those four numbers were passed through a formula that adjusted for undecided, turnout, and other factors, our projection of the national vote was Ronald Reagan 50 percent, Jimmy Carter 41.5 percent, and John Anderson 9.5 percent.

The analysis of state-by-state results on that Friday before the election was equally encouraging. We looked at every state, where we had done survey research and simulated outcomes. We took a look at the survey data and factored in the undecided, projected what we though the turnout was going to be on a state-by-state basis, and came up with a victory for Ronald Reagan. We did several different outcome scenarios, using simulation techniques. One was the best case—if everything we had went our way, what would the outcome be? The other was a worst-case scenario. In the Friday meeting we used only the worst-case scenario because it projected 290 electoral votes. We felt that in light of the national polls, Gallup and Harris, which were projecting the race too close to call in their most recently released survey data, the most prudent projection was also the most conservative. The best case and the expected case simulations of electoral vote outcomes both projected electoral victories for Ronald Reagan of landslide proportions. We had only talked about those projections in private; we had never mentioned them in public.

The interesting thing about the reaction of the people in the room was that they expected Reagan would win but they also expected the race was going to be very close. Maybe he would win by as much as 2 or 3 percentage points; maybe he would get 280-300 electoral votes. He would win the election but it would indeed be a close race. We made the worst-case projection and everyone left the room that day reasonably optimistic that Reagan would win. Everyone in his own mind had come up with a number; and most of those numbers were very close.

Then the campaign shifted into high gear for the final four or five days. The media and campaign trail blitz went on and those of us doing the research and strategy packed up all the high-tech paraphernalia used these days—computer terminals, printers, disc drives—and put them on an airplane and took them to California. Saturday morning, after flying in Friday night, we set up the strategy room at the Century Plaza Hotel in Los Angeles where the victory party would be held on election night.

We were tracking public opinion every day, both on a national basis and within seventeen key targeted states that were necessary to put together the electoral victory for Reagan-Bush. We felt that Carter's prospects for winning at that point were very bleak. Based on our data it appeared that the only strategy open to Jimmy Carter was what we called a big-state strategy. He did not have enough time left to build the coalition of small or medium-sized states needed to win. He would have to focus all his time and energy in the last days of the campaign on the seven big states—New York, California, Texas, Michigan, Ohio, Pennsylvania, and Illinois. We, on the other hand, could afford to be selective—targeting the

campaign time on two or three states that needed a little last-minute reinforcing.

After we had set up the strategy and survey shop across from the suite
Reagan was going to occupy, we began to reflect over all the data that
was coming in from around the country. Friday night's tracking results
showed that the Reagan lead that we had been watching for some five or
six nights had increased by 2 percent. Saturday night's results showed
another point increase. By Sunday and Monday we were looking at a solid
ten-point lead from the tracking survey results. Clearly, by Monday the
race had been won. On Monday after we had run all the simulations, both
national and state by state, we felt for the very first time that we ought to
go out and publicly announce that, first, Ronald Reagan was not only
going to win on Tuesday but he would probably get 50 percent of the
popular vote in a three-way race—which was a remarkable result.
Secondly, he would win an electoral vote landslide, with well over 390
electoral votes in the electoral college.

We looked around for someone to tell that news to. Now Monday afternoon, on the penthouse floor of the Century Plaza Hotel in Los Angeles,
the only people there were security teams with their dogs. They had a
mild curiosity about the equipment we had put in the strategy room. They
had no interest in the knowledge we possessed; they were only interested
in making sure the floor was secure. So we had to look for someone else
with whom to share our news. Along came two hotel workers who had
been assigned to clean up the room. We had reams of scrap and carbon
paper overflowing the available trash cans. It was just a mess. We decided
that these two hotel workers would be the very first members of the general public to hear from the Reagan campaign that the Reagan candidacy
was going to be a winner on Tuesday. So we cornered them and with all
the enthusiasm that only twenty days of sleepless nights and high adrena-
line could generate we told them all this wonderful news. They were very
accommodating, and smiled and nodded their heads and said, "No hablo
inglés."

After that experience we located the plane and talked to several people
who traveled with Ronald Reagan. We reported to them that it looked like
not only would we win but it would be a landslide victory. We were
amazed that no one wanted to hear that. They all preferred to believe that
the race was very close and they must work very hard until the election
was over. They did not want to hear that they were going to win a
landslide victory. This wonderful information was disclosed to only a few
with very specific instructions not to discuss it with anyone else. We had
to sit through the next thirty hours or so until the first election results

made it evident that indeed a Reagan landslide was forming and that in terms of electoral votes, Ronald Reagan would be elected by well over 400 electoral votes of the 535 votes available.

What is a campaign strategy? A campaign strategy identifies the barriers to winning an election. It answers the questions of who, what, and why for the campaign—who must vote for us, what will we say that will encourage/discourage their vote, and why is one group, issue, or part of the country more important than others. A strategy is a conceptualization of the campaign process and as such should provide an action frame of reference rather than a simple "how to" operations manual. It must be flexible and evolve through interaction with the environment without surrendering its basic objectives set at the outset of the campaign—unless new information proves those objectives in error.

The most fundamental assumption underlying the strategy we developed was that Ronald Reagan was the best electronic media candidate in American political history. Politics has changed and politicians have been forced to change with it. Not more than twenty-five years ago the great politicians were those who could deliver impassioned speeches that would have the audience on their feet and cheering. That is no longer true. The great politicians of today's environment are electronic communicators; people who can effectively transmit their ideas, feelings, thoughts, desires, and aspirations to their constituency in a way that communicates with the average voter—and do it all in 30- or 60-second TV spots. Ronald Reagan had mastered the electronic medium.

Even so, there were a number of hurdles to his election that the strategy was forced to deal with. First, Ronald Reagan was well known, but not known well. Second, he was perceived as considerably more conservative than the average voter. Third, he was challenging a political incumbent who occupied the middle of the ideological spectrum, a very good place to be if you are trying to garner votes. Fourth, while Reagan had been politically active for many years he did not have a strong linkage to the Republican Party power structure. Fifth, his candidacy hinged on expanding a relatively narrow political base among conservatives and Republic partisans, expanding to include constituencies which in the past had been traditionally Democratic. This is an important point. He must do this again, to be president for four more years. Sixth, John Anderson's independent candidacy made the campaign much more difficult because it rendered many conventional political axioms irrelevant. Lastly, no constituency could be taken for granted or counted on for the entire course of the campaign. Those were the hurdles the campaign faced and the use of survey research was relevant to each.

Each hurdle was addressed in a series of strategic memoranda which evolved into something called "the black book." I suppose it was called the "black book" because you do not call a strategic document that is going to guide a presidential campaign the "white" book. The black book became something of a controversial document because so many people in and out of the campaign wanted to get their hands on it. It was kept under lock and key accessible only to key members of the inner circle of decision makers in the Reagan campaign. It was kept very confidential because it contained the strategic steps that went into the presidential effort. For example, in that document we recorded the seven conditions for victory that we thought were critical to winning the presidency for Ronald Reagan.

First, without alienating the Reagan base of Western, Republican, and conservative votes we could beat Jimmy Carter only if we continued to expand our base to include more independent Anderson voters and disaffected Democrats to weaken the incumbency advantage. Without breaking any new major issue ground, the thrust of our speeches to accomplish this condition was directed toward inflation, jobs, economic growth, and a more responsible and efficient federal government.

Second, we should allocate all campaign resources carefully against targeted battleground states. Keep in mind that the outcome of any presidential election has nothing to do with popular votes. It has everything to do with the electoral vote count. Electoral votes are based on the number of elected federal respresentatives from each state. If you look at all the states, there are seven states that have the bulk of electoral votes— California, Texas, New York, Michigan, Illinois, Ohio, and Pennsylvania. Those states get a disproportionate allocation of resources—you allocate more resources to those states than their electoral vote numbers warrant. You do so because when you win in the big states it has a magnetic effect. The strategy was to impact the South, attempting to capitalize on the large state of Texas by targeting Florida, Texas, and Virginia, and putting our resources into those three states, hoping they would carry over into states such as Louisiana, Mississippi, and the Carolinas. As the campaign unfolded, this strategy worked very well. By putting fewer resources into the smaller Southern states and working very hard in the large Southern states of Texas, Florida, and Virginia, we were able to maximize impact in the South. In 1984 a similar strategy was used with disproportionate allocations in Reagan's time and campaign resources going into the large states across the country to produce this magnetic effect.

The third condition for victory focused on Reagan's image strengths that embodied presidential values we knew a majority of Americans thought important—leadership, competence, strength, and decisiveness. At the same time we needed to minimize the perception that he was dangerous and uncaring. These perceptions of Ronald Reagan had been around for a long time. If you go back to when he was governor and asked what people thought of Ronald Reagan, he always got his highest marks on leadership, strength, and decisiveness and his lowest marks on caring and safety. Those perceptions go back fifteen years with Ronald Reagan. They were very much in evidence in 1976, in 1980, and again in the campaign of 1984. Things have not changed all that much.

The fourth condition necessary for victory was that we had to reinforce Carter's major weaknesses through our media. We had to add an attack strategy. It has become vital in campaigns today that you not only present all the reasons why people ought to vote for you, but you also have an obligation to present the reasons why they should not vote for the opponent. Hence the negative campaign or the attack strategy becomes an essential part of any campaign operation. Carter's major weaknesses that we chose to reinforce in the media were the following: that he was ineffective and a poor leader; that he was incapable of implementing policies; that he was too willing to use his presidential power politically; and that he was vacillating in foreign policy and hence created a climate of crisis.

A fifth element stressed the need to neutralize Carter's "October Surprise," which was a term we coined during the course of the campaign to innoculate the electorate from whatever the incumbent president might do in those final two weeks to help his own campaign. You may remember reading in *Time* magazine the article about the "October Surprise" which came out in September. It was clear to us that there were certain levers that the White House controlled, particularly in the foreign policy area, that were simply unavailable to a challenger. If the White House chose to pull those levers shortly before the election, they could indeed surprise the electorate into shifting its support. The obvious surprise would have been to get the hostages home from Iran during that period.

We had determined in the summer of 1980 that if Carter were able to negotiate a return for the American hostages, that would have been worth something in the neighborhood of 8-10 percentage points to the Carter vote. If you projected that into the last two weeks of the campaign, it was evident to us that had the Carter White House been able to get the hostages freed during that time, Carter probably would have won the election, other things being equal. Hence, we turned to a strategy called "innoculation." When you go to the doctor's office and you get a shot of flu virus which has been diminished in strength, you get a mini case of the flu to build immunity so when the active bug comes along either you do not get it or you get a very light case. Political innoculation is very much the same. You plant an idea, a notion, a perception among the electorate, that somehow in late October the White House was going to surprise everyone by doing something that would change the outcome of the election. You do not say what or how, you just start commenting about the levers of power and how they can be used to manipulate the outcome of the election during the last couple of weeks. In 1980 the press began to pick up on the notion of the October surprise and speculate about what would happen if the hostages were brought home during the last two weeks of the campaign.

What we saw happen as a result of the innoculation strategy against the return of the hostages was that from a campaign advantage, as measured earlier, the impact among the electorate dropped off to nearly neglible proportions. They had been innoculated well enough that people then thought about the hostages coming home during the last days of the campaign and it made no difference in their support for Jimmy Carter. There was even some evidence that Carter would have suffered politically from it because of a growing level of cynicism among voters.

During the last two or three days of the campaign there was a great deal of talk of the Iranian ambassador negotiating with unnamed sources in the government to bring about the release of the hostages. Those headlines, when tested in survey research across country, revealed a tremendous level of antagonism toward any political manipulation of the hostage crisis. Had the hostages been released just before the election was held, Carter would not have benefited from it; he probably would have lost support as a result of it.

The sixth condition to victory was to take advantage of the Anderson vote when the Anderson support began to wane. It was clear that John Anderson's support base came from better educated, more affluent, white-collar, professional voters. These were voters we felt we ought to have at least a 50/50 split with, if not a 60/40 split with Carter when they decided that it was useless to maintain support for John Anderson. Our campaign argued for several weeks, very strongly, that any debate held in the last three or four weeks of the campaign should include John Anderson. That was because we wanted to extend every political courtesy to John Anderson so that when his people began to feel the futility of their support for his candidacy we might be a desirable alternative rather than having made enemies of his supporters. As it turned out, the Anderson vote did split about 60/40 for Reagan when they started to defect.

Lastly, we had to do everything we could to keep the campaign from becoming event-driven during the last two weeks of the campaign. John

Sears described a political campaign as a dinosaur running downhill with the campaign manager and the candidate clinging to the back for dear life. When the dinosaur starts down the hill you can give it some direction: You can move it to the right; you can move it to the left; you can slow it some; but it is hard to stop. We hoped to maintain enough control during that last twenty days to not only be able to hang on, but to avoid making a fatal error of reacting to events that might occur during that period.

Reagan's 1980 coalition is important to Ronald Reagan today because he was able to make inroads into some target coalitions—moderates, blue-collar workers, Catholics, Hispanics, Jewish voters. Many moved into the Reagan column in sizeable numbers which helped us win in 1980. For example, among moderates, self-identified moderates, in June 1980 he had only 26 percent of their support. By election day that had gone to 41 percent. Among independents, in June he had 33 percent; on election day he had 52 percent. Among college graduates, he had 40 percent in June; by election day he had 56 percent. Of people making under $15,000 a year, he had 32 percent in June; on election day he had 46 percent. We saw at almost every turn that the outreach program of the Reagan campaign was able to put together coalitions of nontraditional voting groups to develop support that was important for the campaign.

Let me turn to the gender gap controversy, the fact that Ronald Reagan is consistently eight to twelve points lower in approval among women than he is among men. Is the gender gap anything new for Ronald Reagan? No, it is not. We saw it before 1980. But in 1980, when the issues of the economy dominated as the election day neared, working women believed that Ronald Reagan was the best alternative. Hence, we were able to pick up about 16 percentage points among working women.

Forty-four percent of craftsmen and foremen voted to support Reagan; veteran support was at a 56 percent level. Born-again Christians gave Ronald Reagan 50 percent of their vote. All these groups were not what you would call expected supporters of the Republican ticket, and they combined to produce the kind of victory we were able to enjoy.

One of the uses of survey research in today's presidential politics is to guide the media strategy of the campaign. Again, Ronald Reagan was well known but not known well. Ninety percent of those we talked to in June 1980 could identify Ronald Reagan; only 40 percent could give us anything specific that he had done and when they did so they focused mostly on the fact that he was either an actor or some kind of politician. Neither of these occupations was high on the prestige list of most Americans.

Within the confines of the Reagan campaign there were a large number of people in very important positions who argued that the way to beat

Jimmy Carter was to attack him from the very outset of the campaign all the way through election day. Based on the data we had collected, it was clear that a simple attack strategy would be counterproductive. Before Reagan was in a position to attack he had to establish his own credibility. It was decided to put together a series of TV commercials that featured Ronald Reagan as governor of California. In these commercials Reagan was portrayed as a governor who was concerned about many facets of political life in California and who worked with all kinds of people from labor unions to conservationists, accomplishing many important things. It followed a mini-documentary format. There were versions of it in 5-minute frames and in 60- and 30-second frames. We ran that series of spots over and over again.

What happened politically as we started to run those spots was that the first time Reagan partisans saw them they all stood up and applauded and thought the spots were great. The next times they saw those spots they began to question why they had seen the same spot three times—obviously everyone knew that Ronald Reagan was governor of California and that he had done this and that with health insurance benefits and this and that with labor unions. Everyone knew that, so it was felt that we should start attacking Carter like we should have been from the outset. So within the Reagan campaign there began a hue and cry against those who were keeping this series of documentary spots on the air. It was so bad that in the very high echelons of the campaign there was a clear division between those who wanted these spots to be pulled off the air and replaced by hard-attack spots against Carter, and those who thought we still needed to continue reinforcing the Reagan image. It was very fortunate for the campaign that the latter group was dominant.

Survey data said people were beginning to know more and more about Reagan and had begun to identify specific good things that he had done as governor of California. We continued with this series of minidocumentary spots, keeping them on the air for nearly five weeks which, in political terms, is an extraordinarily long time for running any kind of a spot. We finally ended up with about 60 percent of the people that we interviewed able to give us some specific thing they recalled about Ronald Reagan other than the fact that he was an actor or some politician from out West. I believe these spots turned his image around and then he was in a position to take on Carter and use some effective attack messages.

Let me expand on the relationship of image to issues. If a voter finds out that the candidate is prochoice, pro-ERA, and pro-UN, that voter has a mental picture of the candidate. Conversely, if you hear that the candidate is antiabortion, wants the UN kicked off the American soil, and is far Right on ERA, you also have a mental image of that person. Politically, candidates choose issues which best portray their image. Issues are chosen in the campaign to best reflect the image attributes of the candidate. In the case of Ronald Reagan, he communicated a position in sixty seconds as well as anyone. Most people who listened to Ronald Reagan on the economy, for example, could not give us facts on some specific suggestions he advocated: inflation, tax cuts, and so forth. We chose those issues because they emphasized his leadership of the economy and his attitude.

In 1980 age was also a factor and it was of great concern. It was one reason for choosing the "talking head" spots and body close-ups showing Reagan's physical features. His vigor in office has pretty much laid that issue to rest. Now survey responses very seldom express concern over his age or ability to handle another four years. People believe that Ronald Reagan is physically able to serve another four years without much problem. Age is not a factor now.

The bulk of the media dollars was directed by research. We assessed the impact of advertising through research. We were very concerned that our advertising have a positive impact on the electorate and not come off overly bitter or unfairly negative. We found that both Carter's and Reagan's advertising were just about equally well remembered by voters. But they felt by a significant margin that Reagan's advertising was more positive in content than Carter's advertising. Carter's was frequently characterized as mean and nasty. That got carried over to the Carter image and some of the positive personal characteristics Carter had among voters—that he was a nice man, a good guy—began to flip-flop and during the last two to three weeks of the campaign the Carter image took on a very negative tone in the minds of a very large segment of the electorate.

During the campaign there was a decision made to have Reagan participate in debates. We argued that there should be no debate because at that point Ronald Reagan had about a seven- or eight-point lead; we felt that a debate would be taking an unnecessary risk with the candidate. The Nashua, New Hampshire primary debate turned around an election in which Ronald Reagan was not supposed to have done as well as he did. Debates are highly volatile and potentially explosive; a mistake can cost you five to eight points, just like that. Given the momentum the candidate was building and the consistent eight-point lead our data was registering, we argued conservatively that it was not worth the risk to put him in a context where he could lose support if he made a mistake. Conversely, those who felt that it was imperative to debate, held that this could be the opportunity for Ronald Reagan to demonstrate he was not the gun-toting nut the Carter campaign had portrayed him to be to the American people. A debate could show that he was a rational fellow who understood the

issues and was a safe choice. As it turned out, they were right. The debate
was, on technical grounds, clearly Carter's; he beat Reagan on virtually
all the issues. But Reagan won the debate on style and was helped the
most by it. We did four separate attitude surveys using four separate
firms, all independent of each other. They surveyed the effect of the
debate immediately as it went off the air. In all cases, attitudes
overwhelmingly favored Ronald Reagan and his performance.

We talked to over 35,000 registered voters in more than 100 major surveys and tracking projects. The data was collected both on a national
basis—where the sample was projectable to the entire nation—as well as a
state-by-state basis. You must target the states where you think you have
the best chance of winning to build an electoral vote of 270. In every one
of our targeted seventeen states where we thought we had the best chance
of winning, we were collecting survey research on the average of once
every two weeks. During the last twenty days of the campaign we were
tracking them on a daily basis, so we had surveys of seventeen key target
states every day during that last period. We could tell if we needed to
shift an event for Reagan from Dallas to Chicago by the way the votes
were showing on the tracking system. Scheduling during the last two
weeks of the campaign was often made not more than seventy-two hours
in advance of events.

In 1984 Reagan is the incumbent, not the challenger, and he must run
and defend a record. If the 1984 campaign hinges on the economy, Ronald
Reagan will be reelected president of the United States with relative ease.
If, on the other hand, the agenda of the 1984 campaign includes issues
such as the nuclear freeze and social issues, the race will be much closer.

Ronald Reagan as a candidate campaigns as a conservative. He governs
as a pragmatist. In 1980 we tried to move Reagan but we could not move
his positions. We tried to demonstrate how conservative he was on some
issues, but that he was a safe choice and not a dangerous person. Reagan's
governing stance is a pragmetic one. He will compromise when he has to.
He has certain principles which he has adhered to for fifteen or twenty
years. They have not changed. He took positions when he was governor
of California that have not changed by one word. That is both good and
bad. It is good because it provides consistency of values, a consistency of
message; it is bad because times change. People look for and have higher
expectations for a position on some issues. But Ronald Reagan as a person
will run again in 1984 as a conservative candidate. He will govern from
1985 to 1988 as a pragmatist.

3
Money in Campaigns

Randy Huwa

Jesse Unruh, a long-time politico on the California scene, once said that "money is the mother's milk of politics." He was quoted several years later as saying that money was the mother's milk of politics, but that the milk had become sour and that it was time for a change in the campaign financing system. That is what Common Cause has been about since around 1970.

I would like to begin this discussion of money and politics by going back to 1757, which may be the first reported case of potential campaign financing abuse. That was when George Washington ran for the House of Burgesses in Virginia. According to reports made at the time, there were a number of campaign irregularities. Mr. Washington allegedly purchased 28 gallons of rum, 50 gallons of rum punch, 34 gallons of wine, 46 gallons of beer, and 2 gallons of cider royal. The issue was that there were only 391 constituents in the district in which he was seeking election, which works out to one and a half quarts per capita.

In the 1880s Andrew Jackson ran for president. During that election the Bank of the United States decided to oppose Jackson's candidacy and substantial campaign contributions were made on behalf of his opponent. However, Jackson won. Instead of reforming the campaign finance laws, he abolished the bank. That is a recurring theme throughout American history—it has been difficult to improve our campaign financing laws.

The first such law may have been one in 1867 which said that naval contractors could not make contributions. But after that there was little change in the rules governing the way in which money was raised throughout the 1900s. Teddy Roosevelt in 1905 said we should have public financing and proposed it in his State of the Union message but his proposal was not adopted.

When recently retired congressman Richard Bolling was elected to Congress for the first time in 1948, he spent $2,500 to win. By the time he retired it was not uncommon for candidates to spend twenty times or even 100 times that amount. Bolling commented, "I remember that as we move through the 1960s and through the Johnson administration, there developed an undefinable feeling on Capitol Hill and in Washington—an odor, if you will—that the amount of money flowing in was becoming enormous and that there were some situations developing very rapidly that were just ripe for corruption." We had campaign finance disclosure laws on the books but they were generally ignored. If you wanted to know where a congressional or a presidential candidate was getting the money for his election campaign, you were generally out of luck. We had a situation in which candidates were allowed to create numerous committees. The McGovern campaign had several hundred or perhaps thousands of committees. It is alleged that they created 373 committees simply to accept contributions from one individual, Stewart Mott. Disclosure reports were used to report only funding information that the candidate personally knew about. So there were many candidates in the 1950s and 1960s who were filing reports indicating that they had raised no money and made no expenditures because the candidate did not know about it. The late Hubert Humphrey once said that he felt raising campaign money was the most demeaning and degrading part of being in politics. He talked about going to Atlanta and making a presentation in front of a curtain. Behind the curtain campaign fund-raising was going on. He pretended not to know what was going on behind the curtain.

In 1971 Congress finally decided it was time to shed some light on what really was happening in terms of campaign financing and where candidates were getting their money. They enacted the first campaign financing disclosure law. When the curtain was finally lifted, the first election that we got a look at was the 1972 presidential election. If ever there was a campaign that gave a new meaning to the phrase "embarrassment of riches" it was the reelection campaign of Richard Nixon. Looking at the campaign finance disclosure reports for that campaign one found things like W. Clement Stone, the largest contributor, giving $2 million. There was $200,000 in an attaché case from Robert Vesco. There was $100,000 from Howard Hughes. There was $2 million from the dairy industry and the president's promise to increase dairy price supports. There was at least $750,000 in illegal campaign contributions from corporations that resulted in twenty-one firms being convicted of violations of campaign law. The top ten contributors to Nixon's campaign effort gave $4 million. The top 100 gave over $14 million. In fact, the money that paid the gentlemen who broke into the Watergate complex came from campaign contributions, as did the money that was used to cover up that incident.

There was a tremendous reaction against the excesses of the 1972 campaign, both among the people and in the Congress. And on the very day that Richard Nixon announced he would resign, the House of Representatives passed the first comprehensive campaign financing system that this country had ever seen.

1974 was a two-part system in presidential elec-
⸱ions a system was established to provide match-
vho were running for president. Once a candi-
vas a serious contender for the highest office in
ise a relatively small amount of money ($5,000
n contributions of $250 or less), that candidate
ing funds. For every dollar raised from an indi-
ᶠ up to $250, the candidate would receive a
to $250 from the federal treasury. The money
.omes from the income tax checkoff. That
.leral income tax form since the early 1970s.
federal financing of the general election and
nating conventions. In 1976 candidates Carter
check from the federal treasury which covered
.ipaigns. The same was true for 1980 and 1984.
.ing in presidential primaries and presidential gen-
first time in our country's history.

.ias worked. Most candidates participated in the system. In
₁ɔ⁄6 and 1984 all the candidates participated. In 1980 all the candidates
participated except John Connally who decided to go his own way. Some
have raised constitutional questions about the whole presidential public
financing system. Can we create a system in which we give money to candidates from the federal treasury in exchange for limitations on total
expenditures? That issue was before the Supreme Court in the case of
Buckley vs. Valeo. It was a case brought by an unusual coalition including
the ACLU, Senator Buckley from New York, and former senator
McCarthy—a strange combination of liberals and conservatives who felt
that the campaign financing laws and the public financing provisions of
presidential election laws were unconstitutional. The court upheld the law
and said that it was constitutional to impose limits on spending and on
contributions, and for the federal government to provide funding for
presidential campaigns as part of the public financing system.

The second issue that was argued about public financing is that it is an
incumbent's protection law. It was argued that if you limit the amount of
money the candidates can spend, the incumbent will always win. Former
presidents Carter and Ford are the best examples to demonstrate that the
argument is not true. The fact is that with public financing we had the
first two incumbents turned out of office since Herbert Hoover. It has not
proven to be an incumbent's protection bill.

Closely in line with that argument was the notion that a public financing
system would only nominate front-runners or only well-known candidates.
In 1976 we saw Jimmy Carter come from far back in the pack to become

the presidential nominee. The system allowed that kind of candidate to gather campaign funds and become the nominee.

Third, it was argued that the presidential public financing system was going to weaken the political parties. In fact, presidential public financing has strengthened political parties. In 1972 we saw that there was virtually no connection between the reelection efforts of Richard Nixon and the Republican National Committee. The time, attention, and focus of that campaign were on reelecting the president, and there was very little spill-over effect. Because of changes in the law, we now have a situation where the presidential campaign is paid for from public funding. The Republican and Democratic national committees are no longer responsible for raising money for presidential campaigns. We no longer have presidential candidates competing with the parties for campaign funds. Presidential needs were taken care of and the parties could go out and raise money on their own. We also no longer have a situation in which the national committees were saddled with the debts of the losers. And amendments were adopted in 1979 that gave the parties a far stronger role in presidential elections.

The presidential public financing system is not perfect. There are adjustments which need to be made. The issue of spending limits needs to be looked at. Those limits were set in 1974, and they have been indexed to inflation. But there are those who argue the need to increase. Their arguments particularly relate to the need to increase spending limits for the nominating period. The number of nominating primaries has increased 50 percent since those laws were enacted, and primaries are generally more expensive than caucuses. There are those who say we should increase nominating campaign spending while keeping general election campaign spending the same.

When the law was passed in 1974, limits of $10 million in the primaries and $20 million in the general election were set and future limits were indexed for inflation. For 1984 those numbers doubled to about $20 million for primaries and about $40 million for the general election. Those are adequate amounts. If you speak to Republicans they always talk about the tremendous amount of money being spent by the Republican Party at the state and local levels. In the 1984 general election campaign roughly $120 million was spent on the presidential campaign, with $80 million spent by the two candidates themselves and the rest on the coordinating expenditures and "get-out-to-vote" drives.

Some problems are created by "front loading" in primaries. *Front loading* is a term used to describe a washing machine, but now it is also used to describe our presidential nominating process and the fact that so much that is important or influential occurs so early in the campaign. On March 13, 1984, 505 of the delegates to the Democratic National Convention were selected. Half of the delegates to the Democratic National Convention were selected by mid-April. This may mean that the campaign, the presidential nominating process, is not really too long but possibly too short. The problem is that it begins in February and may be over by the end of April. The campaign financing system as it is now constructed does not provide matching money for presidential candidates until January, and that may be too late.

Third, I think we have a problem with third-party or minor-party candidates. The present system may not be able to get money to them for their campaigns until after the general election. They get retroactive reimbursements. We may need to change that situation, so that a serious independent candidate like John Anderson might be able to get money during the course of the presidential election.

If we are going to provide public financing to a third-party candidate, how do you decide who gets it? This is the problem that Congress wrestled with back in 1974. How can you decide who is going to be a serious third-party candidate? John Anderson ran in 1980 as a real independent. He was not the nominee of any party. He nominated himself, essentially. He clearly demonstrated substantial public support as a serious contender. On the other hand, it is fairly easy to get on the ballot in a lot of states. Should I be entitled to receive public funding because I am on the ballot? I think the kind of compromise we need is to adopt the system we have for the presidential primaries system. If you are going to get money as a presidential primary candidate you have to demonstrate that you are a serious candidate by raising a relatively small amount of money—$5,000 in twenty states in contributions of $250 or less. Once you have cleared that threshold, once you have demonstrated that you are something of a serious campaigner, you can receive federal matching funds, dollar for dollar. I think the same kind of system could be adopted for the general election of third-, minor-, or new-party candidates. If they raise a qualifying threshold, they would be eligible to receive matching funds during the course of the presidential campaign.

In 1980 the problem that John Anderson ran into was that in order to get money under the current law he had to get 5 percent of the vote. Once he got that 5 percent he was eligible to receive retroactive funding. That did not give him any money to run his campaign. What he did was bet that he was going to get 5 percent, so he went to his supporters and said, "Loan me the money, bet with me, bet that I'm going to get more than 5 percent, bet that I'm going to get federal funds once the election is over, and I will repay that loan." There is probably another way to do that, to provide money to serious third-party candidates during the course of the campaign. It is not the easiest system to structure but it can be done.

The largest problem is the role of independent expenditures. If you look at the total percentage PACs (political action committees) contributed to presidential candidates directly, it is only 1 or 2 percent of a candidate's funds. So this does not appear to be a problem. However, if you look at what PACs give to candidates independent of their campaigns, there is a problem.

In 1974, Congress passed a law that said you could limit the amount of money an individual could contribute to a presidential campaign to $1,000 for an individual. Congress also said that there was a limit on the amount of money you could spend on behalf of that campaign. There was a possibility, Congress said, of corruption or the appearance of corruption by a large campaign contribution or a large expenditure on behalf of a presidential campaign. But when that issue was brought before the courts in the context of congressional races, the court held that it was constitutional to limit contributions but not constitutional to limit expenditures. In other words, if you decide to run for Congress and I give you $1,000, there is the possibility of the appearance of or the potential for corruption because I have given you money. But the courts said that if I decide to spend $100,000 on your behalf, independent of your campaign and without your knowledge, there is no danger of corruption. It strikes me as peculiar reasoning, but that was the court's decision.

In 1976, independent expenditures were relatively small, but in 1980 they took on a new significance. Early in the 1980 election year, a number of new groups were formed, announcing that they were going to make expenditures of up to $40 million on behalf of the presidential campaigns. Two of those groups, Americans for Change and Americans for an Effective Presidency, ultimately spent a little under $14 million. But if we compare that amount of money to the total amount—$29.4 million in 1980—the presidential candidate gets from the government, that $14 million makes a significant difference.

What do we do to limit the problems of independent expenditures? First, we need to determine whether some of the efforts have really been independent. In the 1980 election there were cases where independent expenditure groups and the Reagan campaign were using the same campaign consultants and the same mailing house. Once President Reagan called Terry Dolan who is the chairman of the National Conservative Political Action Committee (NCPAC). Terry reportedly said something like "Excuse me Mr. President, but we really can't be talking because we are going to undertake some expenditure ads on your behalf. So we are going to have to terminate this conversation." I may be one of the few times when someone has hung up on the president of the United States. But that was an attempt to maintain this alleged independence.

In practice the distinction between consultation or no consultation does not hold up. During the 1980 campaign Senator Jesse Helms (Republican, North Carolina) had a PAC that was making independent ads and he said, "Well, as you may know, we have an independent effort going on in North Carolina. Uh, the law forbids me to consult with him [Mr. Reagan], and it's been an awkward situation. I've had to, sort of, uh, talk indirectly with Paul Laxalt [Mr. Reagan's campaign chairman] and hope that he would pass along . . . and I . . . I think the messages have gotten through all right." I think there was that kind of information consultation. If you are an independent expenditure PAC, you can find out a lot about what the campaign is thinking by following the campaign schedule. If Ronald Reagan all of a sudden starts making campaign appearances in Tennessee and Alabama, you must conclude that the people in the campaign think that Ronald Reagan has a chance of carrying those two states. If I am a smart campaign expenditure PAC, I will go after them. We made the argument that at the presidential level it is very difficult for major independent expenditures to be made without some sort of consultation. I do not think that is true if I am taking an ad out of my local newspaper or putting up a billboard in my backyard saying, "He's the greatest." But we are not talking about that kind of activity. We are talking about large-scale expenditures.

Second, Common Cause proposes that we need to amend the federal communication statutes to provide some sort of response time, to be sure that candidates have free time to respond to independent committee TV ads.

Third, we mounted a legal challenge because we believe a provision of the Federal Election Campaign Act that the court did not address in the Buckley case, limiting independent expenditures to $1,000 in the context of public finance grants was unconstitutional, and in 1985 the Supreme Court held that this limitation on independent expenditures was unconstitutional.

In 1972 Clement Stone was the largest contributor in the presidential election. In 1976 I was the largest contributor to the presidential election, because I designated $1 in taxes on the income tax checkoff—I and millions of other Americans.

The presidential campaign fund is running a fairly substantial surplus. There is enough money in the checkoff account at this point to fund the 1984 presidential election, the 1984 congressional election, and the 1986 congressional election, given current rates of participation. So we are running a fairly good surplus in that account. The money is there to make reform work. All we have to do is get the mechanism in place. The checkoff rates of participation have been about 27, 28, or 29 percent over the last three tax years. There are an equal number of people who check "No." There are a lot of people who leave it blank. One of the reasons for that is the federal income tax form does not explain what the money is going to be used for. I think it says the money will go to the presidential election fund. Look at the instructions: "This box allows you to designate one dollar of taxes to the presidential election and will not increase your taxes or decrease your refund." Fine, but what is it for? That message is not getting out to the public and most people do not understand it. We need to explain what the checkoff is for, what the money is used for, and the reason for doing it. A lot of people look at it and say "Uh, why should I give a dollar to those guys?" They do not understand the limits—the advantages—of the presidential public financing system.

My personal campaign is to get Ronald Reagan to designate $1 of *his* taxes to the presidential campaign fund. After all, this system provided him about $50 million in presidential funds for 1980 and almost $70 million in 1984. I would think he would have the good grace to designate $1 of his own taxes for that purpose. But it might be easier for me to raise the overall checkoff rather than get that buck because in 1985, as part of his comprehensive tax reform proposal, President Reagan proposed the repeal of the tax dollar checkoff.

In sum, the public financing system for presidential races has worked pretty well. It has provided money to candidates and it has provided enough money to candidates. We have eliminated the role of the large contributor in presidential elections. We have limited the role of special interest money in presidential elections. We have restored some semblance of balance.

I wish I could make the same kind of report to you on what is happening in congressional races, but I cannot. In 1974 when we were talking about this whole wave of reform, Congress decided that public financing of presidential candidates was good but that it was not good for a congressional race. While Congress took steps to fundamentally change the way we fund our presidential campaigns, it failed to take the same steps for its own. They also changed the laws to increase the importance of PACs by removing a provision that had been in the statute for years which kept government contractors from becoming PACs.

So what happened? The number of PACs increased from 600 in 1974 to almost 4,000 today. The amount of money that PACs contributed went from about $12.5 million in 1974 to $83 million in 1982. In the 1984 campaign, 4,000 PACs contributed over $100 million to congressional candidates. What effect does that have on congressional elections? First, there has been a tremendous increase in the amount of money going to the congressional races. The average House candidate got about a third of his funds from PACs. If you examine people who are in positions of leadership—committee chairs, speaker, majority leader—they received on average more than half of their money from PACs. More and more candidates are spending more and more of their time in Washington raising campaign funds. In the last campaign there was a candidate from Kansas who came into Washington raising money, so that he could go back out to Kansas to spend it, so that he could be elected from Kansas to come back to Washington to represent the views of the people of Kansas. Jim Leach, a Republican member of Iowa, stated that Iowa was basically a state of small farmers and small businessmen, but if campaign contributions are examined, they increasingly come from large labor groups and business groups. Some of the large contributors to Iowa congressional campaigns are the maritime unions, stockbrokers, and longshoremen. Recently Leach was testifying before the House Administration Committee and said, "I'm not sure I should be saying this, but I want to let you in on a secret. Iowa has no oceans." There are an increasing number of campaign contributions from groups that have very little to do with the congressional districts.

PAC contributions tend to favor incumbents by a ratio of better than three to one. PACs invest in incumbents because they are safer bets. Most incumbents win, one of the reasons being the advantages they enjoy in terms of campaign financing. Under the present system of funding congressional races those incumbents are doing very well indeed. Perhaps the best example is the chairman of the House Ways and Means Committee. He received a $250,000 in PAC contributions for his 1982 election. It was not a tough race—he won with about 82 percent of the vote in the general election. Now he has a campaign surplus of a half of $500,000. It is not going to be easy to find a candidate to run against him.

The third and maybe most significant effect is that the campaign financing system in congressional races is having an impact on the way Congress operates. I am not talking about PACs buying or selling votes. Instead, PACs make contributions as a way of gaining access and influence with members of Congress. Perhaps the best description of that was provided by Justin Dart, who was a member of President Reagan's unofficial kitchen cabinet. He once said that the dialogue with a politician is "a fine thing but with a little money they hear you better." I think PACs are using money as a way of increasing their access and influence with members of Congress.

Common Cause had done a number of studies about PAC contributions to members of Congress and the effect those contributions have had. Perhaps the best example was the so-called used-car rule. The Federal Trade Commission proposed a bill that would require a dealer to disclose what was wrong with a used car. The National Automobile Dealers' Association did not like that proposal. They were also one of the largest PAC contributors. They contributed over $1 million in campaign funds in 1980. They went to work and Congress turned down that rule. And if you look at those who voted with the National Automobile Dealers' Association in the House, they got five times as much money from that organization as did their fellow congressmen who did not support the dealers.

But the most persuasive evidence and perhaps the most alarming statements are not those being made by Common Cause. They are being made by members of Congress about the influence of PAC contributions and campaign financing on the legislative process. It is one thing for me to complain about the campaign financing system. It is quite another for Senator Thomas Eagleton (Democrat, Missouri) to say that the present campaign financing system "forces members of Congress to go hat in hand, begging for money from special interest groups whose sole purpose for existing is to seek a quid pro quo. The scandal is taking place every day and will continue to do so while the present system is in place." Congressman Tom Downey (Democrat, New York) said, "You can't buy a congressman for $5,000 but you can buy his vote. It's done on a regular basis." Senator Dale Bumpers (Democrat, Arkansas) said, "Money is the number one political problem our country is facing. You can't have a sensible debate about how much is enough for defense when those PACs are contributing so much." Representative Barney Frank (Democrat, Massachusetts) said, "We are the only human beings in the world who are expected to take thousands of dollars from perfect strangers on important matters and not be affected by it." And finally, Senator Robert Dole (Republican, Kansas) said, "When these political action committees give money, they expect something in return other than good government. It is making it much more difficult to legislate. We may reach a point where everybody is buying something with PAC money. We cannot get anything done."

The problem with the congressional races really goes back to what happened and what did not happen in 1974. Congress enacted a system which changed the presidential campaign financing. It is not perfect but it greatly improved what it replaced. We have not totally eliminated the influence of money in presidential elections, but we have fundamentally changed that system by providing enough money for presidential candidates to wage campaigns without going hat in hand to special interest groups. We have not made the same progress in congressional elections.

There is a growing consensus on Capitol Hill that we have fundamental problems with the campaign financing system for congressional races. When Senator Barry Goldwater (Republican, Arizona) testifies before the

Senate Rules Committee and calls the campaign financing system "a crisis of liberty," we are reaching the point where there is agreement that we have a problem. That is not to say we have a consensus about the right solution. Common Cause has been proposing legislation since 1974 that would complete the job started in 1974. We need to extend the public financing system that covered presidential races to cover congressional campaigns as well.

How do you persuade 535 men and women who are winning under the present set of rules to change those rules? It is not easy. But there are increasing numbers of members of Congress who are uncomfortable with the present system. They feel that they are on an endless campaign financing treadmill, particularly in the House of Representatives when they finish one election and need to begin raising money for the next election immediately. There are a number of members of Congress who do not particularly relish the fact that they have to raise $250,000 or $500,000 to run for reelection. A number of members of Congress do not like having the PACs come back to them with some unspoken sense of obligation: "I give you a contribution; therefore, you owe me this one." Ultimately, two things can provoke a change. One is a Watergate-type scandal, which for obvious reasons I hope we can avoid. Second is some sort of public outrage or concern about the way in which congressional campaigns have been financed.

I do not think there is anything under the present system that will cause it to stop. With the past growth trends it appears that more PACs will contribute more money in each congressional election. At some point the system may topple from its own weight, or it may become so firmly entrenched that we will be unable to change it. It is going to involve a lot of citizen work, citizen involvement, and citizen pressure before members of Congress are able to muster the courage to change the system.

It was not an easy battle in 1974. But we were able to change the public financing system and bring about the creation of a Federal Election Commission and limitations on contributions because people were outraged about Watergate. We will only see change in the congressional campaign financing system if we have that same kind of public outrage, that same kind of public concern. I think a consensus for change is building in Congress and I hope such a climate is developing across the country as well. The model for reform is in place. All we need is the political courage to implement it.

4

Television Advertising in the Reagan Campaign

Richard O'Reilly

I was president of Campaign '80, the authorized Reagan advertising agency organized solely for the presidential campaign. My role was the overall supervision of the creation, production, and placement of advertising and promotion. I had a creative media, production, and traffic staff. We worked as a team. I did not personally go out and produce the commercials. We had a production staff for that. I was ultimately responsible for getting the other key campaign officials to approve the advertising and see that it got produced within the budget, as well as the media spending plans. Under the federal laws governing national elections, principals in the campaign have a responsibility for spending the money properly and not exceeding the budget. If we used the money improperly or exceeded the budget, we would be subject to criminal charges, not civil charges. The election spending laws are tough. So I watched the budget very carefully.

Some political media consultants will work for either party. Most work only for Democrats or Republicans. I am not a full-time political consultant. I did not take the presidency of Campaign '80 until I met Reagan and was convinced that I could support him. If I had not thought so then I would not have done it. I could not have worked for Jimmy Carter because I did not want to see Jimmy Carter get elected.

An election campaign in many respects is much like marketing a product. It is a total marketing effort. You must have an overall plan or objective. In this case the objective was to get Reagan elected president. You must have both a good strategy and tactics in the execution of every aspect of the campaign in terms of the candidate going out making visits in the states, having workers in the campaign, and for creating persuasive advertising.

If you are going to communicate effectively you have to both inform and persuade. The difference between how much of it is information and how much is persuasion will vary dramatically depending on the product or service and in politics on the candidate and the political situation.

There are two other important aspects of communication, both rational and emotional. If you were selling a stick of gum you would not need a rational explanation of why people should chew gum. It would be an emotional appeal. When you are dealing with political candidates you need to explain the issues, but there are emotional considerations as well—the candidate. So let us go back and pretend we are at the point at which Reagan had been nominated in July 1980. He is the candidate, and he is going to run against an incumbent. The last elected incumbent to be defeated was Herbert Hoover in 1932. Carter was the first incumbent defeated since then. Therefore, you are faced with the fact that as a nonincumbent you are in an uphill race against any incumbent who has all the advantages of the presidency to get himself reelected. But the polls taken just before the convention showed some very interesting information. They showed Reagan was viewed more favorably than Carter as the next president. He was ahead 47 to 37 in two different major polls. We also knew in the process of planning that there were two important trends to note. Carter's popularity was very volatile. It changed dramatically—by as much as twenty points in a matter of months. So although Carter was down at that point, there was certainly the possibility that he might go way up again. In fact, in March of 1980 he had an approval rating of 53 percent. But now he was down to 22 percent. A lot of things had happened. The hostages were not back. The Russians were not leaving Afghanistan. He refused to send Americans to the Olympics. The economy was bad. Inflation reached a high of 18 percent. Carter had all those things going against him.

What were Reagan's strengths and weaknesses as we put together a plan for the campaign? The first thing we knew was that a very large segment of the population knew almost nothing about him. Forty percent of the people could say, "Yes, I know Ronald Reagan. I know the name. But I don't know anything about him." That takes us back to the point on communication—information and persuasion. We had an important task of providing information to the general electorate. Second, we knew that many independent voters and Republican moderates lacked confidence in Governor Reagan, particularly in foreign affairs. Many thought of him as being trigger happy. We also knew that the number of Republicans in this country, based on registration, constituted less than one in five potential voters and not all of them would vote for Reagan. So while we had a hard core of people, we knew that there was an enormous population out there who had some reservations about Reagan or did not know enough about him. In spite of the fact that he had served two full terms as governor of California, his record in California was not very well known. There was also a general view that he was more conservative than the general electorate. In addition, we knew that there were reservations about how

Reagan would react as president, and this was based on things he had said in the primary campaign. They knew he would cut taxes. They felt strongly that he would increase defense spending. They knew he would be tougher with the Russians, while Carter was perceived as weak in that regard. They assumed he would get tough on welfare.

There are two ways to view these things. On the positive side, he would cut taxes. People like that because it quiets their concern about inflation, but it raises their concern about whether this kind of president would terminate essential services for needy people. Second, while increasing defense spending may make us more secure, it may also start an arms race. Getting tough with the Russians has a positive side of making Americans feel confident again. It has the negative side of the possibility of an armed conflict. Getting tough on welfare might be doing something helpful by making that system more efficient. On the other hand it might show a lack of compassion. We also knew that Carter would try very hard to show that Reagan's ideas for solving problems were very simplistic. And that Reagan was not a very bright man and all those words that rolled so easily off his tongue were not very meaningful. We also knew that Carter would try to dominate the news, that he would certainly try in any way he knew to use political advantage in terms of awarding grants to local communities, and spending millions of dollars in government contracts in the right place at the right time.

Carter had other advantages. Although the hostages were in Iran, the world was largely at peace. There were no American boys fighting or dying anywhere. The Camp David accords had helped normalize relations between Israel and Egypt for the first time in history. He had an energy policy based on the windfall profits tax by which he presumably controlled oil prices. And in human rights he had done some things that had had a positive effect on Jewish emigration from the Soviet Union. So he had many things going for him.

Our research and polling were integrated with our media. We had Richard Wirthlin and Vince Breglio who designed and executed the research and they are extraordinarily competent researchers. In addition to their talent they had a large budget. Good research is not cheap. A lot of people do research and do not spend enough money to get the right answers. We spent $1.5 million on research during the campaign. And we were the only ones to predict the outcome so closely. That is the result of our quality research. The last day of the campaign a Wirthlin poll said we were 11.5 percent ahead. We won by 11.4 percent. Harris predicted a 4 or 5 percent win. Everybody else said it was a toss up. Much research by others was very bad. Good research requires a good design, good execution, and large enough samples to avoid bias in the results. For example, we tested our ads in the field in California. In two small markets in California we ran about three times as much advertising as usual. Our research cost for those two markets was almost $20,000. That was expensive, but we felt it was very important to measure the effectiveness of our advertising.

We created advertising to play up Reagan's strengths and highlight Carter's weaknesses. There was an extraordinary amount of controversy surrounding our advertising. There always is in presidential campaigns. But within the campaign apparatus itself a lot of people said our commercials were boring. Advertising in the Reagan campaign was not spectacular. Neither was it highly creative. We did a lot of research on our ads and I was involved in it. I went to a great many of the research meetings and listened to people talk about the advertising. I did it for a very simple reason. One of the biggest mistakes you can make is get caught up in what is happening at headquarters and not find out what people are thinking and how they are reacting to your messages. I wanted to make sure we knew how people were reacting to this advertising and Carter's advertising as well. And we did learn quite a bit.

In our minds, the target audience, the people we wanted to influence with this advertising, was not the hard-core Republicans or even the moderate Republicans, it was the independent Democrats. All the focus group work we did, emphasized getting people to look at the advertising who had voted for Carter and people who identified themselves as independent Democrats, because we were interested in their points of view and attitudes in terms of our advertising as well as Jimmy Carter's advertising. This was the core group to which most of our advertising was directed.

Many of our ads could be described as "talking head" commercials. They were not too exciting but very straightforward. They proved to be very effective. We were careful with anti-Carter commercials. People saw Jimmy Carter as a well-meaning person and a compassionate man but not as a very good leader. We determined that we would not attack Carter personally and we never did. Reagan, when he talked about the administration, rarely referred to Jimmy Carter. He referred to the administration. That was a basic strategy and a correct one. But many campaign people thought we were dead wrong. They believed a direct attack against Carter would be effective. We did not. When a candidate is not credible, personal attacks may work (I rarely think so, however). The issue with Carter was *competence* and *leadership,* not his personal character and credibility.

We knew we had to attack the Carter presidency in terms of its performance and therefore we did a number of commercials dealing with the issues of inflation and living costs. We knew the principal issues were inflation and unemployment. We were dealing essentially with a domestic economy campaign, not a foreign affairs campaign. I suspect there will be an infinitely greater importance attached to foreign affairs in the 1984 campaign than in 1980.

We knew we would be attacked on the issue of peace and that was why we had Reagan speak out on that issue. As we moved along, our research demonstrated believability, and charm. Carter, in contrast, did not.

In 1972—most people may not remember this—Richard Nixon did not do one single commercial in the entire campaign. His picture was never shown on a commercial talking about his beliefs and issues. Instead, he was shown doing other things. He was shown going off to China. He was shown in Russia. He did not do any voiceovers. The campaign managers decided that he would make his best impression dealing with the kinds of things he was doing as a president, rather than in "talking to the people."

But in 1980 we had a different situation entirely. We had a man toward whom a great many people reacted most positively. Therefore we decided to use him ad infinitum. Thus the "talking heads." We were letting the people see and hear from Reagan on all the issues, speaking in his own manner, with his own special style. Today Reagan is acknowledged as a "great communicator." We knew he was. Thus, about 60 percent of our advertising was simply Reagan talking to the people. It had a powerful favorable effect.

There were some in the campaign who thought we should avoid talking heads because when people saw Reagan talking to them on the screen they might feel he was an actor reading his cue cards. We were concerned about that. There were some in the campaign who said, "If you keep putting Reagan on, the public will think he is just a slick talker." However, while there were some who thought that, it was a relatively small percentage, because Reagan had a conviction about him which caused people to say: "No, he is not just acting. He believes what he says and I really believe him." It was a concern, but we were showing him saying what he really believed.

Let me give you an example. We shot two ads in our first series. One was outdoors with lush trees and an outdoor setting. In the second, Reagan was sitting in a very "Republican" chair, with a very "Republican" plant next to him. It looked slick. In both instances I was more concerned with the nature of the setting rather than with what he was saying. The chair was too shiny. The library looked too plush. We were in that room arguing for five hours about where the table and the chair should be. Did he stand at his desk, did he sit in his chair. It did look slick, but the point of view was that we are putting him in a setting which was cozy and familiar. But it did not come off as a cozy, familiar setting. It was better when you just had a head shot. The outdoors commercial was better. He was also more convincing up close sitting at the edge of the desk because you avoided visual distractions. How the candidate appears best becomes a matter of endless discussion. I would have preferred never to have had him sitting in that chair.

The issue of negative versus positive advertising or negative communication is a very important question. I feel very strongly that one should rarely attack an individual, and we never did attack Carter. Other independent Republican groups did, but we never did in the national campaign. I think a sense of fair play still abounds. The American electorate has a certain resentment about negative spots. If you present a candidate's record objectively, fairly, persuasively, and in a low-key manner as we did, there is a good chance you will get a nod of assent—"Yes, that makes sense." "Yes, that is right." We did that consistency and fairly. Now let us leave what we did for Reagan and let us take a look at Carter.

Several Political Action Committees created negative ads. We did not see the PAC ads in advance because we did not control their budget or their advertising, and if we had, it could have been considered part of our campaign. However, we worked very closely with the senatorial committee and the congressional campaign. The Republican congressional committee advertising was quite effective. They had a budget of $4 million. And they were buying time at the same time we were. We tried to coordinate their effort with ours, which is allowed under the spending laws. We stayed away from them. One PAC campaign was an absolutely vicious anti-Carter campaign. We were upset because we knew they could have an enormous backlash. We had no right to tell them not to run these TV commercials, and no way of directly getting in touch with them. Somehow they got the message through indirect sources that Reagan was upset about the commercials and they never ran. It has been said by the Democrats that the amount of money PACs spend and the volume of that advertising had an enormous effect on the election. It may have had some effect, but I do not think it was considerable.

We researched both Reagan and Carter commercials at the same time. We found that our TV advertising was more appealing, believable, and persuasive than Carter's. This was not the result of just one or two pieces of research. It was the result of considerable research in a variety of cities. The reasons for this were the relatively low appeal of Carter himself; the fact that we tried to be specific and consistent; and the fact that Carter's campaign had no central focus.

They did not research their commercials. They made many small errors that got magnified in the context of a presidential campaign. The electorate is very sophisticated. At focus groups I would sit and listen to the public talk about the advertising and be pleasantly surprised at their knowledge and awareness. For example, there is a commercial about Carter being presidential. They have him walking up the stairs, going through a door and then closing the door behind him. Every time we showed that commercial people laughed because it was obviously staged. Carter did not appear natural and relaxed in many commercials—Reagan did.

Even in retrospect it is hard for me to understand Carter's strategy. I have a feeling that his strategists were saying, "We have to say something anti-Reagan and a way to do that is to say that Reagan is not experienced and is not a man who works hard but that Carter is." The reaction to Carter commercials as a "hard-working" president (tested in a number of different cities) was, "So what! The President is supposed to work hard. Give us something specific to take from these commercials." The commercials were not effective.

Carter produced more commercials, I believe, than have ever been produced by a presidential campaign. They were well produced—the glossiest, the fanciest I have ever seen. They were infinitely more polished and finished than ours. But their "Hollywood production" style turned out to be negative, because many people saw through the glossy presentations. They did not see Carter as a "regular guy"; instead they saw his ads as Hollywood productions, and that did not work in his favor.

In addition to the emphasis on "talking heads," we also placed major emphasis on a series of commercials documenting the effectiveness of the Reagan record as California governor. This was our second major thrust. The Reagan California commercials emphasized his leadership for eight years, his effectiveness in improving the overall economy in California, his social programs, his defeat of an incumbent (Pat Brown) in his first election as the underdog, and his huge victory in the second campaign. We found these commercials to be very effective in demonstrating on-the-line experience, and helped fill in for people much of what they did know about him. They knew the Reagan fame, he told them in the "talking head" commercials his vision of America, and now they knew of his accomplishments in California. They melded well together.

Carter's people tried to mute the effect of this powerful documentary campaign. They spent their dollars in a direct personal attack on Reagan's California record and it did not work. They did street interviews in California with people who said, "Reagan did not do a good job in California." We were delighted with those Carter commercials because they took away any focus from Carter's advertising campaign. And it proved to us what we already knew—that Carter's research showed our California advertising was effective, and they felt they had to respond.

After the campaign, Jerry Rafshoon, Carter's campaign manager, stated in a public forum where I was present that the Carter anti-Reagan California advertising had been effective because their research showed it reduced Reagan's lead in California. Yet Reagan won California by an enormous margin. What they did was hurt themselves by being negative instead of positive about their own candidate's accomplishments.

One of the characteristics of the Carter campaign was a lack of focus— it was chasing our campaign instead. It was heavily weighted toward being anti-Reagan, and that is not the way for an incumbent president to be persuasive and win votes. There were two other campaign elements. We had a lot of pressure from within the campaign to run anti-Carter advertising, directly attacking the president. But we did not want to do that because we believed it was wrong. Nevertheless we were pressed into it; so we did something that to my knowledge had never been done before in the middle of a political campaign. We went into test markets for two weeks and ran it in two of these test markets, and then took two other matched markets where we ran positive Reagan advertising. The research proved that the positive commercials were more effective than those attacking the president. That was the way we answered the question. To my knowledge, no one has ever test-marketed their advertising in the middle of a campaign. This helped quiet our critics and kept our campaign on the right track.

We did have one anti-Carter commercial that ran in a number of markets. It was footage of Ted Kennedy strongly attacking Carter and his poor record during the primary, the key line of which was "no more Jimmy Carter." It was effective and it upset the Carter campaign. This was very close to the election. His campaign officials called stations and told them to take it off the air. There were certain implied threats that if stations did not comply they might have a problem at license renewal time. They were told that "maybe they had better not run these commercials because they might not get very favorable treatment in Washington." It did not surprise us that Carter did not want that Kennedy commercial on the air: We were not attacking President Carter; it was his own "friend" Kennedy. By that time Kennedy had done two testimonial spots supporting Carter, but they were lukewarm in effect as compared to the Kennedy attack.

When a president chases a challenger he is making a fundamental error. If I had been in charge of Carter's campaign I would have dealt with two things: strategy and execution. I have already commented on their execution in critical terms. Their campaign had no focus, no central theme. Instead they often chased our advertising. They had a great opportunity to say something like, "Look, these are hard times. We've had a major oil crisis. We've seen the Russians be more aggressive than they'd been since World War II. We had to go through inflation. We had to go through unemployment, because we have to make the future secure for our children." They could have used this theme very effectively. Second, I would have used Carter less than they did in advertising. I would have used the issues. I do not know exactly how because I have not gone through the executional phases of it, but I would have worked very hard to make the point that this was not the beginning of the end but the end of the beginning. And I would have dealt with it in terms of the *future,* with a major emphasis on the promise of a bright future—a positive attitude and theme.

Jerry Rafshoon, Carter's media adviser, stated after the election that he had not wanted his candidate to be apologetic. There is a difference between apologizing and explaining a situation rationally and in terms of how it can be made better in the future. I am not suggesting that he should have gotten up and said, "I did this wrong. I did that wrong." Although that can work at times. No, I think it had to be the president speaking out in very strong terms: "This is the kind of situation we face. This is the best we can do at this time. We can do better in the future because we have got that behind us." He never said that. Furthermore, it is very hard to take someone like Jimmy Carter and make him seem forceful when he is not. If I had been involved with him I would have tried to give him a kind of posture in a commercial that would have made him seem stronger in the leadership area. It would not have been easy, but certainly worth trying, because he always seemed "sort of down." It was as if he had the malaise he spoke about. And it did not have to be that way. You cannot change a person's fundamental character, but you can certainly improve the way they present themselves, and they missed the opportunity.

We did a very thorough job of research from beginning to end. The advertising, like all campaign elements, followed a specific plan. We stuck with that plan all the way through because we believed our strategy was right. We kept checking and rechecking. We did not run a negative campaign. We felt that a positive campaign would win. We were helped enormously by the lack of a strong, direct Carter strategy. While the international situation and the economy were difficult and the hostages were still in Iran, Carter could still have made a much better race of it with better ads.

5

Radio Advertising in Campaigns

Tony Schwartz

I would like to cover two things. First, political communication and how it functions. Second, the use of media for social purposes, with its current growth and inordinate potential. Let me begin with the political area.

Many people in various fields approach their work in what I call "obsoletely" the right way. People in politics will talk of "packaging the candidate." Yet if you look at the process carefully, that does not seem to be the case. When my six-year-old son left New York for a Massachusetts visit he commented, "When I went to Massachusetts in July I saw the same thing, the same programs on at the same time that I see them in New York. The same programs are on in a lot of places." He said he saw the same programs in Massachusetts at the same time we saw them in New York, and then he observed that the same programs were in many places. This really says that we are not packaging the candidate but the voter. The same media is North, South, East, and West, and in the apartments above and below. We surround the voter.

You often hear people say that television is a visual medium. One part of it is visual but in reality it is an accoustically structured medium. It is the first time that the eye is used by the brain as the ear has been always used by the brain. In sound a word never exists. If I say the word *exists,* by the time I get to the end—the *s*—the *exist* is gone. We hear by the process of registering the current milli-second fleeting vibration, recalling the previous vibration, and expecting the future one. I can show you how we expect parts of sentences. If I say five words you will think of the sixth at electric speed. I will give you five words and you give me the first word that comes to your mind. My words are: "for the rest of your"—you probably inserted "life." This is a model of what we are doing in the communication process.

The average advertising person thinks of recall. They deal with learned recall almost as a teacher who gives a test to see what you remember of what you have been taught. The average advertising firm tries to measure learned recall, what people remember after hearing and seeing a commercial. I have no interest in that. I am interested in evoked recall, which functions a thousand times faster.

We are dealing with evoked recall, and that is an inner trip. We do not do research after we have produced commercials. We research before, or I use the term "presearch" to find out what is in peoples' minds that we can relate to and structure and restructure.

Let me show you how people take an inner trip. You go into you mind for associations to the things you hear. I am going to take an ad and change its last word. I am going to play two versions of the same ad with the two different endings. I am going to play it for one person and you are going to see how the content of that ad changes in relation to her experience with the last word. She is taking an inner trip and what she hears is associated with her experiences with that last word. She brings that meaning to the commercial. [Statement:] "You can learn about prostitution in New York in a probing series of articles starting Monday in the *New York Post.*" [Girl commenting on ad says:] "I suppose that would be a sensationalist, scandalous sort of pseudodocumentary. My guess is that it would just be something that would exploit prostitution in the papers." [Ad again:] "You can learn about prostitution in New York in a probing series of articles starting Monday in the *New York Times.*" [Girl commenting again:] "I feel that would be more of a sociological document, something I could rely on as being informative and filled with data." The contents of that spot is the sum of what she hears of the stimuli and stored information in her mind. Marshall McLuhan states: "One of the major changes that has come into the world with the electronic environment is that the audience becomes a work force instead of being targeted for campaigns."

I can show you how the audience functions as a work force in a political campaign. I did commercials during the last two months of the first Carter campaign in 1976. Carter and Ford were closer to each other in the polls than Mondale and Dole. Mondale was way in front of Dole as a possible vice-presidential choice. I wanted to show how to take these facts or feelings people had and make them work for Carter. Here is how I did it. "Have you thought about the vice-presidential candidate? What do you think of Mondale? What do you think of Dole? What kind of men are they? When you know that four out of the last six vice-presidents have wound up being presidents, who would you want to see a heartbeat away from the presidency?" You should only say, "What do you think of Mondale?" and "What do you think of Dole?" when you know what people think of them and how they will answer.

Here is one ad I did in Michigan for Bob Carr when he was running against Charles Chamberlain. If you examined the research and asked voters to name anything that Chamberlain had done in twelve years of office, only one person in a hundred could think of anything. When I saw that, I thought of this commercial: "You know there are two men running for Congress in the 6th district—Bob Carr and Charles Chamberlain. Mr. Chamberlain has been in Congress for over twelve years. Let me read you a list of the things he has accomplished. [Long silence.] Did I leave anything out? You see, that's exactly why this is paid for by a growing number of Republicans and Democrats who want Robert Carr elected to Congress."

I have been called "a master of negative commercials." That comment shows little recognition of the atmosphere surrounding the political process. Is it negative in a prize fight for someone to get involved in a clean fight? Politics is a fight. You have candidates spending thousands, to hundreds of thousands, to millions of dollars to defeat the other candidate. The public's reaction is very similar to what takes place in a prize fight. No one likes a dirty fighter. And no one likes a nonfighter. They boo a dirty fighter and they will boo a fighter who is just moving around or not doing anything. They will applaud a good, hard, clean fight. The same is true in politics. You also have to recognize the fact that with two candidates people can vote four ways. They can vote for or against either candidate. And if there are things that are negative in relation to one candidate, those negatives can make people vote for the other candidate if you expose those things. For instance when McGovern ran for president his ads did not attack Nixon but tried to show McGovern's good points. He would have had a better chance of getting more votes using Nixon's weaknesses than his own assets.

You also hear people talk about the image of a candidate. Image is a passé concept. In today's world it is much more workable to exchange the word *attitude* for *image*. The image of any candidate, product, or company is the sum of people's attitudes toward it. We can study where attitudes come from and why people have them and we can work with that. But when you say "image" the only thing we can do with a wrong image is try to retouch it. That does not work as well as dealing with attitudes.

People say, "How do you deal with the clutter question at election time?" There are so many commercials on the air for so many politicians, and then there is all the product advertising. The word *clutter* is very much like the words *noise* and *weed*. A weed is a plant growing in the wrong place. Noise is unwanted sound. The noisiest party is the one on your floor that you are not invited to. Exchange the word *noise* for *sound* and you will see the meaning. There is "noise" from a piano and "sound" from a piano, or the "sound" of children versus the "noise" of children. There are editorial words. "Clutter" is something that you are not interested in. You will never find any advertiser who says that his commercial is clutter. It is always another commercial or the program, but it is not his commercial.

There are a lot of commercials on, and the average person is not interested in most of them so he calls it clutter. Since we do not have ear lids—what determines what we hear? It is a very simple thing. We hear what interests us. Again this sets up the reason for presearch. Presearch allows you to find what people are concerned with. You can also presearch the media habits of people and find out what stations they listen to at what time. You can cross-index your polling on your computer print-out to find the percentage of people feeling a certain way about something and the percentage of those listening to certain stations. Say a person feels this way about the phone company: "I hate the phone company!! I'm helpless. No matter what happens I've got to go along with them or they could take my phone away from me and I don't want to lose my telephone!" If people who feel that way have their radios on while there is a commercial that starts out like this, you know they are going to *hear* it: "Tell me something. Only tell me the truth. Have you ever felt like getting even with the phone company? Fooling them? That's not easy; not for one person. But when the phone company comes along with a proposed 26 percent rate increase you really feel like doing something, right? Well one man did. A suit was filed and argued by a congressman from New York." You know that will interest those people with such feelings. That is a way of cutting through clutter. When I was trying to get a mortgage for my home, I *heard* many mortgage commercials. But the day I got my mortgage "they stopped running them." It is really interest that determines what you hear.

Most people think that candidates have to be in commercials and give answer to people's problems. But strangely it does not work that way. People tend to identify with and understand things they have experienced before. One thing that few people have experienced is the answers to their problems. So the candidate who can make people believe that he understands how they feel about things is the one who will most likely get them to identify with him. If people feel he is qualified for the office they can say, "Gee, he feels the way I do about it. He'll do the right thing." So very often rather than giving the answer to a problem, I try to convey how deeply the candidate feels about it. Many times you do it directly with the candidate speaking about the problem. I do a lot of those kinds of commercials. But here is an unusual one. When I was doing the first successful race for Jay Rockefeller in West Virginia, his research showed that the major concerns of people were (1) jobs and the economy, (2) high utility rates, and (3) bad roads. Rather than have Jay Rockefeller give his answer to what he would do about the roads, I designed a commercial which brought him up 33 points after running it for a week. "Did you ever notice those ads on TV for tires or shock absorbers? You know, where they have cars going over rocky roads in Colorado or over the Mohave desert to show how strong the tires are? Well, have you noticed that they never come to West Virginia? Because our roads are so bad no tires could hold up for long. By the way, this is not a commercial for tires. It is a commercial for better roads in West Virginia. We need them! Paid for by West Virginians for Rockefeller." When I say it brought him up 33 points, it brought him up 33 points on that concern. You see how the process works.

Some say I can get the mayor to speak for me, or I can get the governor to do a testimonial commercial, or I can get another congressman to do a commercial for me. I always say, "I'm not necessarily interested in who they are but in how well they communicate electronically." Often the person who may be a meaningful person in name will come on the air and read his statement mechanically. I would rather have someone who conveys emotion. An important part of the content of the electronic media is the emotion involved. It is a much more emotional medium than print. Here is a good example. This woman knew the candidate very well and you could tell from listening to her. The voters did not know her. But it did not seem to matter as much as feeling that she really knew the candidate and was speaking from her heart about him. [Announcer and woman speaking:] "Jim Speinhower knows people. When a man is running for governor it is good to know what people who know him think about him. 'I would crawl on my hands and knees from here to Jefferson City if I thought that it would help Jim Speinhower to be governor and I'm a woman 75 years old.' And that's why this was paid for by Missourians for Speinhower, Walt Wilson, treasurer. 'And Jim, if you're listening to me, wherever you are, bless your heart.'" That comes across in a more potent way than someone just mechanically reading a spot.

Another important thing is to try to use concepts people can relate to. Certain commercials almost become the stars of a campaign. The one you heard with this woman was an important one. This one was a very important one in the race for controller for the city of New York. One day the controller was telling me something he had been doing. It impressed me and I asked, "Did you initiate this?" He said, "No, every controller has been doing it." But no one ever communicated it. Here is the commercial I did with that fact: "What do you do with your money at night before you go to sleep? Well, like most of us you probably leave your wallet or purse on your dresser or the night table. But that's not what our city controller, Harrison J. Golden, does with the city's money. Before he leaves the controller's office at night he invests every dollar that lies around to earn money for the city, and last year that program of investing the city's cash overnight before it's used to pay bills produced more than $110 million in additional revenues for New York City. And now Mayor Koch has announced that we can finally afford to hire 2,300 more police. Do you think there's any connection between Mayor Koch's announcement that we are going to hire 2,300 more police and controller Golden's nightly investment program? *We* do. That is why this is paid for by New Yorkers who want a capable controller, Harrison J. Golden."

One very important fact about social control in societies is that in primitive cultures one of the most effective means of social control was shame. Here is anthropologist Edmund Carpenter speaking of the role of shame in primitive society: "In primitive culture shame is the primary means of social control. The power of public opinion is used to force a means of behavior. They don't have a means for prisons or punishment. They can't spare people like that, so they will turn the power of the community and simply direct it, focus it, on the person, or it can go to ritual condemnation, in which the man is publicly condemned. In some well-documented cases we know that individuals actually die as a result of this. The human mind cannot survive the dissolution of the social personality. In other cases you will find a strong individual, or perhaps a brave one will simply flee. But then he is gone and so there is no evidence left of anyone who has ever survived this condemnation.

You can use shame in political commercials. For instance, here is a commercial I did in Minnesota: "Did you ever have an uncle who took up golf thirty years ago and still plays just as badly as the first year he picked up a golf club? Your congressmen Don Fraser wants you to think he's had sixteen years' experience in Washington. Well, he *has* been in Washington for sixteen years, but he's still playing the game just like your uncle, like the first year he went to Congress. He's still voting year after year for more government not less, more expenditures not less, the same old policies, same old decisions. You see, he still hasn't caught on to the fact that times have changed. They call for new decisions, new policies. Don Fraser hasn't had sixteen years' experience. He's had one year's experience and he has repeated it fifteen times. Bob Short knows that what worked sixteen years ago won't work today, and that is why this message was paid for and authorized by the Bob Short for Senate Committee."

When people speak of a negative commercial they generally think of the commercial I did for Lyndon Johnson against Barry Goldwater. I would like to go into this because I think it relates to many things that are relevant today. Let me show you what I mean. First let us listen to the soundtrack from the Daisy commercial I did for President Johnson in 1964: "[Birds chirping, little girl speaking:] One, 2, 3, 4, 5, 6, 7, 8, 9, 12, 13, 16, 18, 10! [Announcer:] Ten, 9, 8, 7, 6, 5, 4, 3, 2, 1, 0 blast off! [Blast sound, then Johnson's voice:] These are the stakes: To make a world in which all of God's children can live, or to go into the dark. We must either love each other or we must die." I think that is one of the most moral statements ever made, and I am serious about that. Let me show you. Here is the statement by President Johnson: "These are the stakes: To make a world in which all of God's children can live, or to go into the dark. We must either love each other or we must die." And here is the statement of the pope on the same subject: "The life of humanity today is seriously in danger by the arms race. It must be our solemn wish for the children of all nations on earth to make such catastrophes impossible." They are both saying the same thing, i.e., with the horror of atomic nuclear weapons we have to learn to love each other or die. The people of the earth have to learn to get along or they will destroy everything and everybody. I think that is a very moral statement in today's world. What made it negative was that it was almost like a Rorschach pattern. We saw the same thing in the movie *The Day After,* which was a conservative illustration of the aftereffects of atomic warfare on our population. The Reverend Jerry Falwell and others who take his position see this film as outright propaganda against the installation of atomic missiles in Europe for possible use against the Soviet Union. They claim that the film carries the message that deterrence has failed. On the other side you find groups who favor a freeze on the production of atomic weapons and who feel that this film favors their cause. *The Day After* was a national Rorschach test. The political situation of the day determines how people relate to it and judge it. That is what happened with the Daisy commercial and this is what happened with *The Day After.*

A few years after the Goldwater campaign I met Clifford White, who was one of the top Republican political consultants and campaign managers. He told me his reaction to the Daisy spot and you will notice he says "anything that hurts you call foul or dirty." And here is his comment: "The immediate kind of political reaction you have against anything that hurts is that it is illegal, unethical, and improper, but clearly this was an impactive commercial. It was the most interesting experience because I would have very intelligent people say, 'Cliff, we just cannot use atomic weapons,' and I would then say to them, 'Well, you know what Goldwater said.' 'Yeah, he said he was going to use the atomic bomb.' I said, 'No, he didn't say he was going to use the atomic bomb. He said that one of the weapons we could use in the Vietnam war was a tactical nuclear weapon for defoliating the forest. A tactical nuclear weapon is like a small bomb, not a big one—small. Its purpose is to defoliate, to take the leaves off.' All the while I am going through this exclamation, the person is standing there nodding his head. 'Yeah, but we can't drop the bomb, Cliff!' It was so totally emotional."

It was so totally emotional and yet the average citizen was more right than Barry Goldwater was. Barry Goldwater spoke for the use of tactical atomic weapons. He said one of the weapons we could use were tactical nuclear weapons to defoliate the jungles of Vietnam. I recently met Admiral Gayler who was the commander-in-chief of the Pacific forces and was involved with the use of atomic weapons on Japan. He has been involved with targeting all our country's nuclear weapons. I asked him whether there was any such thing as a bomb that could defoliate the jungle and leave people unhurt and here is his answer: "The notion that you would use tactical nuclear weapons or any other kind of nuclear weapons to defoliate without hurting people is quite literally absurd. Anyone who knows anything about the weapons' effects, the terrible thermal pulse, the burst of gamma radiation, the blast, and all the rest of those things, to believe that you could strip the leaves off trees and not hurt people underneath them is absurd."

This 1964 commercial was really a Rorschach pattern, because I have seen articles that say, "The commercial asks firmly, who's finger do you want on the trigger?" The commercial never mentioned Goldwater but it was played at a time when people were asking themselves, "Whose finger do *I* want on the trigger?" The commercial prompted them to ask that question against the background of what was out in the public. Johnson spoke against the use of atomic weapons and Goldwater spoke *for* them. And that is why Goldwater's campaign and the people reacted the way they did.

Shame can function very meaningfully in commercials. One day I went to pick up my wife at the dentist. While I was waiting in the car outside the dentist's brownstone I saw a man allow his dog to "go" right in front of the doorway. I got out of the car and said, "Excuse me sir, did you ever think that some parents might step in that and then walk on the rug and the baby would play on the rug?" He looked at me and said, "Everybody does it." So I got back in the car and while I continued waiting I thought, "If I knew where that man listens to the radio, what could I do to make him change his behavior?" So I wrote this spot and later had a meeting with E.G. Marshall on a commercial I was working on for him. I asked him if he would read this spot for me and here it is: "Let me ask you something. Have you ever seen someone allow his dog to "go" on the sidewalk, right in front of the doorway? Maybe *your* doorway? Did it make you angry? Well, don't get angry at the poor soul; feel sorry for him. He is just a person who is unable to train his dog. He is just incapable of it. In fact, after he has had his dog for a short time—do you know what happens? The dog trains *him*. So the next time you see a person like that out on the street, take a good look at him, and while you are looking feel sorry for him, because you know he just can't help himself even though he might like to. Some people are strong enough and smart enough to train their dogs to take a few steps off the sidewalk; other people aren't. It makes you wonder, doesn't it, whether the master is at the top of the leash or the bottom of the leash." So the process of shame can work very well. Media can do many wonderful things in our society and can be used for social causes. For instance, my office is right across the street from John Jay College of Criminal Justice. In 1976, the Board of Higher Education voted fourteen colleges in New York City out of existence. It just decided to close down fourteen colleges or combine them with other schools. I went across the street to the college and saw the vice-president there and I said, "Would you like to save your school?" And he said, "Yes." I said, "Okay, we are now a committee to save your school," and we shook hands. I said, "You get some money and I'll do some media." The first thing I did was call in a researcher to do some polling on how people valued the services of the city. Since this college trained police and firefighters I thought I would like to know how they valued this school. Well, people put police protection first, fire second, higher education third, and sanitation fourth. This college combined the first three, so I used it in this way and here is one of the commercials: "Did you ever wish there were some way to check on whether politicians keep their promises? In their last campaign both Mayor Beam and Governor Carey promised to fight crime. That was the promise. And today we can check that promise in a very real way. The Board of Higher Education is planning to close John Jay College of Criminal Justice, the best crime-fighting school in the country and the school that trains over 4,000 of the policemen we still have left. Will Mayor Beam and Governor Carey speak to the members of the Board of Higher Education, which they appointed, and ask them to save John Jay, or will the governor and the mayor forget about their promise to the public about crime and let John Jay die? Paid for by concerned citizens who support John Jay College of Criminal Justice."

Well within an hour of the running of that commercial the deputy mayor was in my office telling me that the mayor had said that the commercial must be taken off the air. I replied that only he could by saving the school. The next day the governor had a representative in my office saying that the governor wanted it taken off the air. I told him the same thing—that only the governor could by saving the school. Well, they both said they had nothing to do with it, but I knew all the members of the Board of Higher Education were appointed by the governor and the mayor, so I did not take the commercial off. Two days later I got a call from Chancellor Kibby of the Board of Higher Education who said he would like to come and see me. He came over and said that if we took the commercial off the air, they would save the school. And they did save the school. I said I would take it off after it was finally saved. It was the only one of the fourteen schools that was not combined or killed. That is how the process system works for social causes.

A week before the 1980 Democratic Convention in New York the city was negotiating the contract of the police, firemen, prison guards, housing police, and transit police. I asked the head of the police union whether he thought there was going to be a strike. He said, "Yes." I asked why. He said, "Because the mayor doesn't want to settle." So I said, "Do you want a strike?" He said "No, not at all." So I said, "Okay, let me show you how we can prevent a strike." I prepared three commercials. I only had to run one. Here is the one I ran: "Mayor Koch, remember the great job the city police did during the transit strike? When our city was in deep financial trouble and banks refused to buy our bonds, remember how the uniformed officers bought those bonds with their pension fund money? Remember the 100 uniformed officers who died in the last five years in performance of their duties? Mayor Koch, over the last five years workers in outside industry received an average wage increase of 50 percent. The uniformed services got only 8 percent. We understood that the city was in trouble and we bit the bullet. But we just can't do it anymore. Most of us have to take a second job. Our wives have to work so we can make ends meet. We can't pay our bills, Mr. Mayor. It is as simple as that. We are the people the city calls on when it is in trouble. Now we are calling on you because *we* are in trouble. We get the impression that you want us to strike and we don't deserve that treatment. If we are wrong, prove it by putting a decent and reasonable proposal on the negotiating table. Paid for by the Coalition of Uniformed Services."

Here is the head of the police union telling me what happened after they ran the commercial: "The immediate response when it had hit the air was that we got signals from the mayor's office that they wanted those commercials removed as quickly as possible and that they wanted to sit down and talk about a settlement. So it paid off immediately. He came personally to the negotiations. The reaction was immediate."

Television that night highlighted that Mayor Koch, after spending about ten minutes with the negotiators, told reporters the reason for his visit: "I come to express my appreciation to the Uniformed Services for their rough work and for the sacrifices they have made since the fiscal crisis." He was actually answering our commercial.

In today's world the whole process of social change is itself changing. Years ago the worker's weapon was the strike. We went through a national telephone strike. The workers went out. They lost their pay and we were not deprived of service one moment. Maybe we had to wait a little longer for "information," but we had the ability to use our phones all the time. We had an electrical Con-Edison strike here in New York and the same thing happened. There was not a moment when we did not have electricity. What does this mean? It means that these workers instead of going out on strike might have taken a fraction of their pay and put it into a communications fund. They then could have used the media if the issues that the public could identify with were on their side.

6
Press Conferences in Campaigns

Jerry terHorst

The press conference is a unique institution in the history of American politics and it is also a unique institution in all countries that respect freedom of the press. The first presidential press conference is generally assumed to have begun with Grover Cleveland. He was the first president to meet occasionally with a group of reporters rather than meet with individuals. And press conferences have endured.

I prefer to credit Thomas Jefferson with holding the very first presidential press conference. It seems that Jefferson, early in the morning, liked to wander down from the White House to a little stream that fed into the Potomac River called Iver Creek. In those days it was customary to go bathing in the altogether. So one particular morning after bathing, he began to climb out of the water and he discovered two young ladies sitting on his clothing—whereupon he went back into the water. One of the ladies was a reporter for a paper run by one of Jefferson's major rivals, Alexander Hamilton, and the other was her friend. She did not want to confront the president alone. So they sat on his clothes until he answered a couple of questions, and then they left. After a discreet moment or two, so the story goes, Jefferson climbed out of the water, dressed, and went back to the White House.

The term "press conference" is self-defining. They occur in politics, business, and academia whenever two factors are present. First, a principal who thinks that he or she has something important to relay to the news media, and second, a number of media persons, at least two or three, who have been persuaded that their attendance will be rewarded with news fit to print or broadcast. The individual or organization that holds a press conference will not succeed in accomplishing their purpose unless they have information worthy of calling a press conference. The calling of a press conference can be overdone. The horror officials live with is, "What if I call a press conference and nobody comes?" One has to be very careful when one decides. Second, the news media has the right to expect that something will be said in the course of the news conference that justifies their presence.

75

If a Soviet official called a news conference he could very well have representatives there. Even if he said nothing more than "hello" they would dutifully report it exactly as he wished it reported. If an American president held a news conference, it is right to assume that the Associated Press, United Press International, and ABC, NBC, CBS, and the *New York Times* would attend. But unlike the Soviets, he cannot command coverage of whatever he said nor can he decree that the news media report only what he wants them to report. That is one of the nice things about American-style politics and American-style press conferences. It is the key to the role that press conferences play in the coverage and conduct of a political campaign.

A press conference plays an important role in a political campaign, but only if the news media are there and agree that what transpires is important for the public to know. The decision to hold a news conference may be up to the candidate or his top advisors, but the judgment of whether holding it was useful is totally up to the media. In other words the press are the jury and the judge.

Given this arrangement, one may readily ask why political candidates ever risk holding news conferences. Why not just make speeches to your supporters, buy time on radio and television, buy advertising space in the newspaper, shake hands in a shopping center, or allow individual interviews with members of the press? Why put yourself at the mercy of group media? Well, they can not escape being at the mercy of the media if they wish to build upon whatever they say directly to the public or to an individual journalist.

In journalism it is hard nowadays to come up with a big scoop or an exclusive. Nothing is worse than being exclusive too long. If your journalistic colleagues do not pick up your exclusive and repeat it, you can conclude that your scoop is going nowhere. The same is true among politicians. Nothing is more deflating than to say something you think is important to a journalist and then have that important something disappear into a void because the journalist missed that point or did not cover it the way you had hoped.

Let me give you a couple of examples. In 1980, when I was covering the Bush campaign in New England, George Bush was constantly asked about Reagan's economic proposal, but Bush could not quite get a handle on how to disparage it. He wanted to, felt it was necessary, but could not quite get it all together. Well, one night in a motel in Manchester, New Hampshire, his press secretary came up with the idea that Reagan economics was voodoo economics because there was not much to it, just a lot of smoke and symbolism, all things related to voodoo. Bush liked that. They tried it out on a reporter for the *New York Times* but the reporter did not even take a note. So they launched the "voodoo economics" at a news conference the next day, and, lo and behold, the networks picked it up, the national press picked it up, the wire service picked it up. To this day George Bush is still trying to live down his press-conference remark about voodoo economics. That is one tangible example of what can happen at a news conference if it is properly programmed and gets to the right number of people. There is a lot of pack journalism going on. It had failed to make the *New York Times* in an exclusive the day before, but the *New York Times* did pick it up after it came out in the news conference.

In 1984, Gary Hart beat Walter Mondale in New Hampshire. The next morning, Mondale held a very significant news conference after spending a good deal of the night with his key staff people. He made the decision that he would have to go out and fight one-on-one with Gary Hart in order to get back in the race. He announced that decision at his press conference the following morning.

In each example, news was made. The press conference served its dual purpose. It rewarded the person who held the news conference and it rewarded the press for attending, and probably rewarded the public. I will also give you an example of a news conference that failed miserably. In 1964 at Knott's Berry Farm Barry Goldwater decided to hold a news conference in the amphitheater where he was going to give a speech. The people were filing in, so the news conference became a prespeech. Goldwater put a couple of new opening paragraphs up front, hoping to entice some local reporter to write about it. But the national press had heard it many times and could almost repeat it word for word. There was a huge crowd; many older women were standing beside the press area and they were diehard Goldwater supporters. When they saw the national reporters not taking notes, they would nudge us saying, "Take that down!" Then Barry Goldwater would let fly with another classic Goldwaterism and again some other person would look askance at us brash young reporters and say, "Take that down!" After the speech, we were talking to Carl Hess, Goldwater's press secretary, when a young man came running out and said excitedly to Mr. Hess, "I have to talk to you, sir!" Hess replied, "Well, just a minute, let me finish talking with these reporters and I'll be with you." The young man said, "No! I have to talk to you right now. It's about what's happening inside the arena." Hess asked, "All right, what's the problem?" And he said, "There are reporters in there taking down everything Barry Goldwater is saying!"

So on the one hand we had the little old ladies saying "Take that down," and on the other there was this chap who was so sure that Goldwater was speaking only to the faithful that he was afraid the word was going to leak to the public. Often a campaign press conference is handled this way: A member of the candidate's staff will call up and say, "We're going to have a press conference tomorrow at 10:00 in such and such a room at the hotel." If you are on the road you say, "Oh gee, that's tough because we are going to be watching another program that's going to come on at 10:00." And they say, "Oh, well, we didn't know that was going to be on at the same time. We'll arrange something else and get back to you."

So the media is not just being invited to the press conference, the press conference is being arranged to suit the media. This is an important distinction. It happens all the time. Politicians today do not call press conferences and expect coverage. They now look to see if there is a window of opportunity in the electronic spectrum where they can get their story out without competing with a speech by somebody else, a space shot or an important athletic event. Have you heard of a press conference on a Saturday afternoon in the middle of a football game? Never! You will not have them on Sunday mornings, either. Press conferences since the advent of television are arranged to reach the media at a time when they think the media needs something. It is no longer a case of whether television observes the event, it is whether television sometimes creates the event—because candidates feel they must cater to television. If they held the Boston Tea Party now, it would have to be done in prime time.

We in the media constantly get criticism about concentrating on the bad news—writing stories about how old Gary Hart is, whether his name was changed, and whether he has something to say. It boils down to whether the press, in its right to be free, has to be irresponsible—or whether a free press also has the duty to be responsible in its coverage.

The concept is both philosophical and practical. If you look at the first amendment, nothing in it says that a free press has to be a responsible press. That is because the founding fathers in their wisdom knew that the moment someone began to set up the precise rules of freedom you would end up limiting freedom. Who would define what was responsible or irresponsible? So free speech and its technical extension—a free press—may give man a full opportunity to air his ideas whether they are popular or not.

The free press has a responsibility to be free of tangling relationships with the government or with any other persuasive force in society, including business. A free press needs to be independent. It ought to be free to support or criticize the government. The responsibility of the press at a news conference was best put by Walter Lippmann years ago when he said that the news media had the duty to present a picture of reality on which men can act. He was not altogether sure that it could be done, however. Reality implies an awareness of truth, and news and truth are not necessarily the same thing. The function of news merely signals an event. The function of truth is to bring to life hidden facts, to set them into relationships to each other so that men may see this reality. There are times, hopefully most of the time, when news is true. That is not always the case, even when those who convey it think it is.

When I was press secretary to President Ford, I conveyed news on one occasion that I discovered later was not the whole truth. It concerned the Nixon pardon. Based on information given to me by the presidential aide then in charge, I told an inquiring reporter that the presence of a White House lawyer at San Clemente—where former president Nixon had been living after his departure from the White House—was merely to work out a legal arrangement for the disposition of the Nixon tapes and papers that were still in government custody. Two days later I informed the same reporter that my news to him had been incomplete, that one of the hidden facts was that this White House lawyer was also working out the technicalities of a pardon for the former president. Well, my correction was not likely to help the reporter, because that was also the day President Ford publicly announced the Nixon pardon.

My resignation on that day did not occur because I had been misled. I believed, in time, that I could educate my fellow Ford aides to accept the notion that when a press secretary is not fully informed, he ends up misinforming the public. As a reporter, I learned long ago that if I were to quit a job simply because someone had not told me the truth I would be looking for work every week. No, I resigned because my conscience simply could not accept the pardon. It interfered with my concept of equal justice under law. I felt that Mr. Nixon was not "more equal" than others involved in Watergate.

In resigning I made some news, although that was not my intent. I had hoped to slip away quietly and let the assistant press secretary take over. My resignation also tells us something about news. The message is that news by nature tends to be negative. It tends to be a break with prevailing public expectations. That is what makes it so difficult for us, in America, when things get hot and heavy and our hearts and emotions are torn in one direction or another. This is especially true in campaign years.

A news conference during a campaign is probably the most important tool a candidate has on the road to signal a change or a new departure from what happened yesterday in his campaign. But often I have discovered, after a few more days on the road, that nothing had really changed at all. All that happened was that the candidate got a story at a time when he figured the press was hungry for one. So while we imparted news, we had not imparted much wisdom or light—and probably not very much truth either.

President Reagan has made some experiments with changing the format of his news conferences—e.g., lotteries, and not jumping up and yelling. They used to be messy to watch: all those journalists jumping up and down, waving their hands, and shouting for the president. It did not look very respectful. I never did like the business of jumping up and down—partly because I am short and I always got stuck behind people like Clark Mollenhoff who is 6 feet 5 and weighs 300 pounds! While I did not always get questions in, I still do not think we should mess with the formats. During a Nixon press conference I was trying hard to ask a question of the president. I was in the second row, had a good seat, but did not get recognized. I finished writing my story, hurried home, and took my daughter out to do some shopping. The phone rang at home and my wife picked it up. A voice said, "It's the White House calling for Jerry terHorst." My wife said, "He's not here right now. I'll have him call." The operator said, "The president will talk to you." So the next thing Richard Nixon is talking to my wife! He said, "I just wanted to tell Jerry that the next time he asks a question when I point in his direction he should make sure some other clown doesn't stand up first."

Lotteries do not work very well. If the purpose of a news conference is to produce the best questions on the most serious subject of the moment, a lottery is the least likely way to catch those kinds of questions from the reporters who may know most about those issues. If you want to go that far—why not just assign questions? Have the press secretary say, "The president today would like to be asked about this, this, and this; please do not ask him about this, that, and the other.

Seating at presidential press conferences is handled by the White House. They have the final say on where people sit. The favored seats are given to those who cover the White House day in and day out, which is fair enough. The front row in press conferences is always occupied by the wire services, by the TV networks, and by the *New York Times,* the *Washington Post,* and the *Wall Street Journal*—papers that pay attention to the business of the White House on a day-to-day basis. Behind them are what are called the semiregulars, the papers and radio and TV stations that are there half the time. The rest of the room is open to anybody on a first-come, first-served basis. The seats in the front are assigned and your name is on the seat. It gets to be a matter of real pride to have a seat in the front row. For one thing you are more likely to be called on because the president can see you.

As a person who has worked on both sides of the podium, I now have greater insight into how press conferences are set up. Every morning in the White House there is a meeting of senior staff people and that includes the press secretary. They sit down for a half hour and each person represents his area—national security, or domestic policy. At various points the press secretary will ask, "How do you want to handle that? Will the president sit still for photographers to come in and take pictures or not? Does he want to make a statement? (Yes, he does.) Who is writing the statement? How long will it take before we get it? Well, there is no reason for me to call the press in if it won't be ready. (It won't be ready until 2:00 p.m.) the press will go crazy! They're not going to sit around and wait until 2:00. Can't we do it at noon?" So you barter back and forth, trying to be responsive to people in the press that you have to deal with daily and hourly and at the same time be able to mirror accurately what the White House wants said.

You can take almost any policy and somebody will say, "This is the reason that we are doing all this, but I'm not so sure we ought to go public with the reason. Why don't we wait to see if we're asked about it?" So I would go out there and say, "This is what we're doing," and if a response came up as to "Well, isn't the senate already working on this?" or "Is this a response to a senator's request?" I would say, "Yes, it is." They: "To what degree?" And I: "Why don't you ask the senators involved and see if this meets their specifications?" I handled it in that fashion in my discussions with White House staff. It is bartering things, making a decision on what to give out and what not to give out. Sometimes you have to stand up and say to the staff, "Well that won't fly. I can't take that reasoning in to the press room. They'd laugh me off the podium. It just won't wash."

I have asked myself whether I liked the inside work better than outside work. I liked them both but, to tell the truth, they were so different that I liked them in differing ways. As press secretary it was very rewarding to be able to be part of the policymaking team, to have some input on issues before a policy was enunciated. You do get an internal reward about having a say in national affairs. On the other hand, I also had responsibility for it afterward. If it did not fly, fell apart, or did not work, you can bet that there would be plenty of people who would remark, "That was a dumb idea you had last week." So you have to be willing to bear the risk. Whereas the fun of being a journalist is that you feel no particular responsibility for what you are covering. As a reporter I felt my responsibility was merely to report it accurately and try to deal with it as a news event, to try to round up comments pro or con, and to make sure my quotes were accurate and that I quoted the right people. After that I was through. If it went down the drain, that was no personal concern of mine.

My tenure as press secretary under President Ford was different from others for several reasons. First, I was the first member of the press to become press secretary in a number of years. I was following Ron

Ziegler. I do not think there were many tears in the press room because of his departure. I did start out with a lot of goodwill and a fair amount of respect from my former colleagues. That also rubbed off on Ford—the fact that he was willing to assign the White House press secretary's job to a working reporter. The other plus was that I was dealing with a brand new president, and everybody without exception hoped he would succeed. I was there during the first thirty days when everybody thought Ford was doing well. He was making his own English muffins in the morning instead of having them brought to him on a silver platter by a navy steward. Relations with the press took a decided downward turn the day after the pardon, because the members of the press felt, as Mary McGrory wrote at the time, that "it was as if Ford had suddenly torn a scab off a wound that was beginning to heal."

There is a curious phenomenon with Reagan press conferences. Reagan is the best public speaker as president that we have had in a long time. So one would think that press conferences would come naturally and easily, as a result of his work experience in meeting with the public and his lifetime career in acting. Well, this turned out not to be the case. He often seemed ill at ease in his news conferences. He was not at his best— certainly not as good as when delivering a prepared speech. I attribute that to two things. One, that he does not hold news conferences often enough, so that the buildup of events between news conferences is so large and he has so much material to absorb that it is just too formidable. The other reason is that the president is a better developer of policy than an explainer of policy. He is perhaps too much the chairman of the board and not enough the operating officer of government. Maybe the truth lies somewhere in between. Most presidents manage to carry off press conferences rather well.

Currently reporters' questions seem long. A good part of the problem is that press conferences are televised. I started covering the White House in 1957, and under Eisenhower the questions were usually short and terse. Reporters were less conscious of their sentence formulation. They were not required, as they were required in televised conferences under Kennedy, to give their name and affiliation. There was none of that. As a result, the questions at these pre-TV press conferences were probably only half as long as those that occur under the glare of lights. A good number of reporters, and I know I felt this way, thought that if you were asking a question in front of a national audience, you ought to elaborate a little for the benefit of the audience as to why you were asking the question. As a result, the questions got longer and fewer questions were asked during the course of a press conference. News conferences generally last only thirty minutes. That time limit, plus the show business aspect of some reporters using it as their moment in the spotlight, make for longer and fewer questions. I do not see any reason why press conferences could not go on for forty-five minutes, particularly if presidents do not hold them any more frequently than they do.

There is perhaps not a more disorganized or unorganized body than the White House press association. They are all individuals, unwilling to surrender prerogatives or a right to this or that. Traditionally and historically the association has been unable to get its act together to do anything collectively, except once a year to elect its officers, who then face all the problems of previous officers.

There are always peer leaders within groups and the White House press corps is no different. In my day as a White House correspondent I think Peter Lisagor was probably the guy in the press that everybody thought well of. One of the current gurus is Sam Donaldson. Sam is loud and brash but he is also, when air time comes, very fair. He gets his share of stories but he is not confrontational in a mean way. He is challenging. He has a voice that penetrates. He can shout through a mass of reporters and get his question asked in a way that will catch the president's good ear. Sam adds to the mix. The president makes a lot of jokes about him, and plays Sam off against the American people. I am sure Sam gets his share of hate mail asking, "Why are you so terrible to our great president?"

But there are other people too, in a more quiet way. Richard Strout (*Christian Science Monitor*) who wrote the TRB column for *The New Republic*, was highly regarded by his peers. He would say, "This looks to me like a bad policy," and then would explain it in a lucid fashion which all of us envied. He was a leader without showing off.

It is wise to neither be too confrontational nor act as the house lackey. The White House has learned not to try to plant any questions, because word gets out and then you get another story which says the White House yesterday attempted to plant three questions with members of the press. That generates another bad column about White House efforts to manipulate and manage the news.

Persons who ask truly confrontational questions do not have a good rapport with the White House staff. If you are known as a person who asks "mean" questions, the White House staff is not going to alert you to a briefing. You are going to have to find out the hard way. They are going to regard you as an enemy or a problem. On the other hand, if you are solicitous or even obsequious (and some reporters are obsequious because they want so badly to hold their job at the White House), such people are pushovers. You can peddle stuff to these people. But it does not last forever. Sooner or later they miss stories. They buy too much from the White House and lose perspective. Neither one of these types is liked by the press that covers the White House regularly.

7

Television Network News in Campaigns

Roger Mudd

My Topic is: "The Influence of TV Network News Coverage on a Campaign." My answer is—there is too much of it! We are all once again embarked on America's quadrennial, longest-running, preplanned special event—the campaign for the White House. It lasts, every four years, from January to January, from the Iowa caucuses to the inauguration.

The politicians and their parties will spend perhaps $180 million this year on TV advertising. The three commercial TV news departments will spend about $125 million to cover the politicians. With that kind of money committed, politics will block out most of the rest of the news. In 1980, one out of every six minutes of TV network news was political.

The story in 1984 will become almost an end in itself. That is, the competition among the networks and the anchor people will become almost more important than the story itself. For example, look at what happened in 1980 when CBS kept nominating Ronald Reagan and Gerald Ford as running mates.

Probably as a consequence of heavy coverage the public's interest has diminished: voter turnout has fallen and the TV audience has declined. Something is wrong, and it may be because once again the networks have tried to make themselves and their ratings superior to their obligations of informing the public.

It was not always that way. Back in the 1940s and 1950s, television and politics were almost strangers. TV reporting was rudimentary coverage of conventions mainly designed to sell TV sets. ABC did not even broadcast the 1952 conventions; NBC's anchorman was Bill Henry; CBS's was Walter Cronkite. Delegates were told to wear blue shirts.

But both politicians and network managers quickly realized the stake each had in the other. Politicians saw access to an enormous and approving audience if only they could control their own images. Networks saw a growing audience, and therefore growing profits, if only the politicians could be made exciting. By 1960, the presidential nominating conventions were being broadcast gavel-to-gavel and convention coverage had become TV news' Super Bowl.

But the arrival of the cameras in force took much of the excitement out of politics. Candidates began to realize that they had to look good and sound good; they had to smile; they had to avoid offending. Convention rules were modified to accommodate television's viewing schedule; convention managers tried to minimize party conflicts; potential conflicts were scheduled early or late.

Politicians' fear was that the TV audience might conclude that a political party which could not control its own convention could not be expected to control the White House. Therefore, much of the drama went out of the conventions—no more dirty linen, no more endless roll calls.

How many can remember the last time a presidential convention roll call went beyond the first ballot? It was thirty-two years ago in 1952 at the Democratic Convention in Chicago when Averell Harriman of New York and Paul Deaver of Massachusetts withdrew and Adlai Stevenson of Illinois was nominated on the third ballot defeating Estes Kefauver of Tennessee and Richard Russell of Georgia. Since then every presidential nominee has been chosen on the first ballot or by acclamation.

And if you did not know the answer to that question, you probably can not remember what election night used to be like back in the 1930s, 1940s, and 1950s. It meant staying up until three and four o'clock in the morning, listening to H.V. Kaltenborn say that when the vote from upstate New York came in and when the farm belt was heard from the picture would change. Those were the days when radio and television had to wait for the wire services to report the vote totals. And the wire services had to wait for each election board and each board had to wait for each precinct.

Now all that has changed and election night seems to end before we can even get our feet up and our beer open. It began to change because television wanted to speed up the process; television wanted to condense and intensify the excitement and eliminate the long and expensive all-night vigils.

It was in 1961 during the New York mayoral race between Robert Wagner and Louis Lefkowitz when NBC decided to send a reporter to each of New York's police precincts, where the votes were counted, and call in the results directly to NBC. They thus short-circuited the process of waiting for the board to certify the numbers and the wire services to transmit them. NBC clobbered CBS and ABC that night on local television in New York. The next morning the race was on to figure out a way legally to get into the ballot box and report the returns before the competition.

CBS hired Lou Harris, the political polling expert who had worked for John Kennedy in 1960. Harris developed a system called "vote profile analysis" (VPA). Harris built a political miniature of each state in the Union using an average of thirty key precincts for each state. Each precinct was selected so that their sum would accurately reflect the demographic and political composition of the state in terms of its urban/rural, ethnic, racial, religious, and economic makeup. On election day 1964, CBS hired 6,000 reporters for the day and sent one of them to each of the 6,000 key precincts in the country. As soon as the polls closed at each precinct, the reporter would telephone in the result and the computers back in Manhattan would begin to build their models of each of the fifty states. When enough of the key precincts in a state had called in, CBS could report even before all the votes had been counted in South Carolina, that Barry Goldwater had carried South Carolina.

CBS had found a way to beat NBC. It had found a way to report the returns accurately on a national basis even before all the polls in the West had closed. It meant in terms of TV programming and costs, that the networks could have election night wrapped up by midnight. Only a tight presidential race or some critical Western state Senate race, which had a bearing on party control of the congress, would drag the coverage out much longer.

But in the process of speeding up reporting, the networks incurred the wrath of many politicians who said it was neither fair nor necessary to project the outcome of a race before everyone had voted. And the networks incurred the enmity of the country's political junkies who saw their most exciting night of the year being stripped of its drama and who felt that it was arrogant of broadcasters to invade the sanctity of the most hallowed symbol of our political religion—the ballot box. But vote projections became the networks' standard operating procedure, and by the 1966 off-year elections, all three networks had developed their own projecting techniques.

By 1972 they were looking for new ways to compete. In 1972 the networks added a new wrinkle to their vote profile technique of breaking out the vote early. It came to be called "postpolling" or "exit polling." It involved having those key precinct reporters stop and question voters *after* they had left the polls. For whom had they voted? What issues had they voted on? How old were they? What was their economic status? What was their party affiliation?

The networks found that about 20 percent of those they stopped refused to answer the questions, but they also felt that the remaining 80 percent who answered were telling the truth about whom they had just voted for and why. Exit-polling meant that by early afternoon, well before most Americans had voted, well before the polls had closed, well before the VPA/key precinct had taken over, the networks had what they regarded as a rough guide to where the precincts were going and why.

While exit polling was not finely developed enough to be relied on during a very close race, the networks thought it would be invaluable for spotting early trends toward a landslide. It also would give the broadcasters plenty to chew on early in the evening and it might give one of them even a leg up on the competition. CBS first used exit polling nationally in 1968, NBC in 1974, and ABC in 1976; but none of the networks used the data to predict or project the outcome of a race. It was simply thought too risky and unreliable. After all, those were not actual votes. They were just second-hand votes with people telling you how they had voted. However, on election night 1980, NBC broke the mold. At 8:15 p.m. eastern standard time—before millions on the West Coast, where it was 5:15 p.m., had even started for the polls—the NBC screen flashed: "Reagan Wins."

NBC later insisted it had used exit polls plus actual returns from the East and Midwest before making its call. But CBS and ABC not only did not believe it, but they were also furious. In the harsh competitive world of election night coverage, NBC had scored a major beat. ABC did not predict a Reagan victory until 9:52 that night. And even Jimmy Carter beat CBS at predicting the outcome when he conceded the election forty minutes before Walter Cronkite did.

Politicians on the West Coast, and Western Democrats specifically, thought that the reduced turnout had cost them some close elections. Oregon's secretary of state said: "I regret the fact that you can sit in Oregon and hear what happened on the East Coast." And there were voters who claimed network predictions of a Reagan victory stopped them in their tracks. A librarian in California said: "You come home from work and find you don't have to go to the polls." A printer in Seattle said: "They told me on the radio there was no sense in my voting."

The networks privately knew they had a problem, a "societal problem," they called it, and they became defensive. They said they were only reporting what they regarded as reliable information as quickly as they could. To delay such news would be "inconsistent with journalistic standards." Besides, any evidence that early predictions of a Reagan victory had seriously affected the process or the outcome was scanty. The evidence was scanty. But that explanation is a self-fulfilling prophesy. It is a sleight of hand game with journalistic standards because the standards kept changing to meet the new definition of reportable news.

Nonetheless, the State of Washington passed a law prohibiting reporters from interviewing voters within 300 feet of the polls, and that effectively outlawed exit polling in Washington. Last summer the House of Representatives held hearings designed to force the networks into voluntarily delaying their exit polling while the voting was still in progress. The networks refused. The *New York Times* and the *Washington Post* joined in a law suit challenging the legality of the Washington exit polling law on First Amendment grounds. I think the networks and the press have a good case in challenging that law, but the law is a measure of the growing animosity among a significant number of politicians and citizens toward the media.

The emphasis in 1984 is again going to be on speed. None of the networks will forswear exit polling. They have all been asked in congressional hearings, "Would you give it up? Would you withhold this projecting stuff?" They would not. They said it was journalistically unsound and would continue to do it. Once again, if it is another Reagan landslide, all three will come on at 8:20 p.m. and say Reagan has won. Once again the Rocky Mountains and the West Coast will not have finished voting. I do not expect much different behavior on the part of the networks come November.

If ever the press needed public support to deflect or resist the spread of government censorship, it is now. There are many more serious threats to freedom of the press every day for the networks to squander needlessly its waning credibility, its good name, over a so-called right to televise projections based on how people *say* they voted rather than on how they *voted*.

But the networks are on another roll. We are all gearing up as if we were approaching Armageddon, preparing for another overkill, another eight to ten months of saturation reporting that seems to trivialize everything in our path. Once again, the networks are covering the Democratic campaign as though it were a two-man race. Mondale versus Glenn with Jesse Jackson added for suspense. Two-man races are easier to cover than eight-man races. Two or three heads simply fit into the screen more easily. Two-man debates require fewer microphones and are more confrontational. Reporting on two or three candidates on the evening news is a lot more manageable than reporting on seven or eight.

Coverage of the night of and the morning after the New Hampshire debate, three weeks ago, came down mainly to reporting about how Walter Mondale and John Glenn stood up and pointed at each other. Perhaps Gary Hart caught the attention of a few reporters who had not noticed him before; maybe Ernest Hollings came across as a loose canon on the Democratic deck; Jesse Jackson may have impressed some with his newly acquired presidential dignity. But most of the press was watching Mondale and Glenn.

Of course, the media has always watched the front-runners closely. It has to because everybody else is. But suppose you are not a front-runner. Suppose you are a back-runner struggling to break out of the pack? How do you get the attention, the space, the time of television to get the voters to take you seriously? Suppose you were Alan Cranston who is a smart, experienced Democrat, with a reputation as a strong senator, a practical, sensible liberal who knows how to count, a candidate who decided that the destruction of our planet is a bigger issue than a budget freeze.

Suppose you were Alan Cranston and the three network reporters assigned to you were Meredith Viera of CBS, Dan Blackburn of NBC, and Steve Shepard of ABC. What would that tell you? Or suppose you were Reubin Askew and covering you from the networks were Rene Ferguson of CBS, Mike Maus of NBC, and Rebecca Chase of ABC? What would *that* tell you? They are all hard-working reporters, but they are not first-line political reporters, and that tells Cranston and Askew that the networks have already decided that they did not have much chance of winning. And thus, even a lesser chance of getting much coverage on the evening news.

Why should Cranston not get roughly the same coverage as Mondale, at least until the voters themselves have had a chance to speak? Mondale may be younger, he may be slightly better looking, he may not dye his hair, but certainly he is no smarter, no more dedicated, no more serious than Alan Cranston. What if the polls have Mondale ahead? What if the teachers, the unions, and a bunch of politicians have endorsed Walter Mondale? So what? Nobody had endorsed McGovern in 1972 or Jimmy Carter in 1976 before they started winning.

We do not know how popular Alan Cranston is at this point. We do not know whether Alan Cranston's message about the nuclear freeze is getting through. We do not know whether people really think that is the most important issue, and that there is no more important thing than the preservation of our planet. We do not know that yet. Until the people in Iowa, New Hampshire, and Massachusetts make some judgment on that, we have no way of knowing. We ought to avoid practicing front-runnerism for about sixty days until the people tell us who they think the front-runners are. It may be that given the choice, given the chance to vote for Cranston, he will come in fourth. But he could come in a strong third. You do not know. The science of journalism, the science of getting into your mind ahead of time before you have made up your mind, is an imprecise science. We are doing the process a disservice and we are doing Cranston, Askew, McGovern, and all who may follow a disservice by not giving them a fair chance.

In the interest of fairness and the precarious nature of the democratic system, journalists, networks, and newspapers ought to exercise some self-restraint until the American people have sorted things out. It is this period that we are in now that is so critical. It is critical to people like Hart, Askew, Cranston, and McGovern because we go around as journalists and say, "You're going to win and you'll be second, and if you don't get a good third you're out of it." And they never had a chance. Those guys might have made terrific presidents! We are not electing a president. *You* are! We ought to just back off for sixty days from about the first of January in every election year and let the people sort it out. And then after they have decided in the Iowa caucuses, voted in New Hampshire, and have gone through a couple primaries on Super Tuesday with six or eight states, then you zero in on the front-runners.

No one is really sure about the absolute effect of television on politics. There are only opinions. My opinion is that television killed the party structure and replaced the old bosses with media consultants, so that a candidate's image is at least as important as his position. The networks have speeded up the vote-counting process to such an extent that many Americans feel that their vote has been debased. The networks have helped strip conventions of their drama, have called elections before they were over, and have made life difficult for all but the front-runners.

The networks have become too intimately involved in the electoral process. We are heading for a presidential campaign that within the next twelve years will take place either within a TV studio or at least within television's special confines. I am not sure I know what to do about it.

There is one step the networks could take and one law Congress could pass that might relieve some of the problems of election night. It is too much to ask of the networks that they withhold legitimate vote counts or key precinct returns from the East until the polls have closed in the West. It makes no sense to deny an audience the complete-vote in Rhode Island until the voters in Alaska have reported. The answer would be for all the polls to close at the same time—say in the East at 9:00 p.m. and in the West at 6:00 p.m. That would mean Eastern voters would go to the pools from 9:00 a.m. to 9:00 p.m., the Midwest from 8:00 a.m. to 8:00 p.m., Rocky Mountain from 7:00 a.m. to 7:00 p.m., and the Pacific from 6:00 a.m. to 6:00 p.m. The East and the West would be the most inconvienced, but that disruption would be relatively minor.

A poll-closing law would be the congressional contribution. The network contribution would be to foreswear the use of all exit polls until after the polls had closed. That would mean that no broadcaster could say before 9:00 p.m. in the East that Reagan was leading, was winning, or had won.

Election night then really would not begin until nine o'clock. But with all the polls closing at nine and all the returns from those precincts arriving together, the next two to three hours would be very intense. The networks doubtless would have to hire two to three times the number of computers and operators to handle the avalanche of votes.

No longer would election night be the old stately transcontinental and transitional march from Connecticut and Kentucky westward through Ohio and Arkansas, onto Wyoming and Colorado, and ending with Arizona and California, with the big electronic map showing the Reagan states popping up in blue and the Carter ones in red. Henceforth the big map would pop up red and blue; according to how quickly the votes could be counted, how quickly the key precincts could be fed into the network computers, and how quickly the computers could tell their anchor people.

Based on past election nights, the states reporting their returns most quickly are always Kentucky, Indiana, and Connecticut, in that order, followed by California, Arizona, and New Jersey. So within the first five minutes with all the polls closing at 9:00 p.m. in the East and 6:00 p.m. in the West, there would be an interesting mix of states to give us an early indication from urban East to rural South, to republican Midwest and an unpredictable Pacific Coast.

The great bulge of states, from New York and Pennsylvania to Florida, Michigan, and Oregon would be reporting during the next ninety or 120 minutes. Henceforth, the wait would *not* be for the Pacific states but for the traditionally paper-ballot rural states—Alaska, Arkansas, Georgia, South Carolina, and bless its heart, Cook County, Illinois.

Election night for the landslides like Eisenhower in 1952, Johnson in 1964, and Reagan in 1980 would be over by midnight at the latest. The close ones—Kennedy in 1960, Nixon in 1968, and Carter in 1976—would need more time. But at least the American viewers would come to realize that the networks were not trifling with their vote. That a California, Oregon, or Rhode Island ballot was worth as much in the computer as the one from Greenwich, Connecticut or Trenton, New Jersey; that networks believed enough in the integrity of the ballot that they would report only real votes and not projected ones; and that the networks felt as strongly about the national functioning of the political process as they did about the natural functioning of the ratings system.

Too much is packed into the nightly news. We insist on doing fifteen stories rather than six stories well. Also each network ought to have a weekly broadcast that gives some air to the candidates. There ought to be a weekly report of thirty minutes on the campaign. There ought to be debates. And there should be a nightly report on the two candidates every night of the week. Where we trivialize the election process is between now and then. There is nothing more important than the campaign itself. I believe that our tendency is not to give the process the time it needs to perform naturally.

8

Columnists in Campaigns

David Broder

As far as I know, there are no written rules anywhere in journalism as to what columnists are supposed to do or what kind of role they are supposed to play in relationship to campaigns. I suppose if Dear Abby decided in her column a week before the election to endorse a presidential candidate it would have a great impact on the campaign. It would be unexpected, out of character, and because of her credibility with millions of readers, it would have a marked impact. We know for example that the piece she wrote recently about the so-called notch problem in social security benefits by itself has made that a major subject for congressional mail. On the other hand if Bill Buckley came out in a column tomorrow for the renomination and reelection of Ronald Reagan or if Tom Wicker said that Alan Cranston makes a lot of sense on the subject of the dangers of nuclear war, I do not know how much impact that would have because those columnists would be saying exactly what most readers expect them to say. And it would probably be discounted because that is what you expect to be hearing from them on that subject.

There are columnists who do intensive political campaign coverage and build their columns on the intensity of their reporting work in campaigns. The dispatches they file from the political battlefront affect those in the political community who rely on them to be their eyes and ears on the scene. I am thinking of people like Jack Germond and Jules Whitcover, or Bob Novak and Rolly Evans in their columns. But even with them, there is limited influence. Germond, for example, wrote on the day that George Bush made his formal announcement of his presidential candidacy that the Bush campaign had peaked on the day he had announced it. It did not keep Bush from winning the Iowa caucuses or being Reagan's most persistent challenger. And it certainly did not keep him from winding up on the ticket and in the vice-presidency. There is a wonderful story that Bob Novak tells about himself which would suggest the limits of his political acumen and influence. Before Novak discovered the wonders of Jack Kemp, he had another enthusiastic young man who was on his way up in politics, a fellow by the name of Ben Barnes who was then lieutenant governor of Texas. Novak thought that Ben Barnes was probably the future leader of the free world. This was back during the Vietnam War, when aside from promoting Ben Barnes, the Evans and Novak column was very hawkish about the whole subject of U.S. involvement in Vietnam. Unfortunately for Barnes he got caught up in something called the "Sharp Zone" scandal in Texas. In the election in which he should have been nominated and elected as governor of Texas he found himself very much on the defensive and running an uphill and ultimately a losing campaign in the Texas Democratic gubernatorial primary. The last night of that campaign, as Novak tells the story, he went with Barnes to the latter's last rally. Afterward they had a few drinks together and they were leaning on each other. As they weaved their way back to the motel in whatever Texas city the last rally was held, Barnes supporting Novak said, "Well, you were with me when I was doing well and you are with me at the end, and I really appreciate that." And Novak said, "Well Ben, I am still with you but I have got to tell you I still believe in the South Vietnamese army too." So there is a bit of self-awareness about the limited impact even from those columnists who are out there everyday reporting on politics.

Other columnists hardly ever set foot on the campaign bus. They deal with weightier items—world topics, international topics, topics of major domestic policy. The extent that a Joe Kraft, a Tony Lewis, a Jack Kilpatrick, or a George Will influence campaigns would be measured by the general influence they have on the intellectual or political climate of the time. Some people feel that we are experiencing a conservative era in this country. I think that today the most popular and probably the most influential columns are being written by people of a generally conservative stripe. George Will, Bill Buckley, Jack Kilpatrick, and Bill Saffire probably have, in terms of their combined circulation influence and firepower, probably no counterparts on the Left or liberal side of the political spectrum on the op-ed pages of American newspapers today. The Republicans have won three of the last four presidential elections and have given major importance to the direction of governmental policy in the last fifteen years in this country. Maybe there is a connection between the influence of conservative columnists and the pattern of the outcome of recent campaigns and the general direction of our government. But my own guess is that both the popularity of those columnists and the success of conservative politicians probably are a symptom of deeper changes that are taking place in this country, rather than one being the cause of the other.

If you are under the impression that I am somewhat skeptical about the overall power and influence of columnists in determining the outcome of specific campaigns or the general direction of politics and policy in this country, you are right. I am inclined toward the position that the impact of columnists is about what the late Senator Dirksen used to say in that phrase of his about his power and influence—"about as influential as a snowflake falling on the broad bosom of the Potomac River." That is how most columns and most columnists' impact can be measured.

When columnists chose to play a direct role in intervening into political campaigns they botch the job almost always in incredible ways. Journalist make the worst political strategists. And the political advice that journalists sometimes feel compelled to give tends to be the worst advice those candidates ever get. During 1960, in the first campaign I covered, I recall the distinguished columnist Joseph Alsop in that wonderful almost British tone of his going around in West Virginia and saying, "Madame, are you going to vote for Senator Kennedy or are you a bigot?" It is true that Senator Kennedy carried the West Virginia primary, but I do not know of any people in the Kennedy campaign who felt they were particularly helped by Mr. Alsop's inquiries into that cause. I was witness to a wonderful incident on the Goldwater campaign in 1964 involving my friend Clark Mollenhoff who was a great investigative journalist for the *Des Moines Register.* He was a columnist for that paper and for other papers. Mollenhoff firmly believed that the key to Goldwater's victory in the 1964 election lay in the proper exploitation of something called the Otepka Case. Otto Otepka was a minor functionary in the Department of State who became well known because he was convinced that we were taking great security risks by allowing people to come into this country who had, in his view, dangerous Communist links. He would go from time to time to Capitol Hill to sympathetic senators with cases that he thought the State Department senior brass had been just terribly negligent about allowing people to come into this country that he thought should not have been allowed. He did this often enough that finally he got fired from the State Department. He became a hero and a cause célèbre for conservatives. And Mollenhoff was sure that if Goldwater would just deal with the Otepka case and use it as the key issue in his campaign, he would turn the election around and defeat Lyndon Johnson. He badgered them to the point they finally said, "all right Clark, you write a speech and we will get Goldwater to deliver it." As often happens in presidential campaigns, there were two or three different streams of decision making going on simultaneously which were totally unaware of each other. A different stream of the campaign was trying to get Goldwater to make a pitch for the Chicano vote or the Hispanic vote as it was called then. On a whistle-stop train trip from Los Angeles to San Diego Goldwater made a stop at a little town called Pico Rivera. They had brought in a great number of Mexican-Americans by bus to hear Senator Goldwater. By a wonderful coincidence it was at this very stop that they shoved Mollenhoff's Otepka speech into Goldwater's hands to deliver. Here was Goldwater talking about this hero and martyr who had been driven from office by the State Department. In the Goldwater administration Otepka would be a man of honor and not one pilloried for his patriotism. The audience kept hearing over and over this strange name Otto Otepka and as it was a complicated story, it was hard to follow. Goldwater had never seen the speech before and as he kept talking there was total silence, no reaction. People were getting more and more embarrassed and nervous. Finally after hearing this strange and foreign sounding name Otepka for about the fifth time, somebody in the crowd seeking to be helpful hollered out, "Fire him!" That was the end of the great Otepka strategy in the Goldwater campaign. And most advice that columnists and journalists give to candidates is about as helpful.

Most columnists try to keep their mouths shut about what campaigns ought to be doing, perhaps because we know our own limits and that neither the candidates nor the voters really depend on us for wisdom as to what to do.

The things that draw you to Washington as a journalist—interest in the kind of gossip, political maneuvering, and all the plotting and counterplotting that goes on—are the same things that draw the politicians and lobbyists there. We are all junkies of the same sort of nutty political world. When you have that kind of community of interest it is the easiest thing in the world for friendships and associations to develop. That is a problem. It is a great pleasure because you meet some very interesting, lively, funny, and fascinating people that way. It is a problem journalistically because at some point you have to deal with these people not as social buddies but as news sources and as actors in the play that you are writing about. You have to write about them. And when you sit down and write about them you cannot worry first and foremost about the consequences of that story on their ambitions, hopes, careers, plans, or dreams. You have to think about your responsibility to that reader who may be somebody you do not know at all but who has a certain degree of reliance on you that you are going to tell them the story as accurately, directly, and fairly as you can.

My solution is that I do little intimate socializing with the people I write about. I do not spend my evenings at dinner parties at their homes, or when we have a dinner at our home the table is not likely to be filled with politicians that I write about. Obviously in the course of a campaign you drink with people on the campaign staff and you get to know them outside of working hours, but you do not build your life around them. You have to be very professional in your relationship with them and make it clear at all times when you are dealing with them as a reporter that you are not coming as an old friend to shoot the breeze with them. You are coming as a reporter who is interested in a story. One of the advantages of working in Washington is that most of the people that you are dealing with are on the political side are professionals. They know something of the inhibitions and the character of this relationship between politicians and reporters. They understand that there is tension and an adversarial element to the relationship no matter how much you may enjoy yourself. The level of tension really depends on the personality of the candidate and that of the reporter. Some people in politics are more prone than others to divide up the world between those who are with us and those who are against us. If a politician is prone to divide the world that way, almost certainly I will wind up as a reporter who is against them. Most politicians are professional enough to understand that tension or an adversarial relationship is built into this situation and they can deal with it well. For example Ronald Reagan is not someone who either expects or particularly desires to have a lot of cheerleading in the press corps. He understands that is not our function. He does not seem the least bit troubled by the fact that there are many stories that question or poke holes in his arguments or assertions. Other presidents have had much more trouble dealing with that situation.

If journalism does anything in a campaign it is not telling people what to think. What we may be able to do by focusing on a particular subject or individual for a time is give people some clues as to what to think about. At any time in this country there are a hundred, maybe a thousand ambitious politicians all clamoring for attention. There are a hundred issues fighting for attention on the public agenda. It is the role and responsibility of the press to try to sort out that clutter and focus peoples' attention on individuals or issues and give views as to what topics and people may be worth spending some time and thought on. Another way of saying the same thing is that columnists particularly have a degree of discretion about keep a story going or letting it die. They can help build momentum for a candidate, particularly a candidate who has just won some kind of a victory. They can keep an issue going once that issue is launched in a campaign.

But even when they are playing that kind of a role, it is a secondary role. Columnists by themselves cannot get people interested in somebody who is not in the real world of politics scoring some kind of success or doing something tangible that seems to merit peoples' interest. Columnists by themselves cannot force people to become interested in a topic that is not a matter of real concern to them or is not a matter of real debate in the political world.

My hunch is that the role of the columnist has diminished a good deal since the era of H.L. Menken and Walter Lippmann. What they were writing probably was, at that time, the dominant force in shaping the thinking of the country. Certainly all of us on the print side of journalism are aware of the fact that the role of the press, the writing press, has changed and diminished since television became the prime channel of communication in this country. I want to make a couple of observations to back up that point, but I see more changes in my own job as a reporter on the reporting staff of the *Washington Post* than the subsidiary role I have as a twice-a-week columnist. I spend most of my time as a reporter.

If I have learned anything about journalism it is that you are better off spending your time reporting than you are writing. Unless you are a marvelous stylist, as few people in the business are, your reader is not going to value your work for its literary content. So I am inclined to spend much more of my time reporting than writing. You do not have a lot of time to spend meditating on what you are going to do. For the most part stories define themselves after you have been in business for a while. You know what the lead is. It jumps out at you. It is that kind of reflexive news judgment that gets pounded into your head during your period of apprenticeship in the newspaper business. There is a situation, a quote, an event that jumps out at you saying that this is what the story is about. You know that you are not going to deal with everything, so you pick out what you think is the most interesting, significant, or newsworthy part of that story. It really becomes a reflexive reaction.

I try to write in terms that are understandable. But I do not assume either in the news stories or columns that I write for the *Washington Post* that I am writing for someone who is politically ignorant. A view of journalism that I share was expressed many years ago by Bill Hobby who was then running the *Houston Post*. At a journalistic meeting I went to, he said that the best writing and the best reporting in most newspapers was found on the sports page. When a reporter sits down to write a story about a game, he does not have to take four paragraphs to provide a background for the reader. He does not need to say that baseball is a game played on a diamond-shaped flat surface between two teams of nine men each in which the object is to hit the ball and advance runners around the bases. He assumes as a sports writer that the reader knows that or he would not be reading the story in the first place. So he spends his time writing about the nuances, pecularities, and events of that particular game and the performance of players in a way that is interesting to people interested in baseball. That is the way I write about politics—to make it interesting to somebody who is interested in politics.

It is in my role as a reporter rather than as a columnist that I want to examine the changes that have taken place in the role of newspapers in covering campaigns and in influencing them. Television has changed the political world, and therefore, has changed the world of journalists who cover politics. Television has brought candidates into the living room, and by so doing has given people a sense of direct, first-hand knowledge of those candidates that they did not have before. Among the many effects of this technological change is that it has fed the public demand for direct participation in the process of choosing the candidates. Americans by and large are no longer satisfied to wait patiently until November of the presidential year and then mark their ballots between the two candidates of the two major parties. Many Americans want to get into the game at a much earlier stage and help the parties pick the candidates who will be on the ballot in the general election. As a partial result of television's direct exposure of candidates in the living room, we have moved to a much more open nominating system with much greater public participation in the process. In 1984 we have something that comes as close to being a national presidential primary as we have ever had, because in a span of about ten days in the middle of March, twenty or more state will be choosing delegates. As a result there have been a number of other important institutional changes which have had direct impact on journalism and particularly on political journalism.

Direct participation by the public in the nominating process and the domination of that process by direct primaries has changed political conventions. Political conventions used to be the great playground for newspaper reporting of politics—H.L. Menken wrote those classic pieces out of convention halls. Conventions themselves have become much less important as a device for picking presidential candidates and for taking care of the other work of the political party. The convention hall itself is dominated by those overhanging TV booths. It is hard sometimes to tell from TV coverage of a convention whether it has become a showcase for politicians or for the networks to display their competing teams of floor reporters and anchormen.

Television has changed the nature of issue communication in the campaign. It has lessened the emphasis on formal speeches of substantial length given to large audiences with a direct and identifiable interest in a particular subject—for example the defense speech that was traditional at the American Legion or VFW convention or the farm speech at the National Plowing Contest. All these speeches used to dominate the schedule of candidates, provide the grist for many newspaper stories and follow-up columns and analyses. Instead of communicating about the issues in that kind of formal speech, candidates now deliver their issue messages either in relatively brief paid TV commercials or in carefully staged TV settings designed to supply what they know television needs for the evening news shows. So they have compressed their issue messages into a format that television can accept.

Reporters used to worry a great deal about developing contacts with professional politicians and establishing a basis of confidentiality and intimacy with them. That is much less useful to reporters now because those professional politicians are far less influential in the presidential nominating process than they used to be. There are no longer any smoke-filled rooms to penetrate at the convention halls. The knowledge of the back channels of the convention decision making and of behind the scenes manipulators is much less useful to reporters than was formerly the case.

Similarly, the time reporters spend on the campaign plane or bus is much less significant now in terms of what we can get out of it because the substantive content of the campaign planes is much less than it was previously. We still keep reporters on those planes and buses because we do need to monitor what the candidates are saying. And there is always the chance that some candidate on some day will go off on his own and say something that is not in the script and you need to be around if that happens.

Increasingly, the press, particularly newspaper reporters, have shifted their focus and priorities from tracking the candidates to tracking the public. We spend much more of our time talking to voters and much less of our time listening to and writing about the candidates. Fortunately we have been given in the last twenty years some wonderful tools which we did not have before to monitor the process by which the American people reach that election decision. Survey research has gone from being nonexistent to being handled increasingly with care, sophistication, and utility by newspapers and news organizations. We have become more skillful in handling the polls done by professional pollsters. Many news organizations, including the one I work for, have developed their own in-house polling capacity. With exit polls and all the other devices that have become familiar just in the last ten to twelve years, we are able to do things in tracking the dynamic of public decision making that was simply not within out capacity before we had those polls. I will give you a specific example. It is possible that a very intuitive and shrewd reporter with nothing more than a reporter's instinct and abilities might have been able to do in 1980 the job of reporting the dynamics of the Democratic presidential nomination fight. But it was only because of the availability of exit polls that we are able to say with a good deal of certainty what was happening in the Democratic electorate during that process of the Kennedy/Carter primaries of 1980. It was only because of the exit polls that we were able to say with some degree of confidence that most of the people taking part in the Democratic primaries agreed with Senator Kennedy on criticism of the record, policies, and approach of the Carter administration. But also that many of those people, whenever they thought there was a real possibility that Senator Kennedy might emerge as the Democratic nominee, were pulling back from a decision to support Senator Kennedy. This was because of a deep and largely personal difficulty and antipathy they felt toward him as a prospective presidential candidate and president of the United States. A fairly complex and sophisticated kind of ambivalence was at work in those primaries. Intuitively some reporters talking to cab drivers, barbers, and ordinary citizens under the old system of reporting might have been able to guess what was taking place. But that reporter had a very hard time in backing that hunch with evidence until we had the kind of information exit polls gave us.

We still do a good deal of monitoring of the words and actions of the candidates. I would like to think that we still do that essential job of keeping the candidate relatively honest in talking about the issues. For example Senator Glenn made the comment that Walter Mondale had personal responsibility for the economic conditions of the country because of what he called the failed policies of the Carter-Mondale administration. It only took one cycle for newspapers and other news organizations to point out that Senator Glenn in 1980 had endorsed President Carter for renomination and endorsed him specifically by saying that he was in agreement with the economic policies of the Carter administration and believed that those policies were bringing the country out of its economic difficulties. There is a good deal of that kind of monitoring.

The kind of nominating and election system we have now is a more open and participating system. If offers much greater opportunity for individual Americans to make their voices and wishes felt. My own subjective judgment is that as the system has become more open, the quality of the candidates has declined. I do not think it has worked to improve the quality of the candidates that are being nominated for the presidency of the United States. I admit my own preference and bias. I liked the closed system. I would rather cover a caucus or a convention than a primary. A caucus and a convention have in newspaper terms the kind of dramatic unity—of time, place, and characters—to provide the story with a beginning, a middle, and an end. And it is all confined to one building in one place and usually takes one or two days. That makes for better storytelling than a primary election which spreads all over a state or a primary election season which spreads over three or four months' time. I would love once before I retire from this beat to have the opportunity to cover a national nominating convention which went on for more than one night. That would be a very exciting story to cover. But I am not sure that I will ever be able to do so.

I want to put my worst bias and prejudice on the table. I have spent so much of my adult life covering politicians that I have come to believe that whatever their failings might be, politicians are very good judges of other politicians. If you go into any state legislature in the country and ask the first ten legislators you meet who are the best people in the legislature at that point whose judgment they trust, you will get a consensus pretty quickly on the best people in that legislature. Similarly, if you ask the question of senators about other senators, representatives about other representatives, or governors about other governors, you will get good answers. I will give you a very specific example. Neither Jimmy Carter nor Ronald Reagan was rated very highly by their colleagues in the governorships of this country when they were contemporaries in office. Neither Carter nor Reagan was ever chosen by their fellow governors for a leadership position in the National Governors Association. They were not rated that highly. Under a relatively closed system of nominating where governors have power because they control state delegations, the judgments of those political peers on the attributes of those two particular presidents would then have been a matter of great significance. But under the kind of nominating system we have today a governor is just one more vote in a caucus or one more vote in a presidential primary. I am elitist enough to think that those governors have a better basis for judging the quality of those two men than most of the rest of us. They certainly have a better basis for making that judgment than the newspaper people who cover those candidates. People who are in politics are pretty good judges of other people in politics. My preference would be to have a system where those who have a special knowledge, intimacy, or acquaintance with those candidates have more than one vote and a larger than equal voice in the choice of those nominees. If that does not convict me of being a rotten, elitist pig, I do not know what will. I have been on this beat for a long time. The presidents chosen under the old system, from Franklin Roosevelt to John Kennedy (myths to the contrary notwithstanding) were chosen by the bosses. Kennedy ran in four contested primaries in 1960 and 90 percent of the votes he got were in a very old-fashioned way of brokering with political bosses—the Mayor Daleys and the David Lawrences of this world. In my lifetime, looking at the set of candidates nominated by the bosses against those nominated by the people, I think the bosses have it all over the people.

Under the present system, the first thing you do is get out of public office. You do not try to do anything else. You do what Ronald Reagan,

Jimmy Carter, or Walter Mondale did to be successful. You take two, three, four years out of your life and run for president. If you want to have an open system that means you have to introduce yourself to a lot of people who have never met you before. And you have to do it at a time that is convenient for *them,* not when it is convenient for *you.* This is a big country and people complain about the length of the presidential campaign. The reason campaigns are long is that these candidates have to go around introducing themselves to people who have never heard of them before. The fact that you were governor of California for eight years or majority leader of the U.S. Senate for six years does not really make you a familiar figure to many people in this country. We are only casually interested in politics.

Thanks to the Campaign Finance Reform Act it also takes you a lot of time now to raise the money to run for president, because you cannot go to three people who happen to believe deeply in you or your principles and programs and say, "Give me $100,000 to start my campaign." We have made that impossible. Now you have to go convince 1,000 or 100,000 people to give you $5, $10, or $100 each if you want to run for president. That is also very time-consuming.

Howard Baker who has been, without being too partisan, one of the most effective majority leaders of the U.S. Senate has made the perfect rational decision. Having tried it once the other way he has to quit that job and go run for president for four years. That carries a fairly high cost to the country, because Howard Baker may or may not become president. But one thing that is sure is that he is not going to be majority leader. If you feel the value of having that kind of direct participatory process is worthwhile, you have to accept the price. Other people looking at this system say, "Who needs it, I am not prepared to leave my family, my job, my occupation, or anything else for two, three, or four years and go chase the brass ring." Those people are not going to run for president under this system.

I use my column to write about each of the candidates. In almost every case it has been a kind of "who is this person" piece. The unstated question is who is this person and what is there about him that gives him the nerve to think that he should be president of the United States. With the current Democratic field there are qualities that they have that do not make it preposterous, in my view, to consider themselves of sufficient stature to run for president. I have written that kind of column about almost all of them. And I have written several columns saying this is not a bad field of candidates. I can remember not very long ago covering campaigns in which we had people like Vance Harke and Sam Yorty running for president or as part of the presidential debate in New Hampshire, Mr.

Cole from Connecticut, dangling a dead rat from his fingers. This is a pretty classy field compared to some we have seen in the past. As a reporter and columnist and as a voter, I hope we continue to have classy candidates to write about and vote for in 1988 and in years to come.

9

Newspapers in Campaigns

David Nyhan

I should warn you that among the colleagues at the *Boston Globe* I am referred to as "Dave Nyhan—often wrong but never in doubt." I will probably stay true to that label in discussing my views regarding the influence of newspapers in a campaign. It is a treat for me to share my views because the journalists who preceded me, people like David Broder and Roger Mudd, are fellows for whom I have the highest esteem. In our profession they are regarded as reliable people with great integrity. I have seen what they have done in political campaigns. They are extremely influential people. I happened to be standing in front of Ed Muskie that day in 1972 when he stood on a flatbed truck outside the Manchester, New Hampshire *Union Leader* and launched what he thought was going to be a decisive counterattack in his campaign. Muskie denounced publisher William Loeb as a "gutless coward," but it was snowing that day, and the moisture caught up with Ed, and he started to give a little sob. The article David Broder wrote in the Sunday *Washington Post* was probably the single most influential thing that knocked Muskie out of the race and helped reelect Richard Nixon.

Similarly, the interview Roger Mudd did with Senator Ted Kennedy on the eve of the 1980 campaign was the single most effective bit of journalism of that campaign cycle. It gave exposure to Kennedy's lack of preparation. When a candidate cannot answer the question of why he wants to be president it shows he is unprepared. Kennedy was unable to field the questions. So journalists are influential.

I would like to examine the political press and how it affects the race. First, who are the political press? What do we do right? What do we do wrong? And what should we be doing better? Then I am going to discuss the press in the context of New Hampshire, because that is where I have spent at least two days a week every week this year.

Who are the political press? They are only a handful of newspaper reporters in this country and a few TV correspondents who get substantial amounts of air time to cover a campaign every four years. This does not include most newspapers or TV stations in this country. There are only fifty to 100 journalists who make their living writing about national politics year round. Some are columnists who do not write news stories. It is the papers that you immediately think of—the *New York Times,* the *Washington Post,* the *Wall Street Journal*—and a few you do not think of on the East Coast, like the *Los Angeles Times,* which has a Washington bureau of nearly forty people now. And it is a few regional papers like the *Boston Globe* and the *Philadelphia Enquirer.* It is a relative handful among the 1,700 daily newspapers in this country, most of which rely on wire service reports. And it is very difficult for the wire services to have the time or the resources to invest in political campaigning like a successful national or regional paper.

What are we doing right? If you take to heart what I said about how few people do it, how few papers invest resources in this kind of thing, and if you are lucky enough to be a reader of those kinds of papers, then you are well served. Readers are well served by newspapers that make a major commitment to covering the campaign. Some newspapers give readers more information than they can handle. Nobody can keep up with these papers. The Sunday *New York Times* or *Boston Globe* weigh four or five pounds—a couple of million words. Nobody can digest it. Nobody can devote forty-five minutes or an hour a day to reading a series of newspapers. I get ten newspapers every day. I turn a lot of pages, but I cannot say that I read everything in them. There is an information glut, and the average voter cannot absorb what is printed and written about the candidates and delivered on his doorstep if he gets one of these good papers. So they pick and choose. A newspaper is really a supermarket. The papers give you rows and rows of shelves with hundreds of different stories to sample from. We cannot make you read them. But we try to make it entertaining and accurate.

It is true that the bulk of the people get most of their information through television, but advertisers, opinion-makers, and handlers of candidates will tell you that people they want to get to and influence are the ones who read intellectually respectable newspapers. And the successful papers are successful commercially. It feeds on itself. One reason the *Boston Globe,* the *New York Times,* or the *Los Angeles Times* can spend tons of money on political coverage is that they are dominant in their markets and they make an information product as well as advertising packaging. And while it is true that more people hear about more things on television, many people that you want to influence read newspapers.

Readers, viewers, and voters have been well served if they have exposure to the political press. Most people in this country do not get to read that kind of material, because it takes a tremendous commitment by publishers to make the space available and to pay people to go out, report it, prepare it, and put it in the paper. More papers should do what leading

papers do in terms of political coverage. The fact that they do ɪ
lot to do with ideology. Most papers are extremely conservativ
not like to rouse the rabble by giving readers a wide variety of v
and stands on issues from which to pick and choose. There is n
spread in political coverage in papers across the country.

I learned something about political coverage in 1980 after th
vania primary, when it became apparent that George Bush waꜱ   g
to topple Reagan even though Bush had won in Pennsylvani   ɪat
Teddy Kennedy, likewise having won in Pennsylvania, was n   , to
topple Jimmy Carter. I cast about for a new way to do my   ʌs a
national political reporter. I decided to spend a lot of time res.   g the
influence of the New Right. I wound up doing a series of thirty   n articles and columns for my paper between May and December 1980 just on
the New Right and the kind of influence and impact it was having. One of
the things I discovered was that the New Right was most powerful in
states that did not have a dominant newspaper. In such states the New
Right had a field day. The single-issue attacks—principally on incumbent
Democratic liberal senators in places like Idaho and Iowa—were far more
effective when you did not have a big paper to sort out the issues and let
people realize just what was happening.

The political newspapers set the agenda for the political campaign. We
cannot herd the candidates in a particular direction. We follow the bell
cow. This year it has been Walter Mondale. He is the incumbent in this
group. The papers that cover the campaign police the action. We make
sure that the rules are applied, more or less fairly and equitably. We tell
you where their money is coming from and what they are spending it on.
We tell you if their TV advertising is misleading. We are like the referee
in a heavyweight title fight. We tell you what is fair and what is foul. And
what we say about those details is generally picked up and magnified and
its impact increased manifold by national television.

This is an expensive proposition for newspapers and only the pros-
perous ones can afford to do it. I have been in New Hampshire every
week this year. The other night in a hotel bar I happened to have a drink
with the helicopter pilot for CBS News, who brought his chopper and is
permanently stationed at the Manchester airport. He told me that in the
whole month of January he had flown only twenty-one hours, and even a
print reporter can figure out that is less than an hour a day. The cost of
bringing a helicopter up, paying the pilot, getting hangar space, and doing
all the maintenance is a tremendous investment for a TV network, and
they just wanted him there. They did not really use him. He was there
for a few aerial shots, to carry a little bit of film, maybe ferry a couple
crews around. CBS is going to come close to spending in New Hampshire

perhaps what Walter Mondale is allowed to spend in New Hampshire to win that primary election. That is about $400,000.

The *Boston Globe* has seven reporters on the road more or less full-time covering different candidates in different primary states because this is such a front-loaded year. We will have been in Iowa, New Hampshire, Maine, Vermont, Massachusetts, Rhode Island, and seven other states all before St. Patrick's Day. If Glenn, Hart, or someone else does not show some strength against Mondale, it will be over early. We make a tremendous monetary investment in this. Yet the candidates are limited to spending not more than $400,000 legally in New Hampshire. There are many ways they get around that. They bill a lot of their services and advertising through Massachusetts. And I would be very surprised if you could total up the accurate figure. I would bet that more than $1 million will have been spent on Mondale's behalf in New Hampshire, not just by his campaign, but by the labor unions and independent expenditure groups doing other things before this is over. And the policing, reporting, and sorting out of the details is done by this political press, this relative handful of reporters who discover and publish items and then have an added impact when television picks them up.

We also develop the issues. We do not tell the candidates what they have to say, but we point out to readers when candidates are ducking issues. Much has been made in the last couple of days of the fact that Gary Hart shrewdly asked Mondale in the Iowa debate last Saturday night. "Can you name me one issue that you have taken a stand on that was opposed by the leaders of labor unions?" Mondale ducked it that night. His nonanswer was reminiscent of the time Dwight Eisenhower was president and was asked to name one thing that Richard Nixon had achieved as vice-president, and he said, "Well, give me a week and I'll think of something." It took "Fritz" about three days, and he came up with some examples of some things that he had stood for that labor had opposed. But it is the press that picks up a charge by one candidate or another, and we give it the megaphone. We magnify it, and then when Mondale responds, we report that as well. In politics you always get this two-cushioned shot: charge and countercharge, accusation and response. It is not just one-way. It goes out there. It bounces. And it echoes back.

What we have not had a chance to do this year, that we did in years past, is one of the things we do best. And I say this with a certain amount of relish. We pounce on mistakes. I talked earlier about Broder's pouncing on the now-famous "crying incident" in New Hampshire in 1972, and the Mudd interview with Teddy Kennedy which reverberated around, because in both cases you had an incumbent president who was desperate to foil a challenger and exhorted the media to pick up and magnify these gaffes.

In 1972, we learned many years later, it was a frightened and paranoid Richard Nixon exhorting the networks and major papers to get tough on Ed Muskie. To report that he would not stand up to the Russians; that he was a wimp. And in 1980, the Carter people used all their considerable influence to encourage the media to speculate on Kennedy's alleged character flaws.

There have not been many mistakes this year for a couple of reasons. First, there is a pretty good crop of Democratic candidates. No matter what you think of their particular ideology, they are uniformly intelligent and articulate. There are no rogues or villains among them. You had a similarly solid, although not quite so spotless group of Republicans, in 1980. John Connally had a bit of a checkered past, but in 1980 and 1984 they were not a bad group. They are not famous. They may not all be charismatic. They are not terribly charming and they may not kindle passion and devotion among the electorate. But they are a responsible, articulate group of men with considerable experience. They have not messed up, so we have not had a chance to pounce. But when they do, the press will pounce with a venegeance. These people have been fortunate so far, and they have been restrained and disciplined among themselves. But, there is no pressure on a public figure like that which builds during a presidential campaign. And it gets even tougher in the fall than it is during the primary season. When one of them does make a mistake, or is perceived as having done so, the political press will be there and you will be the first to know. You can read it in your newspaper.

What do we in the media do that is wrong, or that is not so good, or that we could be doing better? You hear that the press makes too much of the polls. And there are responsible newspaper editors who say that we should not use polls, that it is the devil's tool, that you cannot trust them, and that it is only a snapshot in time. All that is true. My own feelings on polls are: Politicians use them; why should we not use them? Even if we do not pay thousands for our own polls, we wind up reporting the polls of others. The networks can afford to do it. The national polls sometimes do not zero in on a state, like Massachusetts, New Hampshire, or Rhode Island, the way a regional newspaper might, but my own feeling is that polls are a legitimate journalistic tool because they are a method of analysis. It does give you a snapshot. I am a defender of the use of polls, even though some people criticize them saying they influence too many people and dry up campaign money for candidates perceived as trailing. Neither the press nor the polls make candidates or presidents. If either was the case, Ed Muskie would have been president. In my business we often talk about "the President Muskie system." As you all know, he never became president, but it was not for lack of favorable polls or media coverage. The polls did not create Jimmy Carter in 1976 when he came from nowhere. Certainly the press did not make Richard Nixon president. The influence of the polls and of the media is often overstated.

We hear that the press is biased. We hear that, at least, the writers and reporters are flaming, liberal, commies and that the publishers are good old, reliable, stouthearted, free-enterprise conservatives, who do not know that the inmates are running their asylum. And while they are totting up the profits, their hair-brained liberal dreamers who do the reporting are taking the country down the road to ruin.

In 1972 something like 90 percent or more of the newspapers in this country of 1,700 dailies endorsed Richard Nixon, not George McGovern. Few newspapers had the courage to stand up against what was going on in those days. I am very proud to say that my paper was one of them. We endorsed McGovern and I am proud of it to this day. By and large, the press is biased and distorted. But it is distorted in favor of the conservatives, of the right wing, of the business and managerial class—and it is against liberals. It is against those who would share the wealth, those who favor a bigger role for government, and those who favor government regulation.

The vast majority of editorial and op-ed pages in this country is dominated by conservative-to-far-right forces, not by liberals. There are a few liberal columnists in this country, very few. There are far more conservatives, because by far the bulk of newspapers proprietors in this country favor the conservative political viewpoint. So if there is bias in the press in general, I would submit that it is a bias on behalf of the Right against the Left in the majority of American newspapers. I would have to concede that papers like the *Washington Post,* the *New York Times,* and the *Boston Globe* are liberal by most newspaper standards. The vast majority of reporters who work in this business are liberal. Most of them would be considered liberal because it is hard not to be a liberal when you see how society works up close and how power can influence.

Another thing the press does wrong is the tendency to be too respectful of incumbents. It is not just true of President Reagan. It was true of Carter. I was a White House correspondent in 1975 and 1976 right after Jerry Ford had taken over for Nixon. At that time, the press was too hard on Jerry Ford. We were slow to get Nixon, so we said, "Let's take it out on Ford. He's a meathead."

Ford is a big, tall, graceful man. He was a skier, an athlete. He was a big-time college football player. He is an open-minded, open-hearted guy, a small-town Republican who lucked out. Nixon had to pick a vice-president after Agnew went in the tank. He grabbed Ford because Ford meant an easy confirmation vote in the House. Congress would easily approve one of their own. Nixon needed somebody to stand at his back as he was going into the tigers' den with Watergate. So he picked Ford, who never expected to be president.

Ford never got a break from the press because there was this delayed reaction: Nixon had picked him so he must be something evil; there must be something wrong with him. Jimmy Carter played this very skillfully. Carter unfairly charged and the press reported, unfair accusations against Ford and some ties with funny money right at the end of the 1976 campaign that hurt Ford. That was an example of less than scrupulous fairness by the media toward the end of that campaign.

With the exception of Ford, the press is not tough enough on incumbents. Ronald Reagan is a wonderful candidate. Philosophically, he is too far to the Right for me. But he is a terrific human being and a marvelous speaker. He is a man of great courage, verve, spontaneity, and self-confidence. But let us not kid ourselves. You know Ron does not put in a full day. I do not know anybody, not even people who work for him, who think that he is good for more than four or five hours at a crack. Now he is seventy-three years old. He cannot really focus.

Carter went the other way. Carter used to check out the White House tennis court. There is a lot to be said for Reagan's self-confidence, optimism, and his ability to inspire people with his speeches, which has rendered him untouchable by current standards of political criticism. But the press lets him get away with murder: 270 marines dead in Lebanon. Forget it. Granada, here we come. He neutralized it. By invading Granada he neutralized the political fallout from Beirut. He is a guy who has always been lucky. But he also makes his own luck. He has "submarined" the arms control process. Every president we have had has been dedicated to arms control in a way that Reagan is not, and I think the press has let him off the hook on that. On the fairness issue, you can argue both ways. There are many people in this country—voters I talked to—who think they are better off thanks to Reagan. He controlled inflation. They feel, "Sure, a few people went out of work, but I'm all right. I've got my tax refund and he restored the economy." I think he gets a lot of credit for that, and I think he deserves a good deal of credit for what he did with the economy. But he can be attacked on the fairness issue. The press, after Watergate, decided that it had to pull in its horns, because people began to feel that the press had become too powerful and influential, and we were maybe bullying people. We had to chasten ourselves a little. We had the Janet Cook incident with the *Washington Post*. Every time you mess something up in the paper and you have to run a correction, your own credibility as an institution diminishes. We have some dirty laundry in our own profession, and one of the results of that has been that incumbents get generally better treatment than they deserve from the press. Reagan is extremely well protected on this count because he is no goon on television. He is so disarming and likeable. People just love the guy, and they do not want to read that maybe Ron does not have it all together on this, or he cannot figure out what to do about the deficit, and that he will not even listen to his own chairman of the Council of Economic Advisors, and even a majority of the influential Republican senators in this country think he has gone a little haywire on defense spending. It is very hard to get at him because he lives in a cocoon that the press allows to exist. The president is a father figure. He is an authority figure in our national life. After Nixon, the press decided to think long and hard before taking out after a guy. This is true for Reagan. It did not happen to be true for Carter, who seemed to lose his self-confidence and then became fair game for the press. Carter invited a lot of attack upon himself in a way that Reagan has not.

Another thing the political press may be faulted on is making too much of a horse race of primary campaigns. We did it with the Republicans in 1980, and we can be faulted for doing the same thing now. We concentrate too much on who is ahead now, or who has the best machine. A couple of weeks ago I was in New Hampshire with David Sawyer, who is doing Glenn's advertising campaign. He said, "Why are all you political writers writing about Mondale's political machine as if it were the White House and he were running an administration expertly, cleverly, and skillfully?" Sawyer had a point in that Mondale is getting great credit for assembling this marvelous political machine, this Rolls Royce, this IBM of campaign apparatuses, while Glenn is perceived as an incompetent bumbler by many people, unequipped to be president and ill-qualified in large measure because his campaign has been afflicted by fits and starts and reorganizations. The press has become enamored of political machines, more so than issues, records, or the character and personality of the individual. I do not think that is true of readers. There may be an upset in New Hampshire because Glenn and Hart will do a lot better in New Hampshire than the wise guys of the press think. Voters are a lot less impressed by the reputation or efficiency of a political machine than they are with their subjective, personal, and emotional estimates of character and personality. Once we sense an upset, once we sense a guy has made a mistake, once a front-runner has been humbled, get out of the way, because the press is going to stampede. In 1976 it was Jimmy Carter in Iowa, Jimmy Carter in New Hampshire. *Time* cover, *Newsweek* cover, network specials. We are easily spooked. And if it happens this way, for a John Glenn, Gary Hart, or Jesse Jackson, get out of the way, because there is going to be an avalanche of news coverage. It is not really pack journalism, it is a reaction to a stimulus. All the press will rush from one side of the boat, from covering Mondale, to covering whomever the new star is, and the whole media ship is going to tip.

I try in my writing not to plant things. Let me give you an example. A week ago or so I came back home and I said, "I am convinced this Glenn thing is going to happen." And my wife said to me, "Oh, come on. You must be biased toward Glenn and that's why you talk about it." Maybe I am, but I see this out there. I sense it is there. It is not reported a great deal, and the thrust from most of the stories tend to write him off. He messed up. He is going nowhere. And this is part of the game—to put your training, instincts, and skills as a reporter to match against the conventional wisdom. Fortunately I am in a senior position in my newspaper. I have two columns a week. I can write what I want, and if they do not like my judgment, they can get a new boy.

Let me give you my impressions about what is happening in New Hampshire. It is probably going to be the single most important election held in this country before November. New Hampshire may be Glenn's last stand, in a sense. It is also Mondale's first opportunity to prove that it is not just the bosses and the union chiefs who love him, but that he can get some votes on his own. I believe Mondale is overrated in New Hampshire, that the electorate up there is much more conservative than the profile of a Mondale vote nationally. I am increasingly struck by that, and I have been there every week since Christmas. Every time I go out and talk to voters I find people who say they are going to vote for Glenn, that the other candidates are too liberal. Generally, they do not like Mondale's ties to labor, and they think he has been bought and paid for. And they are going to vote for Reagan in the fall, because they are convinced that Glenn is not going anywhere. You never see anybody who is in love with Mondale, other than the Mondale staff. It is very interesting. I never met a Glenn staffer who said, "I really like Glenn. I really admire Glenn. He's a terrific guy." They are respectful, but they do not love him. The Mondale people love their guy: "Fritz is a nice guy. He's terrific. He's always been great to me. I think he's a wonderful man." I do not see passion from voters in New Hampshire for Mondale. There is a resigned atmosphere. The New Hampshire people are more independent and more conservative than the Democrats are nationally. I would give Gary Hart third place on the basis of a good organization, but he lacks a galvanizing issue. I do not think there is an issue in New Hampshire, other than the personality and character of the men involved. I really cannot figure out Jesse Jackson. I think if he gets 10 percent of the vote up there it will be tremendous achievement. Somebody counted it up the other day, there are something like 2,351 registered Black voters or identified Black voters in the whole state. Jesse is "the candidate of the professionally disillusioned." He is a message, a voice. He is a way to shake them up.

I was thinking how I would compare the New Hampshire election of this year with that of other years. It is not like in 1968, when the war was decisive and Gene McCarthy was up there, the young people were organizing, and Lyndon Johnson was forced out essentially by McCarthy's very strong showing in New Hampshire. It is not like in 1972 when George McGovern carried the war issue and eventually toppled Muskie for the nomination. It is not like in 1980, when Jimmy Carter and Teddy Kennedy went to war, and everybody was unhappy with the result on both sides. It is like in 1976, when we had a group of essentially nameless and faceless Democrats who decided to go to the voters in Iowa and New Hampshire—show them what they had to offer and play on "I ain't Richard Nixon, I'm new. I'm fresh. I'm clean. I'm honest. Believe me." And Jimmy Carter was the best at that.

In 1984 we have eight guys who are not too familiar to the American people. So far they have held up extremely well. Since the middle of last year, the majority of the eight Democratic candidates have met in debates, in dinner forums, in formats where they were examined and questioned by people and judged by the press. They have now done this more than thirty times. This has never happened before in the history of this country, that so many candidates had so many appearances together where they were judged one against another in public. The political press has done a good job in bringing you the details of their stands and positions.

In the case of a political correspondent, a presidential campaign means a year out of your life, you are traveling a great deal. You are in a different hotel all the time, eating out all the time. Most political writers do it because they love the action. They love the game. They love the chase. I talked to a lot of high-school kids who are very direct and naive. They have very good questions to ask. They say, "Do you have to do it, or do you enjoy doing it?" I do not enjoy being away from my family. It can get wearisome listening to a candidate give the same speech ten times and you can become immune. But if I were rich, I would do it for nothing, because it is tremendous fun. There is nothing more important. I do not share the feeling of loneliness, boredom, or helplessness, or the feeling of being drawn along by the tide, or that my voice does not count or is not heard. I have a little sliver of access to the media, and I can reflect the concerns that I run into. I have a typical American sympathy for the underdog. I like to see a good fight, and call foul if I see it.

I like to highlight issues. The ability to highlight an issue, to focus it, and force politicians to respond to it, is a big power. The *Globe* decided last fall to try and organize a candidate's debate. We did it in conjunction with the Kennedy School at Harvard. It was not Harvard that delivered the candidates for that debate. It was the *Globe*. It was our idea to do it because in advance of the New Hampshire primary we said, "We can get these candidates to come and we can get them to talk about foreign policy. And we can get them on television. And once we can get Mondale to come Glenn will have to come. And once Glenn comes, everybody comes. And we can sit them down for an hour and a half and drill them on foreign policy in an intellectual, demanding, rigorous format and make them address things in a way they might not in a stump speech." When you can do that you do not feel helpless. So it is rewarding to be a political journalist.

You just do not work for your editors. You work for the approval of your peers, who are often your competition. And if you are "snookered," to use a John Glenn phrase, or if you are seduced into writing something that proves to be ill-conceived, you lose esteem within the political writing fraternity. This is a powerful force for correcting abuses before they happen, but it also has a tendency to make reporters think twice about whether they should go with their instinct. In a paper like mine, we run something like twenty-eight or thirty different political columns every week. There is a great range of opinion, and people are allowed to write what they really think. Editors, at least at my paper, are not trying to stamp out spontaneity, fresh insight, or a different point of view, just because standards are applied involving fairness and questions of whether this is really accurate or presents a fair picture.

Reporters who are sentenced to ride the plane, to sit in the fuselage, to watch the body, are in a cocoon. They do not get out. They do not talk to people of opposing viewpoints. They only see the candidate they are following and that candidate's crowds. That is not how we do it. On my paper we staff Mondale. We staff Jesse Jackson full-time. We have other people out with other candidates. We have Curtis Wilkie full-time in Iowa. I have been full-time in New Hampshire, along with a woman named Chris Black. Frequently we have two *Boston Globe* reporters with the candidate, or I might see Glenn and Mondale or Hart and Jackson in the same day. I am in the state. I cover the state really, not just one particular campaign.

The press is unfair. Much of the press is biased in one way or another, and also hostile. Many reporters abuse their powers and a lot of unfair things are written. Politics is not pristine. It takes place in the hurly-burly of the marketplace. It is Darwinian, survival of the fittest, and you have to have a certain resilience, strength, instinct, courage, character, luck, charm, and appeal. There are a lot of things that go into it. All I can say is, by the time the candidate gets to the voters, he has been through the wringer a few times with the press, and you see him, more or less, warts and all. It may not be fair. It may look like we are picking on him, but nobody every stuck a gun to his head and said, "Gary Hart, your sentence for your crime is that you have to run for president." They want to be there. They welcome it. They come to the media and say, "Put my name in the paper."

We cover television and its impact on politics better than television covers newspapers and their impact on politics, because television is like a rich kid who is big, strong, and wealthy and can do anything he wants but does not know what to do. Papers and the people who work for them are not as rich and as famous, but I think it is easier to have an idea of what you are about and want to do if you work in the print media. I have a great respect for a lot of people in television. Ted Koppel's show, *ABC News Nightline,* has been a great public service for this country. The *McNeil/Lehrer Newshour* is very good. Individual correspondents like Roger Mudd or Ken Bode of NBC are esteemed by their print colleagues as well as their industry's news directors. But it is just harder for television.

The good TV people, Roger Mudd and people like that, the major TV anchors and the network political correspondents, are very good. They are more highly paid than newspaper people. But they have less freedom, less ability to initiate, and less control over their product than does a senior reporter or columnist. They are the prisoners of their format more so than we are.

In newspapers you can be critical. It is easier for me because the *Globe* is a liberal paper. If you are in television you cannot be critical. If you are the White House correspondent for CBS, which is the senior TV job in the White House, you cannot be as argumentative as you can be in print. You cannot go much in depth. The evening news is twenty-four minutes of headlines illustrated by pictures. It is not a 1,000-word column selecting every detail the way you want. Watch Dan Rather on the *CBS Evening News* and then listen to his commentaries on the radio around 4:30 every afternoon. And it was the same with Cronkite. His radio spots were designed to help the CBS radio network and also to give the anchor a chance to let off a little steam, to be a little more liberal, opinionated, and critical. When he is on camera he cannot raise an eyebrow, or snarl. What would you think if Dan Rather came on and said, "Jesus, can you believe this? This is what Reagan said today. That the homeless are there by choice. This guy is tapioca." You can do that in print. Maybe Rather will say in his commentary on radio, "You know? I think the president was wrong." But put him on television, and he is right down the middle, and straight. No sensible person can believe with a straight face what they have to report, and often they just give you the deadpan, "The president said today . . ." They are hoping you will read between the lines. But the people out there in TV land, the mush heads and those who do not really pay attention—what we in the newspaper business call the lipreaders—they do not get the subtlety. Television is not a subtle medium.

Television is like a giant cyclops. It is a huge giant in everybody's path, but it only has one eye. That is the only way it can see. A print reporter can report in many different ways. The sarcasm you can use in print would be unthinkable for a TV reporter. Many TV people started out in newspapers, but they will all tell you uniformly the flaws of their own medium. What I have attempted to do is to explain the strengths and flaws of newspaper coverage as I see it and practice it.

10
News Magazines in Campaigns

John Mashek

Before I dazzle you with my brilliance and perspicacity as a political writer, let me relate an experience from the 1976 campaign. The Democrats had practically a batallion running for president that year. *U.S. News and World Report* had all of them come in from time to time on background to find out what made such forgetable candidates as Fred Harris, Lloyd Benson, and "Scoop" Jackson tick. I had a phone call one day from a guy who identified himself as Jody Powell and he said, calling from Atlanta, "I understand you're having all these candidates in and you haven't had Governor Carter in." I repressed the impulse to say, "Jimmy who?" and I said, "Sure." Carter stood at 1 percent in the polls at that time. So about three weeks later Jody brought Jimmy in and we sat down and had lunch. As my editor and I were walking back to the office after the lunch he turned to me and said, "Well. I was pretty impressed. Carter obviously did his homework on all the issues. Mashek, you're supposed to be the political expert, what do you think?" And I said, "Jimmy Carter has about as much chance of being elected president as a Pole does of being the next pope." Well, we know what happened. We have the Polish Pope and we had Jimmy Carter.

In discussing the role of news magazines and their impact or lack thereof on political campaigns, and I am going to be focusing more on my own magazine. But I can also give perspective on the roles of *Time* and *Newsweek*. First, you have the circulation of news magazines to contend with. No presidential campaign or candidate is going to sneeze at a total 9,000,000 circulation plus a 20 to 30 million readership for news magazines. *Time* sales are about 3.2 million, *Newsweek* 2.9 million, and *U.S. News* 2.2 million. We brag that we have a circulation figure of 2.2 million but a readership of 10 million including the pass-along readership. I sometimes wonder how all that is figured; but, if they say 10 million, I say 10 million. That's not to be sneezed at. It's a substantial readership. The important thing to keep in mind is timing. We are a weekly deadline publication the same as *Time* and *Newsweek*. unlike the minute to minute deadlines of radio, the wire, services, TV to some extent, and the daily deadlines of newspapers. So we have to approach things in a different way.

Take as an example a week during the primary campaign. Our magazine emphasizes a stage-setting to its stories. If the Iowa caucus has just happened but the New Hampshire primary is about to happen, we will emphasize New Hampshire. We will carry a story on the results of Iowa but that will be secondary to a look ahead. The results are important but we focus on what the results mean in New Hampshire, or on Super Tuesday when the Democrats select over 600 delegates. Our timing and focus are very important. We focus more on what is ahead than on the past which is already old news.

Time and *Newsweek* have later deadlines than we do. They can even go into Sundays. Our deadline is 8:00 p.m. eastern standard time Friday night. That is *it*. If something happens on Saturday, we are dead. As writers we have to keep in mind that the readers are going to be looking at this next Monday. There has to be some freshening of the angle for us to explore because there is no sense in repeating what people have already seen or heard about a week before. It is history. That crystalizes the importance of planning sessions and always keeping the calendar in mind. It was frustrating to be a White House correspondent and take a trip with Ford or Carter leaving on a Friday and coming back on a Sunday or Monday. That is really a down time for us. I felt sometimes I was there just as a guard in case there was an assassination attempt. Many presidential trips were over as news by the time we got back. Thus, there had to be something important and meaningful coming out of them for us to use.

There are things we do well and things we do not do so well. On the positive side, news magazines can take an issue and probe it more deeply than television with its 60 90-second takes. Walter Cronkite said it very well at the University of Texas a few years ago: "I hope the American voter or the American citizen does not get all his information from TV because he is cheating himself or herself if they do because they are just seeing a snapshot and they really do need to read newspapers and magazines if you are going to get depth." So that is one thing we can do that newspapers and television cannot do well. We can take an issue and really examine it—not just in politics but in business, finance, or space.

In the middle of 1983, when we knew the Democratic field was going to be large, we decided that we were not going to be swept up with what the polls were dictating because the two best-known candidates, Walter Mondale and John Glenn, were far out in front. We would give all the candidates a three-page front story. Not a story that was some sort of a puff piece, but a biographical story with some critical analysis to tell our readers exactly what made these people tick and where they stood on the issues. We felt that this background would help readers and voters stay informed. I wrote four or five of them and went out with the candidate several times even though I had been out with him many times before in some cases, just to get a feel of what they were saying and how audiences were reacting to them. Those long stories formed the backbone of our political coverage in 1983. We made up our mind that we were not going to be swept up by dinners, forums, and state cattle shows making us run around and using all our budget to follow the candidates of meaningless straw polls. There was a straw poll in Alabama that is a good example. Cranston won a young Democrats poll in Alabama. Twenty-five people showed up. To even mention that in more than one paragraph is a disservice. Does anybody really think that Alan Cranston would carry Alabama? Yet some of the media paid attention to that. I did one story on straw polls and went to Atlanta, Georgia, and did a story on the anatomy of a straw poll. I stressed how a cattle show is put together getting the candidates there and raising money for the state party. I was not making fun of it but putting it into a better perspective. That it was to some an important political event. But a lot of the press did a disservice to readers and voters by lifting those events into something they were not.

There was no Republican contest in 1984. Yet we were not ignoring Reagan. We assumed he would run. Many in the press got swept up into the "Is he going to run?" "Isn't he going to run?" The assumption should have been made that he was going to run and leave it alone, because there was too much press focus on something that people really were not taking note of. I do not think there is a lot of political interest the year before an election. People do not focus on politics.

We attach a lot of importance in the magazine to what might be called "side bar" stories in the daily press. For example, one of the pieces we ran was "Campaign Advertising, Is It Effective or Isn't It?" We take a candidate, as an example, who has some good, professionally done TV commercials. Then we examine whether they have helped him. Well, if you take Iowa as a gauge, good commercials certainly did not help Glenn. In campaign advertising so much money is spent—50 to 60 percent of campaign budgets. Who are these people? How are these commercials made? What does the campaign consultant think about when he is producing these ads? This is what we try to do in our side bar stories. Another side bar might be the debates and their history. How important are they? How effective? How do candidates use them?

The issues are important. The press, not just magazines, but newspapers and television have taken the rap of, "You don't say anything about the issues; all you do is focus on the personalities." I have heard that until I am blue in the face and I am defensive about it. Invariably during campaigns we devote lots of space—several pages—to where the candidates stand (in their own words) on every issue from the Middle East to budget deficits. I sometimes wonder whether the same people who are criticizing us for not having stories about where the candidate stands are bored to tears with them and do not read them. They are more swept up into the personality cult of politics than we are.

There is one story I want to refer to because some of my colleagues kid me about it. We published a piece called "The ABCs of Electing a President." One of my competitors said, "Well, that's just a primer that you could get in a civics lesson at any school." The piece was about eight or ten pages and was very basic. You would be amazed at how many people who are close to this process would flunk an examination on some very basic questions. For example, what is a favorite son candidate, or what is a bandwagon candidate? We often take too much for granted before we sit down to write a story that the reader knows a great deal about the subject. I am not saying we should go out and reinvent the wheel, but there is a time for basics. As a writer, I am not writing these stories for my colleagues, the guys on the bus, I am writing them for the readers. And if it takes getting a little basic now and then, I think it is important because you are going to lose a lot of people if you write over their heads and give them only inside information. I feel very strongly about this. All of journalism is losing sight of this. Incidentally, we had requests for 200,000 reprints for those "ABCs" last year, so somebody out there must have liked it.

I do not think anything is too basic. Obviously you are not going to rewrite the constitution every week and explain it to people. Maybe I am being a little defensive because of needling from my colleagues on the "ABCs" story. I like to watch people on airplanes—watch their habits in reading newspapers and magazines because I write politics. I see a lot of people just skim. By covering a lot of the basics of government and politics you are not going to interest all readers, but you owe it to readers and subscribers to explain the basics. In Iowa, what is a caucus? An editor asked me that before I went out just to test me. He said, "I think we ought to do a story on Iowa about a caucus." My first reaction was, "What! Who gives a damn?" And he said, "Well, that's what they're having out there, aren't they?" And the more he talked I thought, "This guy makes sense." I went out and talked to a few precinct captains for Mondale and Cranston. I asked, "What do you do? How are you getting your people to your caucus?" And one guy just said, "Well, I'm just going to call my friends. They'd better show up. They're my friends." The Cranston guy was a farmer in the northeastern part of the state, sixty-six years old, and had never worked in politics before. His candidate had finished fourth, but this guy was emotionally wrapped up in the peace issue and he thought Cranston was right. I asked, "Well, how many people do you think he'll get to the caucus?" And he said, "Oh, about twelve." My editor was right. It was important to tell our readers what the caucus system was about as opposed to a primary. You do not spend thousands of words on it but it still explains something very important.

Reporters can lose a lot of perspective if they crowd a candidate. That is fun to do when you are younger. It is no fun anymore to be gone from Labor Day until election day. We are going to have reporters with the presidential candidates, but my assignment is not simply to cover the candidates but to talk to voters, to local people, businessmen, labor leaders, and local editors. You can learn a lot about what is going on in the campaign and who is going to win that way. I should have listened to my instincts in 1980. I knew Reagan was going to win but I did not believe what I heard in states like Pennsylvania, Ohio, and New York. I heard it but did not believe statements like, "You know, Carter is not doing well here." The polls were so much closer than that and they made me disregard my first-hand experience. Next time around I am going to listen to my own instincts and continue to talk to people and not just to candidates.

What do we need to do better or what are we missing? The thing that bothers me the most is that we are too much into the horse race aspect of a campaign. As the political editor of *U.S. News* I am trying to avoid that, but you get swept up and you have to say who wins and who loses. I think getting into the horse race aspect way ahead of Iowa is a mistake.

The reliance on polls bothers me, because for every accurate poll there is an inaccurate one. Every story ought to qualify the poll ahead of time with some disclaimer. We get taken in with polls that have shown to have been inaccurate down the line. I think we ought to be very careful in television with exit polls. During the 1984 primary season, Iowa was called by NBC two minutes after the caucus opened on the basis of two precincts.

News magazines feature analysis. They can do that better than newspapers or the evening news. But we seem to be better as scene setters than at postelection analysis. Why did one candidate get only 3 percent? Or why did another, who was apparently the best organized, do so poorly? It is almost like the Superbowl. There must be "yards" written about the Superbowl leading up to the game, yet little insightful stuff afterward. Yet I would have a difficult time selling the editors on an "after" piece unless there were something really meaningful, mainly because it looks back and is by that time old news.

News magazine stories are tightly edited. That is one of the tough sides of the business. Those pages are valuable and there is a lot of competition for that space. When I am doing a story and told what I thought was going to be a three-page story becomes a two-page story, I am crushed because I have to go in and edit. You think everything in there is so good you die a thousand deaths loving that page.

TV news has a formula format, meaning the three networks do not necessarily break new ground by spending five minutes on a story when competitors spend a minute and a half. There are three major news magazines. Each has a profitable and successful formula. There is probably too much comfort in the way we write. We write not for profit but out of habit. It has to do with how we did it four years ago or eight years ago or how our magazines do it today.

What are the differences among *Time, Newsweek,* and *U.S. News?* The one thing I have to say is that what they do, they do well. They are more colorful. They entertain. Their publications use more adjectives and adverbs. Our mission is more to inform. Therefore, there are more nouns and verbs in *U.S. News.* Some people say we are dull. But some people like reading writing that is not that flashy.

Time and *Newsweek* consider themselves competitive. They look at us as the little guy down the block. We are based in Washington whereas *Time* and *Newsweek* are based in New York. That is one difference. With later deadlines, if something happens on a Saturday, they can change covers. We can change covers only until Friday morning. We started our press run Friday morning when Andropov's death was reported and had to throw about 400,000 magazines out because of the cover. But that is the investment you have to make.

How am I influenced? I read *Time* and *Newsweek* but not until late in the week. And I am amazed sometimes at the same types of stories we have and where they give more time to it and we give less or vice versa. But they have no influence. I am interested in how they cover something a little differently. I run into *Time* and *Newsweek* reporters, but there is no comparing of notes or the like, only friendly rivalry. When you see them you want to know what story they are working on. But I am really not influenced by them. I get mad sometimes when I see a story they have that I wish we had. That gives me pause. But there is no collusion.

11

Local Television News in Campaigns: Boston

Kirby Perkins

In major media markets such as Boston there is a lot of competition among stations. There is as much interest in their competitive coverage as in the campaign itself. In the Boston market Channel 5 probably did more coverage than anyone else. But it was not hard issue-oriented reporting. It was more of the profile variety that played to give people some information about the candidates. Early in the race the networks are not as important to a candidacy as the local stations are. One of the reasons for this is that more people watch local news than network news. What happens in the New Hampshire primary, especially for the Boston TV stations, is that Boston stations can show what they can do. Each station sets up its own operation in New Hampshire.

Local reporters tend to be more deferential to a candidate. The main reason for that is the "boys on the bus" travel with the candidate day after day. They know the candidates better. They know what they said yesterday and what they said today. It is easier for those people to get a line on what is happening.

How do we in Boston cover a campaign and how does that coverage affect what happens? All of us had our own studios in New Hampshire. Coverage from the Iowa caucus to the primary consisted of about twelve minutes a night. Twelve minutes may not sound like a lot, but it is an enormous amount of time for a local TV station that has approximately thirty-five minutes out of an hour dedicated to news. TV stations are attempting to cover a story because there is a public interest to be served in covering that story. Second, there is a very intense competitive situation for the coverage.

When Walter Mondale arrived in New Hampshire he was covered like the imperial candidate, the favorite, the invincible juggernaut. How did we know he was invincible? We local reporters are not dummies. We read the *Boston Globe*, the *New York Times,* and the *Washington Post.* We know a smooth, well-organized political machine when we see one. He was covered that way. When you cover a campaign you have to report what you see. Mondale's campaign organization was an incredibly impressive gathering of people. The consensus was that Walter Mondale probably could not be beaten.

The principal vehicle for discussing the campaign is the horse race. I do not say that with a great deal of admiration and pride, but it is basically a horse race story. Who is winning? Why are they winning? It was not until the Sunday before the Tuesday primary that it became clearer to me—and I suspect to everyone else who was watching him—that Gary Hart was going to do far better than we had thought. I covered him on Sunday and saw him at a senior citizens' luncheon in Nashua and the people were out the back door. It was packed and they were enthusiastic. Previously every other time I had been with him it had been he and I and a cameraman in a barber shop. But still the perception continued that the best he could do was second. After you have heard it for so long, you believe it. So when we were still covering the horse race the question was how in the world was he going to finish second, and could he get close enough to Mondale to be perceived as actually winning. So if we were covering a horse race, how did we miss the big story? How did everyone in New Hampshire miss the fact that Gary Hart was going to win there when no one thought he could do it? The first explanation lies in the notion of the safety of the journalistic pack. Unless you have compelling reasons to believe otherwise, what is thought to be true tends to be what is reported by almost everyone. The line of reporting tends to be fairly consistent from newspaper to newspaper, TV network to network, and station to station. The next reason everyone missed the story was in the nature of day to day journalism. We get paid to determine what is new today from yesterday. It was not easy to figure that out, this idea that there is a generation of Americans who started to say, "We're looking for something new." It was missed. It was missed in New Hampshire. All of a sudden it was there, and the only time we saw it was in the last exit poll done by ABC news. ABC news and the *Washington Post* saw it and they actually backed off themselves. The night before the primary their polling data showed that Gary Hart was going to win; they were so flabbergasted that they had to call it a dead heat. At that point everybody got up in the morning on Tuesday and they were all convinced that Gary Hart might win, but we could not believe it.

The second answer is somewhat more subjective, reflective, and nonempirical, but I think most people love a good fight and that is especially true in New Hampshire. It is a better story. American voters and the American media all love to believe in an ill-defined notion of the American dream. We like to think that you cannot be taken for granted. Just through tenacious work people can make themselves into something that everyone thought they could not be. There was a generalized belief in

New Hampshire among reporters and also campaign people that in the end Walter Mondale took it for granted and Gary Hart worked very hard for it and that was one of the main reasons he was able to pull off that victory.

All of us who cover local politics thought that Massachusetts was going to be the next challenge after New Hampshire, but all of a sudden we found out that everyone had gone South on us and we were left with no one to cover other than the noble but somewhat nostalgic George McGovern who was making his last stand in Massachusetts. Everyone else left the state. Now all of us who had been in New Hampshire in what was a very competitive and intense battle to see who would provide the best coverage had to figure out what to do. In Boston we were able to spend some money and chase the candidates. I was dispatched to Georgia, while our other reporters went to Alabama and Florida. Our Super Tuesday coverage instead of being principally a Massachusetts story wound up being an Alabama, Florida, and Georgia story. That was a classic example of the relationship between a campaign and the people who cover it. The "boys on the bus," the national press, and the big city local press always go with the candidates. Now we local reporters go with the candidates as well.

With one hour rather than thirty minutes we can spend ten or twelve minutes on political coverage as opposed to network news. Local stations have the opportunity to spend seven minutes on Gary Hart. The national news is not going to spend seven minutes examining Gary Hart's "new ideas." They are going to wait for the *New York Times* to do that. But even though we have the opportunity to devote seven minutes to Hart's issues we do not do it.

If asked to defend the dearth of issue coverage on TV news I will not. Right after Gary Hart won the Maine caucus and Massachusetts was thought to be the next battleground before they all went South, I tried for two days to get the "Gary Hart and his new ideas" story on the air and could not. The reason I could not get it on the air was because the most dedicated political station in Boston was simply unwilling to do it due to the amount of time that would have required. It was a mistake. In the day to day process they say, "Oh, but you got him at Quincy Market." My point is that this whole idea of issue-oriented coverage always sounds good, but in the day to day mix of the local and network TV stations it always finds its way to the back burner. That is an unfortunate admission. Generally political coverage gets 3, 4, or 5 minutes out of the hour newscast, which only has thirty-five minutes worth of news to begin with. It tends to be very spot-oriented coverage. If Walter Mondale came to town to Boston that day and said, "What are Gary Hart's "new ideas?" and he listed three examples of inconsistencies, that would be the story of the day. The candidates tend to determine the day to day turf that we report on. The *New York Times* had one of its Washington reporters explore Gary Hart's Senate record. They published a very thoughtful piece on Gary Hart, "The Genesis of New Ideas"—to what extent are they new—and they simply analyzed his entire Senate voting record. So you think Channel 5 is going to send me to Washington to do that? I doubt it. I do not say that with pride but regret, but that is reality.

Newspapers like to have people keep reading, so they like to have good writing. We like to have them keep watching, and unfortunately action tends to be an inducement to keep watching, so we give them pictures of the day's events.

Local TV stations in major markets live and die financially with the financial success of their news operations. That is why competitive considerations are so important. In a city like Boston if you get one more rating point it probably means $3, $4, or $5 million in revenue. So they spent money to send us to Illinois, around $12,000. It is a trivial sum given what they think they get back for it. If they do not make enough of those decisions correctly they are out to lunch. For example, I went to Ireland. The reason I went to Ireland with Mayor Flynn was to give Channel 5 exclusivity. Those kinds of decisions are a news director's decision. TV stations are as much a business as anything else.

In Boston's case not covering New Hampshire like we did would probably be the equivalent of a New Bedford station not covering the Big Dan's rape trial or a Providence station not covering the Von Bulow trial. It is a given that you are going to cover it. The question is how well are you going to cover it. The competition between TV stations has a down side and an up side. The up side is that increased competition means that they spend more money to cover stories better. The down side is that the increased competitive pressures sometimes tend to detract from the content of the news. For example, if Gary Hart comes to town, I have to cover him very quickly in the first section of the newscast. It is not going to run any longer than two minutes, regardless of what he does, unless something extraordinary happens. But our station also developed what they call a check point segment which occurs later in the newscast. Those segments tend to be 4, 5, or 6 minutes, which is about all the time you can reasonably fill up in an interesting way, given the requirements of daily journalism. You can in a four to five minute stretch of time get something said that helps people make a decision about who they want to vote for.

The real failure of television in the last ten years is that network newscasts are still only a half hour. Ten years ago the big issue was how could the networks move from a half hour to an hour. They have to take the whole world and telescope it into a half hour. That is absurd. The best campaign coverage on television would occur if ABC, CBS, and NBC all had an hourlong evening newscast. They would do the same thing that local newscasts now do. They would still be fairly hard and fast at the top, but in the back of that hour they would start giving you longer, more thoughtful pieces, because they would have a lot more to work with. With network correspondents, their frustration is that they almost never get on the air. I fight to get more of what I think is important on the air. Other people who have other interest fight to get what *they* think is important on the air. And there are people who run a news operation who tend to referee all of those disputes and make management decisions about what they are going to put on the air.

Government and politics tend not to rank very high when you survey audiences to try to determine interests. At a bar if you watch what people tend to look at, it would not be Gary Hart. They see fire on the screen and people screaming and that attracts their eye. Television is a mass medium, probably more so than any other. With newspapers, you have the option of reading an article or not. You can read the first two paragraphs and say, "See you later." In television you read the first two paragraphs and you also get the third, fourth, and fifth, because it is a linear medium. In television you start at 6:00 p.m. and you end at 7:00 p.m. And there is only one way to get from here to there and that is to keep going straight. There are two options as a viewer. One is to keep watching and the other is to stop watching. That is why there is so much pressure to make reports either overwhelmingly compelling or brief. Out of my audience of 200,000, one-quarter of them are reasonably interested in the story. The other three-quarters do not care about it. So there is enormous pressure to keep it interesting.

If you have Gary Hart in town and you do a two-minute story on him and you have him walking through Quincy Market and doing these other things—just the sheer set-up of the story, just the showing of the pictures takes up 35, 40, or 50 seconds, and you have not even started on the first issue. Some stories lend themselves readily to time and place consistency. If, for example, Gary Hart is at the General Dynamics Shipyard at Quincy, you can make a calculated decision that I am not going to do a report on Gary Hart's views on Central America today. Instead we are going to talk about his relationship to unions and his views on defense. Then you have time and place consistency and the pictures you are showing bear some resemblance to and connection with the issues of being discussed. That is why there is such an overwhelming need in television to get pictures of what you are going to talk about.

Let me give you a classic example from the *CBS Evening News*. El Salvador is currently one of the most compelling international stories. The

CBS news had footage of a cameraman from *Time* getting shot. In terms of importance in the politics of El Salvador it did not rank high, but it was a way to vividly remind people of that story. It was the lead for only one reason—CBS had pictures of it. Had they not, it might have been among the final stories in the newscast.

There is an equal time fairness doctrine that mandates that you have to give candidates equal time on a show like the *Today Show*. News shows are exempt from the equal time provisions of the fairness doctrine. So we are in no sense obligated to do anything other than what we determine to be fair, accurate, and responsible in our newscast. That is why peripheral candidates get less time. It is not that there is a desire to do them in. In terms of news value they are not determined to be as significant as other candidates.

Sometimes candidates do things exclusively for newspapers and they are very important. Gary Hart, for example, had a meeting when he came to Boston with the *Globe* editorial board. We do not get in the *Globe* editorial room and take pictures and listen in while the *Globe's* stable of reporters and a few editors ask questions of Gary Hart. But these events are very important because they help determine the style of coverage and the impressions that a certain influential newspaper has of the candidate. So Gary Hart or Walter Mondale would take very seriously a meeting at the editorial board of the *New York Times*, the *Washington Post*, the *Boston Globe*, or any other major newspaper, because in most cities newspapers set the tone for the coverage in a given city. Even in the electronic era that tends to be the case. The long-term trends covered in a campaign are mostly defined in print. But when they come to town there are always events scheduled with cameras in mind. The candidates know it and do it to accommodate the people who are catering to them. It is a symbiotic relationship. In fact they get pointed out, and after a while it gets absurd because everybody knows it and you just give them a visual backdrop for whatever it is that is being said. If a candidate ever refused to take his campaign to a location that was pleasing to the camera he would be doing himself in. And the people who covered him would be complaining left and right.

The visuals are important, but so is the amount of time devoted to a story. *McNeil/Lehrer* broke the mold a long time ago with its half-hour program. Most people think *Nightline* was a radical innovation, but it was just an 11:30 p.m. version of what *McNeil/Lehrer* had already been doing for seven or eight years. Public television tends to be the workshop of new ideas. My convention has always been, "Fewer stories, better told." But that runs contrary to research that any consulting firm in television will offer you. That is why stories are short—TV journalism now "suffers" from the insights of modern "research" which tells you how to cover the news better. This research purports to tell you what the audience wants. It is like product research—telling you how to build a Chevrolet that will sell, not one that will travel more safely.

Consultant advice on how to make local news profitable has been the big thing for over a decade. I think they have come close to running television! Right now they are advising a station in New York that it is time to go back to news. News will sell now. I have nothing good to say about consultants. If anybody tells you that they are just gathering a little information for you and then putting it on the desk of the news director and saying, "Take a look at these when you get a chance," they are wrong. These consultants, especially in smaller markets, almost run news shops. And that means that you have taken that role away from people who are paid professionals in journalism and who are now less and less in control. I do not know of a consultant anywhere who says, "Give them more political coverage." I have never heard them say that. In fact, I saw a ranking of some of the topics people are most interested in and politics and government were way at the bottom.

12
Local Television News in Campaigns: Providence

Laureen White

Local stations in large media markets like Boston have the resources to develop many specialty units, among them a political unit. WLNE-TV Providence is in a medium-sized market. The news director at Channel 6 decided not to create a unit exclusively devoted to political coverage. Instead, we covered the candidates as they came to town and relied on networks for day to day activities and analysis. We did not spend money to send a crew to New Hampshire for the nation's first primary. The cost of buying satellite time and all the other logistical expenses involved just was not worth it for us. The local NBC affiliate did send a crew to New Hampshire, but they did not trek all over New England and the rest of the country covering every campaign appearance. The management at WLNE felt there was no way our people were going to outdo the CBS network specialists and political producers who had spent the last two years recording every whistle stop. In addition, we were in the midst of covering two major local stories: the infamous New Bedford gang rape trial and the corruption scandals rocking Providence city hall.

Candidates use local TV news as a campaign vehicle. They fly into town, hitting three or four states a day. They hold impromptu news conferences, and they know local TV stations will come running. Candidates realize that when they come to town, the media roll out the red carpet. They are big local news. Their appearances command upward of five minutes on the evening newscasts. While that may not seem like a big chunk of time, it is. Consider that a typical half-hour broadcast devotes approximately ten minutes to "news." The rest of the time is spent on weather, sports, and commercial breaks. For instance, Gary Hart came to town, called a news conference, staged a rally, and walked the streets of Providence flanked by enthusiastic supporters. Each of the three local TV stations spent several minutes that night on the story. That is expensive and useful TV time the candidates could not otherwise buy. It is practically free publicity. They know it is a gold mine because much of it remains unedited. Oftentimes, fundraisers or news conferences are held at

6:00 p.m. to coincide with news time. Political operatives are hoping to generate so-called live coverage. The advantage to that is three to four minutes of unedited campaign rhetoric going directly into the local viewers' living rooms.

Candidates know they are not going to be peppered with a lot of tough questions from local reporters because most stations around the country are in the same position as Channel 6. They do not have experienced political reporters who have spent a lot of time researching, traveling, and becoming informed on the campaigns. They are not going to spot inconsistencies. For the local reporter, it is the next stop after yesterday's apartment house fire and before tomorrow's drug bust. Candidates have probably been asked the same questions dozens of times by other reporters around the country. They have their stock answers. A masterful performance during a live broadcast is what they are after. Local TV stations crave live remotes, as well. In fact, I wish I had a nickel for every time during a morning editorial meeting the question was asked, "What can we do live tonight?"

If a candidate comes to town on a weekend, it is even a bigger story because of the dearth of significant news on Saturdays and Sundays. Recently George McGovern came to town on a Wednesday. He was competing with several big local news items. Consequently, he got very little air time, probably forty-five seconds at best. The other candidates, Hart and Jackson, visited during the weekend. They got close to ten minutes each, spread out over several days.

Walter Mondale was supposed to come to Rhode Island the day of the New Hampshire primary. But as his prospects for victory grew increasingly bleak, he decided to skip this state, where there were only twenty-two delegates at stake, and put his efforts elsewhere. He had by far the most sophisticated local campaign organization. He was the first in our area to introduce the satellite news conference. While he never campaigned here, he sent letters to all the assignment editors saying, "If you want to plug into Walter Mondale, just turn your satellite dish around and you can get Walter Mondale in Alabama or Walter Mondale in Florida and you can even ask him a question." We never took advantage of it. But his organization called several news conferences to sing his praises, sponsored by prominent Democrats in the state, including the governor.

Television carries a tremendous burden, because 65 percent of the viewing public gets most of its news from it. Forty-one percent of the public gets all its news from television. That is certainly no way to make an informed decision, considering the reams of material and analysis published in newspapers and magazines. The chairman of Rhode Island's Republican Party claims less than 15 percent of the population votes according to issues. Less than 15 percent even know where their candidates stand on the issues. WLNE's own market research suggests less than a quarter of all viewers in southeastern New England even care about politics. If you are wondering about their main concern—it is the weather forecast.

As an assignment editor, I am responsible for collecting, sorting, and gathering information on all story possibilities. Early in the morning, I go through the assignment folder for that day and decide with our limited resources what stories we will commit ourselves to and to what extent. We strive for a well-rounded newscast, combining hard news, soft news, and enterprise reporting. It is certainly far from a precise science. You have to use your gut instincts and experience to put together a product that will prove useful and interesting to the viewer. When a presidential candidate comes to town, covering him is a given. The question is, what angle do we pursue that might prove valuable to our viewers? For instance, since Rhode Island is the Ocean State, we might look at the candidate's ideas on cleaning up the bay. Traditionally, TV news crews focus on the horse race, the nuances of the event itself and how the crowd reacted. After the story is shot, the reporter must negotiate with the show producer on how much time will be allotted. Typically, a piece runs anywhere from two to four minutes. If it is a weekend, time constraints are practically nonexistent because very little else of substance is happening.

When TV reporters assemble a story, they must keep two things in mind: what will the narration say, and how can the story be told with the available pictures. The viewers not only are interested in what happened that day and where the candidate went, but they are also curious about how the politician interacts with the crowd. Is he funny; is he stiff; is he quick on his feet; what kinds of clothes does he wear; does he bring his wife along; does he seem comfortable. Naturally, this is a more exciting and telling picture than, perhaps, a static shot of a piece of campaign literature. The bottom line is that the reporter wants you to watch his piece. If you do not have the incentive to look up from your newspaper, the reporter has failed. Pay particular note to the opening and closing shots of the story. The reporter wants to grab your attention from the start and leave you with something to remember.

We have not had a president come to Providence in several years. Most of their on-camera appearances masquerade as official duty. For instance, there may not be anything intrinsically noteworthy about bill signing. But why not invite the cameras in for a bill signing "ceremony"? The end result, oftentimes, is the same: visibility on television. A sitting president wants the viewers to perceive that he is carrying on the rigors of being president. Another advantage the incumbent has is more flexibility with campaign money. The more he can pass off as "official business," the less he needs to spend from his campaign coffers on public appearances. That money can then be spent to purchase TV ads. Generally, you do not have to worry about incumbents getting their due; they get plenty of coverage on network television.

It is a different ball game on the local level. Coverage is dictated by availability. Since our station did not travel around the country following the candidates, we were left with little choice. When the candidates came to town, we were there. Roughly, they all got the same treatment, with the possible exception of George McGovern, who got a little less air time because it was a busy news day. The major networks have a far tougher problem to deal with in terms of fairness. Not only must they keep in mind story quantity, they must also factor in the tone of the story. The political specialists are more apt to turn a tough investigative piece based on their expertise. However, one rarely finds such aggressiveness on the local level.

13
Functions of Presidential Campaigns

Bruce E. Gronbeck

The Federal Election Commission's annual reports for 1980 and 1981 make fascinating reading. From them we learn that: The presidential primaries—excluding money spent by political action groups and other independent agencies—cost almost $63 million; following the primaries, the general election, contested by Reagan, Carter, and Anderson—and again excluding PAC expenditures—cost those candidates' organizations about $67 or $68 million; the Democrats and Republicans each received from the Federal Election Commission over $4.2 million to help finance their conventions; taxpayers, through the checkoff box on income tax forms, provided about $100 million of those dollars in $1 increments; by the last weeks of the campaign, Jimmy Carter was dropping $4 million per week on television, with Reagan spending twice that amount. Overall, adding together governmental matching funds, personal contributions to the candidates and their organizations, the money spent by PACs and other independent groups, and national party organizations, the total amount of money spent on the presidential campaign alone in 1980 ran between $800 million and $1 billion, nearly doubling the estimated $520 million spent in 1976.[1]

These figures are staggering. Why is it that more and more dollars are being spent every four years only to turn out a smaller and smaller percentage of eligible voters in this country? In 1980, only 53 percent of our eligible voters cast ballots.[2] Even my own county in Iowa which is *the* most politically active county in a highly political state, managed to get out only a little over two-thirds of its eligible voters in 1980. Because of Iowa's bellwether position as the earliest caucus state, millions and millions of those dollars were spent there by presidential hopefuls even prior to January 1980. Yet the state turnout, while certainly above the national average, was anything but spectacular—63 percent.[3]

Facts such as these cause candidates and potential candidates to despair, campaign and party organizers to get ulcers, and serious academic scholars to question their explanations for and accounts of political campaigns. Political communication theorists and researchers, in particular, have had to make intellectual adjustments in recent years, as they have realized that thinking about campaigns primarily as mechanisms which just elect a chief executive is narrow- or even wrong-minded thinking. Broader conceptualizations have emerged, and, in the process, functional campaign theories—in particular, dramaturgical versions of functional theory—have begun guiding research.

In this essay I will review the classic "limited effects" model of campaign research, not so much to beat on it once more but to probe its strengths and shortcomings conceptually. Then I will examine general functional alternatives to the limited effects model in order to specify their intellectual strength and pave the way for a look at a particular functional theory of considerable promise, so-called dramaturgical theory.

The Classic Model of Campaign Communication Research

The classical model for campaign communication research has been termed a positivist or social-scientific model which attempts to answer the simple question, "What are the effects of communication upon the outcome of electoral politics?" Answers to that question, beginning in 1948 with the publication of Lazarsfeld, Berelson, and Gaudet's enormously influential *The People's Choice,* have been sought primarily through systematic and controlled survey research. Lazarsfeld and his colleagues employed a panel research technique which allowed them to sample systematically and pursue electoral questions longitudinally. They drew their 1940 sample from Erie County, Ohio, and their 1948 sample from Elmira, New York. Generally, they found movement in voters' preferences in roughly only a quarter to a third of their sample between May and October; more startling for many observers, they discovered that only 5-7 percent of their respondents actually switched their preferences from one party candidate to another.[4]

Further investigation by other researchers produced similar findings. By 1960, these findings were forged into what has been called the "limited effects model" of political mass communication or, a bit more elegantly, "the law of minimal consequences."[5] That law is phrased in the following manner by the man who articulated it, Joseph T. Klapper:

> Within a given audience exposed to particular communications, reinforcement, or at least constancy of opinion, is typically found to be the dominant effect; minor change, as in intensity of opinion, is found to be the next most common; and conversion is typically found to be the most rare. . . . This is in no way to say that major changes and conversions do not occur, nor that under particular conditions they may not be widespread. It is rather to say that by comparison they are rare, and that persuasive mass communication normally tends to serve far more heavily in the interests of reinforcement and of minor change.[6]

Once the law of minimal consequences was articulated, there was scramble by social scientists to account for it: Why do not mass communi. cation messages produce greater changes in attitudes and behavior? While many answers are given, the classic research suggested five explanations, all of which can be grouped under a single statement: "Mass mediated communications have minimal consequences in political campaigns because other variables intervene to reduce the effects of those communications." In 1960, that explanation was composed of five more particular explanations:

Explanation 1: Predispositions and Media Selectivity. Perhaps the most heavily researched explanations focused on audience predispositions and selective exposure, selective perception, and selective retention. As Klapper surveyed twenty-some studies, he noted that voters are much more likely to expose themselves to messages which reinforce what they already believe and value; that they are likely to perceive in messages they do hear only those ideas which are in accord with their present beliefs and values; and that they are likely to remember only those elements in messages which are similar to their predispositions. Hence, the ways in which one's predispositions filter what one listens to and sees, how one comprehends it, and what aspects of it one remembers are highly selective psychological mechanisms. Such personal selectivity can reduce significantly the impact of the most artfully constructed piece of political propaganda.

Explanation 2: Group Norms. The second explanation of minimal consequences was even simpler. Small group research as it was developing in the 1950s demonstrated that, in Katz and Lazarsfeld's words, "ostensibly individual opinions and attitudes . . . [are] primarily social [in] character."[7] That is, the groups to which we belong strongly influence our beliefs and attitudes, and those groups' normative standards of behavior— including voting behavior—govern many of our actions.

Explanation 3: Interpersonal Dissemination of Messages. Some research has shown that mass communication messages often are shared by people who heard or read them with people who did not hear or read them. Such interpersonal sharing of messages more likely occurs between people with similar views than between people with similar views than between people with variant opinion, and hence the interpersonal dimension of mass communications works as another form of selective exposure.

Explanation 4: Opinion Leadership. This is simply another way of discussing what is called "the two-step flow of communications," an idea originally articulated by Lazarsfeld, Berelson, and Gaudet in 1948. Regarding the two-step flow hypothesis, research has demonstrated that opinion leaders—individuals who are influential in their communities and social circles—take and pass on positions to others. Further, in the words of Elihu Katz, "personal contacts appear to have been . . . more effective than the mass media in influencing voting decisions."[8] These leaders expose themselves to mass mediated and other messages, formulate choices, and tell others about those choices, with the others then typically following the advice of those leaders on any number of matters, including political preferences and behavior.

Explanation 5: Ideological Middle-of-the-Roadism in Mass Media. Klapper points to some of his own research as well as that of others who have investigated the content of radio and TV programs. Those studies typically show that electronic media programming tends to reflect the attitudes and values of the dominant culture, and hence tends to avoid strong advocacy and controversial stands. Such reinforcement of the dominant ideology, Klapper argues, occurs because the media are commercial or economic institutions that depend on their abilities to attract large audiences—which, of course, those institutions hope not to alienate. Middle-of-the-roadism is considered the best way to avoid such alienation, and thus in terms of political choices, it generally homogenizes differences between candidates. The ideological conservatism of the mass media almost guarantees that voters will not perceive great differences between candidates, and consequently will have little incentive to change party or candidate allegiances during a campaign.[9]

These five explanations were considered to have enough empirical force behind them to explain the "limited effects" of communicative messages during presidential campaigns. Scholars were driven by the logic of their own research findings to minimize the effects of campaign speeches, ads, printed propaganda, and the like upon the voting public. They *had* to minimize those effects theoretically as well, given the way they conceptualized the notion of "effects of messages." In the classic positivist paradigm, researchers were conditioned to deal with objectifiable, even observable, political behavior. Hence they focused their research on beliefs and attitudes—because they could be "measured" by pencil-and-paper tests—and on such political behavior as voting, because votes could be counted objectively.

Additionally, as these researchers examined the general environment of political campaigns, it seemed that most practitioners of politics *acted as though* the primary function of campaigning was to change beliefs and attitudes in such a way as to change voters' behavior. So, these scholars reasoned, if campaigners *think* they are out to change votes and if vote changes are easily measurable, then political campaign research ought to focus on belief, attitudinal, and behavioral change.

But as noted earlier, the idea that campaigns achieve little or nothing—at least in their mass-mediated manifestations—is an anomalous idea. Surely all of that money spent on presidential campaigns must do *something*. And indeed, candidates who talk to many different audiences and spend comparatively large amounts of money on ads, TV spots, computerized mail, and other sorts of mass media are more likely to emerge victorious than candidates who do not. How can such anomalies be explained?

Since the early 1960s, many political researchers have used two theoretical and research strategies to attack the anomalies of the "law of limited consequences." One group has continued working within the assumptions of the classic model, but has (a) refined its research and measuring techniques, and/or (b) made the idea of reinforcement a positive effect. They have recognized that political campaigns are as much if not more processes producing *political stability* as they are processes aiming at *political change*. They likewise have recognized that they focused in the past two exclusively on the campaign message builders. They now are likely to examine the roles of the media and voters in controlling the effects of campaign messages.[10]

Despite such adjustments, many still were dissatisfied. Beginning in the mid-to-late 1960s, political communication researchers argued that a single-minded focus on observable effects was the result of asking the wrong questions about political campaigning. Instead of asking, "What are the effects of political campaign messages?" they asked, "What are the functions of political campaigns?" or "To what uses can political campaigns and messages be put?" These questions do not seem radically different from the great "effects" question asked by Paul Lazarsfeld and his coresearchers. And actually, the shift being proposed was not a radical shift—but it was intellectually or conceptually significant nonetheless. Asking questions about functions or "uses" is important because of what the new questions demand we think about:

1. Questions about functions or uses recognize that campaigns do more for a country than get a leader elected. They recognize that presidential campaigns not only bring about an orderly change in leadership but also serve a much wider range of difficult-to-observe yet discernible purposes and functions.

2. Questions about functions or uses recognize conceptually that campaigns focus on more than a couple of presidential contenders and their staffs. These questions recognize that campaigns bring with them a general mobilization of significant and varied personal, public, and institutional resources of a society.

3. And questions about functions or uses recognize, ultimately, that campaigns as base comprise or constitute a complex, highly significant, sociopolitical, ritualistic drama. A "presidential campaign," that is, is not simply a series of "Why I want to be president" messages which bombard a society for a few months every four years. Rather, a campaign is able to serve so many different needs of so many different kinds of people because it has all the characteristics of a sociopolitical or ritualistic drama: It is repeatable every four years; it is comprised of distinct acts or phrases; it is ubiquitous; it really is audience- rather than candidate-centered; it works primarily, not simply to get someone elected, but to define the essence of a society's "political culture"; and, by the end, the public is not merely "an audience" to all those speeches and ads, but, instead, a series of actors who, like the candidates, have leading roles to play.

The last series of statements, particularly, demand clarification. Before they can be tackled, however, we need a sharper sense of what is meant by "functional theories of campaign communication." Then we can deal with the analytical and practical force of dramaturgical assumptions more cleanly.

Functional Model of Campaign Research

While the functional model of campaign research exists only in bits and pieces, we can construct its basic tenets, at least, in the following manner: [11]

1. *Audience members receiving communications from others are active, not passive, processors of those messages.* While some researchers working within the class limited-effects model seemed to assume that audiences can be manipulated at the will of message builders, functionalists assume that "real world" audiences have considerable freedom in the ways they use mass mediated messages.
2. *Audience members differ in their individual needs, and those needs determine what use individuals will make of the messages to which they are exposed.* In classic studies of the people who listened to radio soap operas, for example, it was found that some people felt needs to escape from "reality" and hence listened to the soaps for "mere entertainment"; that some people were unsure how they were expected to act publicly, and hence listened to them to learn about other people's social expectations; and that some people wanted to learn more about society in general, and so listened to radio serials for facts about the world, that is, in the same way they would listen to news and public affairs programs. [12]

3. *Given varying human needs, audience members differ in the uses to which they put the communications of others, and hence in the kinds of gratifications they get from their consumption or those communications.* Sometimes we may watch a candidate's TV commercial in hopes that it will help us decide how to vote. At other times or in the case of other people, some may watch that same commercial to figure out what issues are important this year, to examine and judge the cleverness of the candidate's media expert, to poke fun at the opposition, to talk back to the TV set and, indirectly, the candidate, or just to see something other than the mindless sitcom playing on another channel. Depending upon our particular needs—or motives—we can "use" that TV commercial for any number of varying purposes. In the process of viewing that commercial, presumably, we are gaining some sort of gratification which is strong enough to make us watch it again and again.

Any functional theory of communication, then, assumes that receivers are active human beings who are subjecting themselves to communicative messages because certain needs can be satisfied and certain gratifications can be gained from exposure to those messages. The interesting question we are now faced with is: "What are the functions fulfilled for members of the American public by presidential campaigns and campaign messages?" Research on that question is going forward at a tremendous rate every four years. After the 1976 election, I pulled together as much of it as I could find, in order to come up with a list of communication functions in general. As I combed that research, I identified fifteen functions or "uses" to which campaign communications could be put by different people at different times during a campaign.

To avoid a mere laundry list, groupings were sought. First, there were two main groups—one called "instrumental functions" and the other "consummatory functions," drawing on a distinction made by Wallace Fotheringham almost twenty years ago.[13] Put simply, "instrumental functions" are those which serve as a means to some other or secondary end. For example, converting someone to your political beliefs is not really an end in itself if you are a political candidate; that conversion is important to you only if that person actually goes to the polls and votes for you the second Tuesday in November. "Consummatory functions" are those which can be thought of as ends in themselves, as psychological states or pieces of behavior which are in and of themselves gratifying. For example, you might watch the proceedings of a political party convention, not so that you can decide how to vote, but so that you can laugh at the spectacle of silly people wearing garish hats and blowing stadium horns, ironically, in the name of democracy. In this case, the viewing of conventions is a consummatory activity, presumably gratifying in and of itself.

Using this distinction, I found eight instrumental function in one list, and seven consummatory functions in another. To more precisely map the campaign environment, the two lists were subdivided once more. The results led to perhaps awkward labels, but at least the maps were clearer. Let us review them briefly.[14]

Instrumental Functions

Behavioral Activation. The first three functions are termed "behavioral activation," and are drawn from the classic voting studies. Presidential campaigns can affect, to some degree, people's political behavior, reinforcing loyal party members strongly enough to get them to vote, activating a new set or pool of voters from among the general population, and converting some undecided or even other-party members to one's own party cause. Thus, behaviorally, campaign communication can produce *reinforcement, activation, and conversion.*

Cognitive Adjustments. The second group of instrumental functions grew out of various strains of cognitive research—"mapping" and "agenda-setting" research. Because American presidential campaigns are characterized by many multifaceted dialogues—between the candidates as in debates, between individual candidates and audiences as in speeches, and between candidates and representatives of the print and electronic press as in interviews and news conferences—our campaigns are highly interactional. In those interactions, much information about politics and politicians is offered, issues are defined and shaped, political personalities are given contours, and political motives are isolated and evaluated. As a result, the main characters in campaign dramas—the candidates, the press, and the electorate—all learn much about each other and the sociopolitical world.

In the face of such political information, all participants in political processes make a series of cognitive adjustments. Though there are several ways to describe these adjustments in informational maps, I chose three labels. The kinds of adjustments candidates themselves make are called *reflections,* in that candidates are encouraged in those dialogues to more faithfully reflect their constituencies' beliefs, attitudes, judgments, and desires. I called the kinds of adjustments forced on candidates by their opponents *refractions,* in order to stress the kind of bending and twisting of positions which often occurs when candidates face direct attack. And the kind of adjustments voters make are termed *reconstitutions,* so as to recognize the power both candidates and the press have in getting us to think about and rank-order issues, problems, and their solutions in particular ways.[15]

If we stretch the term a bit, reflection, refraction, and reconstitution all represent kinds of cognitive adjustments talked about by scholars interested in "agenda-setting research." That is, the drawn out processes of campaigning slowly but perceptibly drive a citizenry with the aid of the press to identify, discuss, and rank-order its priorities, to make a large-scale "mental map" of the social-political landscape. Such mappings may not directly affect votes this year or the next, although they can; the mappings, however, may well have important long-range effects. For example, John F. Kennedy really did not get accepted or passed legislation he proposed in the name of the New Frontier. Yet he got legislators and constituents thinking along certain lines that converged in Lyndon Johnson's Great Society legislation a few years later. The benefits—or the vices, depending on your political outlook—of the cognitive mapping which occurs during campaigns, therefore, spill over into nonelection years, often affecting the ways society at large thinks about its social-political problems for years to come.

Legitimacy. The third group of instrumental functions is more difficult to describe, but it certainly is important. Not only does campaigning perform a series of functions for the populace, but it likewise can function instrumentally in important ways for presidents themselves. Presidents are assigned or delegated power by the American campaign process. In the words of Louis Koenig, campaigns yield or "reflect a social and political consensus that will sustain constructive programs for major public programs."[16] That sense of social and political consensus can be termed "legitimacy." That label captures the kind of power accorded both the president and the office of the president following the campaign. Because the presidential campaign is a trial or series of tests, like the warriors of old the person actually emerging victorious from that trial is assigned power. So one legitimizing functions of campaigns is to confer the title of "leader" upon the winner.

In a related fashion, the campaign process legitimizes—as Koenig suggested—"constructive programs," that is, it provides *endorsement* for particular social-political programs. That is not to say that what candidate X says he will do in office is what President X always in fact does. But it *is* to say that president after president appeals to the "popular will" or "popular mandate" behind his ideas when proposing legislation. One need only remember that Ronald Reagan spent most of 1981 putting economic and taxation proposals through Congress by reminding people on the Hill of the public's endorsement of those proposals. President after president acts *in the name of* the instrumental endorsements symbolically given to his ideas during election time.

These, then, are eight means to larger ends which flow from presidential campaign communication processes and messages. They have guided political and communication research in various phrasings for over four decades. Yet thinking about people's potential or actual consummatory experiences during campaigns can produce an even more interesting series of functions. What kinds of gratifications can people gain during the course of the campaign from the campaign itself?

Consummatory Functions.

It is something approaching a monumental task, if you think about it, to attempt to list all the possible uses to which people can put presidential campaign communications. Presidential campaigns run, these days, for almost two years. Further, depending on a person's interests or motives, a person's profession, and/or a person's degree of political activity, particular messages can be "used" in multiple ways simultaneously. For example, a journalist might derive many gratifications from a campaign speech. That journalist might be able to write a column for the *New York Times* and hence earn some money, become personally interested in the political fortunes of that candidate, get a good laugh from the humorous anecdotes told, and learn something about some social problem he or she did not know before. That journalist, therefore, could gain professional, political, psychological, and intellectual gratification from a single political message. And if we consider not only journalists but innumerable other categories of people in society, each with their own needs or motives, coming up with a finite list of consummatory functions becomes difficult. Rather than attempt a complete listing of individuated consummatory functions, we should only identify general functions, as have previous researchers. They are listed in two categories.

Political Involvement. Uses and gratifications research focusing on political campaigns has tried to document the ways people use campaign communications in their everyday lives. Under this heading five functions can be grouped. The first is simply *participation,* because once candidates announce their intention to run, set up state, county, and local offices, and begin to make speeches, they signal politically active citizens that it is time to get involved—time to start raising money, licking envelopes, compiling voter lists, and holding barbecues and keg parties. For the political activists in communities across the country, such direct participation is consummatory; "working for the cause" produces direct or immediate gratification (even when the cause produces no winners). A second kind of direct involvement is *self-reflection,* because as particular candidates search for themes, slogans, and issue priorities, they force many people to think about their personal political preferences, social-economic priorities, and willingness to commit themselves to this or that candidate. These people not only learn about issues, but perhaps even change their self-perception in the process. The third sort of involvement has been called *social interaction*, because campaigns give almost all of us a great range of topics to discuss with associates, friends, and even strangers at cocktail parties, work, and on the street. In Eric Berne's terms, presidential campaigns provide a social "pastime" we call, simply, "talking politics."[17]

Fourth, politics can generate a somewhat peculiar kind of involvement called *parasocial interactions*. Politics can provide some people—especially shut-ins or others wholly or partially cut off from social interaction—an opportunity to "talk with" others. Most of us know people who talk back at the TV set, who seemingly cuss out the president when reading an article about him. That is parasocial interaction, and it occurs often enough during campaigns to show up regularly in uses and gratification studies of campaigns. The fifth involving sort of function is labeled *aesthetic experiences*. It represents a whole range of entertainment functions—such things as being entertained by conventions or ads, getting oneself caught up in the high drama or low comedy of campaigns. Indeed, were it not for the aesthetic or dramatic dimensions of our extended political campaigns, few of us would get involved in other, more important ways.[18]

Legitimation. The last two consummatory functions go beyond simple or direct involvement and even beyond the two kinds of instrumental legitimation processes discussed earlier. Frankfurt School critical theorist Juergen Habermas has focused much of his work on the idea of legitimation, more particularly, on the ways political-cultural elites legitimize their actions within cultures. He argues that there is an almost insidious dimension to political processes—they are self-justifying. Whenever we say "we are doing X because that is the way X is done in this society," we are demonstrating the power of such self-justifications.

More technically, then, legitimation processes represent series of behaviors which gain normative power through repetition; the more we engage in such behaviors, the more "natural" they seem—and hence the more powerful they become.[19] Presidential campaigning can be thought of in these terms. The more often this country goes through particular campaign rituals, the more "natural" those rituals seem to be, that is, the more pressure there is applied to particular candidates, representatives of the press, and other political activists to continue traditional behaviors. Hence, the processes of presidential campaigning ultimately justify themselves through sheer repetition. Such legitimation processes create two additional functions fulfilled by campaigns: *acquiescence* and *quiescence*.

First, presidential campaigns and their undergirding rules almost force our citizens to "acquiesce," to recognize that campaigning procedures should not be changed in any radical way because they are "democratic."

Whether true or not, most of us have accepted the political myths which say, among other things, that "anyone can grow up to be president of the United States," that "if anyone wants to change the political system, all he or she has to do is 'get involved' at the grass roots level," and that "in America's extended presidential campaigns we find a winnowing process which guarantees that the 'best' person will emerge victorious." This country, in short, has constructed a campaign process designed to force acquiescence because it is founded on the ideological notion of openness; everything *seems* open, especially since the party reforms of the early 1970s, which put special emphasis on grass roots development of political allegiances. It is extremely difficult for anyone to oppose such apparent openness, and hence acquiescence is the normal reaction.

Related to acquiescence is another notion—quiescence. Not only do our campaign processes more or less convince us that our methods for selecting leaders are fail-safe and ultimately democratic, but they are based on a myth of rationality, and hence are designed to make us "feel good" about them. After all, Americans can say with extreme self-pride, in our system candidates are forced to lay out political programs, to justify those programs publicly, to occasionally engage in direct debate with their opponents, and to stand the tests of press conferences. So, we often conclude, while the American way of electioneering may seem odd and cumbersome to observers from other nations, it certainly is better than alternatives because it leads to comparatively reasoned public decision making. It therefore is comparatively "devil-proof" because it shines the light of critical examination and public accountability on anyone who runs. That can make us quiescent, can make us feel generally happy or content with the process per se. We see ourselves, very often, engaging in one, big New England town meeting via television. Overall, then, campaigns function to produce both acquiescence and quiescence, for we have been thoroughly educated in our myths and ideologies and by now they protect us conceptually.

1. The list of functions comes from several different research models for political communication. Behavioral instrumental functions have been isolated by researchers working in the classic "limited effects" stream of thinking. Cognitive instrumental functions are grounded in agenda-setting research. Legitimizing instrumental functions have been described by class/structural political scientists such as Koenig. Participatory consummatory functions have been investigated by "uses and gratifications" scientists, while processual consummatory functions have been suggested by continental critical theories.

2. The fact that these functions come from so many different streams of thinking indicates that, at present, there is no master or second-order

theory which has been as yet devised to comprehend them all. Functionalism is more a model than a theory as such. The most thoroughly functional research mentioned—"uses and gratifications" research—has been excoriated for its atheoretical nature.[20]

3. The most fruitful theoretical perspective in which to ground functional models of political behavior is the so-called dramaturgical theory of communications.

Dramaturgical Theories of Campaign Communications

Following, then, are six perspectival assumptions to which most scholars of political dramaturgy would assent:[21]

1. *Human beings are social actors.* We are purposive creatures who both reflect standards for action fostered by collectivities and follow prescribed forms or rituals when seeking to express particular ideas and motives. We are actors because, through socialization processes, we are acculturated to follow social rules in our public behavior in order to be understood and in order to avoid public ostracism or other forms of sanction.

2. *As actors, human beings are acculturated so as to play certain roles in certain situations.* For most situations we face in life there are predetermined scripts we are expected to follow as we play those roles. In some situations several scripts are available; for example, there are a variety of scripts available for behaving "properly" or "competently" as a parent, teacher, or student. Yet there probably are only a limited number of such scripts available for any given situation in any given society.

3. *Such scripts generally are reciprocal.* If I adopt script X to act out, say, my role as parent, my offspring assumes script Y in a reciprocal sort of way to play the roles of children. In situations of social harmony, the scripts acted out by various parties to the interaction call for reciprocity.

4. *By implication, the social order in general is negotiated.* As we share meanings with each other—via symbols—we together negotiate commonly understood ideas, behavior patterns, and commonly agreed-upon evaluations of those ideas and behaviors. While there certainly are real objects and forces in the world, much more important to our lives as social creatures is social reality—the descriptions, interpretations, and evaluations we develop together of that brute reality.

5. *Human beings inhabit a physical space and a particular historical epoch. But, more fundamentally, human beings dwell in a social reality, an entangling web of symbolic environments.* Those symbolic environments, within certain limits, dictate our behavior, control the way we perceive and react to our own and others' behaviors, and set

our own and others' expectations of each other. A collectivity's reality, thus, is socially constructed and individually constraining.
6. *A key term to dramaturgical theory is enactment.* Traditional affective psychologists attempted to discover what sorts of forces cause people to act in certain ways. Communication theorists since World War II have attempted to define and explicate the ways human beings interact with each other. But the dramaturgist seeks to understand "enactment," which refers to the kinds of implicit or tacit messages about culture communicated every time two or more people talk. Whenever we talk to each other, we employ culturally sanctioned languages or codes, we use those languages or codes in culturally sanctioned ways, and we naturally assume culturally sanctioned roles and role relationships with others. Hence, our talk with each other is not only about something such as taxes or tonight's plans, but also is an embodiment of culturally sanctioned behaviors. For example, every time you politely say, "Good to see you again, Aunt Matilda," when your aunt walks into the room, you not only are expressing your pleasure (feigned or not!) at seeing a relative, but your words embody a cultural rule of "good manners" which tells you *how* to recognize the copresence of others in your immediate environment. Communicative messages are acts and interactions, but also enactments of roles for living. A dramaturgical theory of campaign communication, if we extend the notion of enactment to the public sphere, calls upon researchers to specify the cultural-political rules which are embodied—even given silent expression, if you will—in the stump speeches, ads, pamphlets, billboards, and placards which surround us every leap year.[22]

These six assumptions lead to a theory of society and individuals' functioning within that society which depicts people as bonded together in a maze of commonly held beliefs, attitudes, values, and rationalizations for both personal and public behavior. In a sense, a dramaturgical theory posits that we are prisoners of culture and language. That, to some, is a bit unsettling. Yet consider the utility of dramaturgical theories of society and communications: They allow us to account for a tremendous variety of human public behavior, especially presidential campaign behavior.

They explain why the sociopolitical drama we call "political campaigns" occur in several different *phases* or *acts*. As in classic dramatic literature, so in sociodrama: Different phases or acts are present because differing social purposes need to be fulfilled. Baldly, the first act (preprimary phase) allows us to identify and examine critically the would-be actors; the second act (primary phase) provides tests of power among those key actors; the third act (conventions) is comprised of celebrations or legitimation rituals for offering adoration of victorious candidates and party platforms; and the final act (the general election) contains the denouement, the struggle for political-institutional life and death among the remaining contenders.[23]

Additionally, dramaturgical theory helps one understand why candidates' "images" have become so important to politics. To many, "image" is a dirty word, for its suggests artifice and manipulation. On the contrary, argues the dramaturgical theorist, a candidate's image is all we can know, and is in reality the only basis we have for making voting and other cognitive or behavioral political decisions. In voting for candidate X instead of candidate Y we are responding to a series of symbolic cues emitted by both candidates, and accentuated in mass-mediated depictions of those candidates.[24] Further, questions of uses and gratification are answered by dramaturgical theory. You and I are spectators, and, as individuated spectators to political dramas, each of us has particular motives governed by our own conceptions of self in society. Some of us are in the front row, are political activists who use political messages as both instrumental and consummatory gratifications. Others are in the middle of the symbolic auditorium, with a modicum of interest even though we might or might not become directly involved. Still others are sitting in the back, maybe watching campaign dramas with detached amusement, maybe attempting to avoid viewing, maybe attempting to avoid viewing altogether.[25]

Finally, dramaturgical theory makes gains in accounting for the length and cost of presidential political campaigns. Because political dramas are larger than life, because they serve a complex variety of functions, they become imbued with a great variety of meanings; and because they serve a complex variety of functions, they demand increasingly more time to play themselves out. As society has become more diversified, as bureaucracy has grown, and as the demand for services from federal agencies has increased, proportionally more resources and time almost of necessity must be invested by the culture in campaigning. The campaign is more important now than it was, even though, paradoxically, fewer and fewer citizens think it is and participate in it. Further, thanks to the growth of communication industries in general and mass media institutions in particular, there now are agencies able to support both general (e.g. broadcast television) and highly targeted (e.g. computerized mail) mediation of political behaviors and ideas. Again then, campaigning becomes more important, if only because it becomes more difficult to avoid, and if only because there are simply more opportunities now than in the past for candidate organizations to spend money for the mediation of their message. In other words, we should not really expect a correlation between money and voter turnout. The call for increased expenditure is predicated upon bureaucratic complexity and availability of media, not voting habits, that is, upon the political economy and not the size of the electorate. And the call for more campaign time is predicated on the growing diversity of citizen needs or motives which has accompanied the growth in campaign activity, not on a need for more information with which to make a rational voting decision.

Hence our presidential campaigns, to the dramaturgist, get leaders elected, yes, but ultimately they also tell us who we as a people are, where we have been, and where we are going. In their size and duration, they separate our culture from all others, teach us about political life, set our individual and collective priorities, entertain us, and provide bases for social interaction. Most fundamentally, because political institutions represent the grandest and most powerful of our social institutions in this century, campaigns define us to ourselves for at least a few years. As campaigns end in the endorsement of political myths, ideologies, and derived programs of action, so also do they end in a large-scale enactment of our collective self. In a perhaps terrifying sense, by the end of the campaign, *we are whom we elect.* We may not like that, especially if we are partisans supporting others, but that is sociopolitical life in the United States. That is the outcome of sociopolitical drama.

Conclusions

Perhaps we should end this chapter on a less metaphysical note. While functionalism is about half a century old, it only recently has been touted as a determinative guide to thinking and research focusing on political communication in general and presidential campaign communication in particular. It is possible to list fifteen (or more) functions, to organize them under headings, and to suggest that they can be accounted for theoretically by a dramaturgical theory of human communication. It is likewise possible to suggest—even demonstrate—that dramaturgical theories are in their elasticity capable of absorbing the classic "limited effects" theories, agenda-setting research, cognitive mapping theory, uses and gratifications research, and even the neorationalistic work of the likes of Lloyd Bitzer.[26] The allure of dramaturgical theories of presidential campaign communication, I suspect, comes from their structuralist foundations. Dramaturgists preface, explicitly or implicitly, their assumptions on a structural view of human life, a view wherein our perceptions of our environments, others, and ourselves form symbolic universes which analogically account for our very thoughts and which psychologically rationalize our very actions. Structuralist assumptions, despite some assaults on them in recent years, nevertheless are mightily attractive.[27]

Much work remains to be done before dramaturgical theories of presidential campaign communication assume an ascendant position across academia. Only the broadest theoretical outlines have been sketched. Researchers operating under the dramaturgical umbrella have just begun to analyze particular types of communicative messages, particular campaign situations and their demands on message builders, the range of myths and ideological tenets or rules which underlie campaign practices, and the varying roles spectators of different types play from campaign act to act. At this point, dramaturgical theory, while attractive, has not yet produced enough specific studies of particular campaigns to concretize its abstract foundations. Such studies must combine information on voters and voter behavior, systematic study of mediated coverage, and critical studies of particular campaign messages if dramaturgical theory is to grow in explanatory power and acuity.

Tradition has it that the sign spanning Shakespeare's Globe Theatre read, "Totus Mundus Agit Histrionem." That may have been simply a market analyst's suggestion for increasing the number of up-scale theatregoers, what with the Latin and all. Or, more intriguingly, it may have been a fundamental statement about life. Perhaps, indeed, "All the world *is* a stage." If you accept that notion and pursue its political ramifications, you may well discover some of the yields of the $800 million presidential campaign in 1980, and why it produced over its burdensome duration an actor acting as president, who, in a reenactment four years later, is looking very presidential.

Notes

1. *Federal Election Commission Annual Report, 1980* (Washington, D.C.: Commission's Office of Publications, 1980); *Federal Election Commission Annual Report, 1981* (Washington, D.C.: Commission's Office of Publications, 1981); Andrew J. Glass, "The Campaign and the Money Game," *New Leader* (6 October 1980): 4–5; John W. Mashek, "$800 Million Price Tag on '80 Election," *U.S. News and World Report* (22 September 1980: 22–23; "Election Tab: A Billion Dollars, and Rising," *U.S. News and World Report* (15 December 1980); 32–33.
2. David M. Alpern, James Doyle, John Walcott, and Christopher Aferton, "How the Land Slid," *Newsweek* (17 November 1980); 32. Worse, as reported in *Psychology Today* (August 1983); 8, that 53 percent turnout put the United States dead last among twenty "democratic" countries whose voter turnouts recently were compared.
3. U.S. Bureau of the Census, *Statistical Abstract of the United States: 1982–83,* 103rd ed. (Washington, D.C.: Government Printing Office, 1982), p. 492.
4. Paul F. Lazarsfeld, Bernard Berelson, and Hazel Gaudet, *The People's Choice* (New York: Columbia University Press, 1948); Bernard Berelson,

Paul F. Lazarsfeld, and William N. McPhee, *Voting: A Study of Opinion Formation in a Presidential Campaign* (Chicago: University of Chicago Press, 1954).

5. The phrase "the law of minimal consequences" was suggested by Hope L. Klapper, according to Kurt and Gladys Engel Lang in their *Voting and Non-voting: Implications of Broadcasting Returns before Polls Are Closed* (Waltham, Mass.: Blaisdell, 1968), p. 4.

6. Joseph T. Klapper, *The Effects of Mass Communication* (Glencoe, Ill.: Free Press, 1960), p. 15.

7. Elihu Katz and Paul F. Lazarsfeld, *Personal Influence: The Part Played by People in the Flow of Mass Communications* (Glencoe, Ill.: Free Press, 1955), p. 63, quoted in Klapper, p. 26.

8. Elihu Katz, "The Two-Step Flow of Communication: An Up-to-Date Report on the Hypothesis," *Public Opinion Quarterly* 21 (1957): 63.

9. Klapper, pp. 38–43. Note that Klapper's argument is not as current as it sounds. His understanding of alienation is highly cognitive, based on a conception of rational choice. It is, therefore, almost completely unrelated to current neo-Marxian research on ideology and hegemony flowing from the pens of the British cultural studies scholars and the "political economy" critics.

10. Perhaps the best example of current research within the classic "limited effects" paradigm is that of Thomas E. Patterson, *The Mass Media Election: How Americans Choose Their President,* Praeger Special Studies (New York: Praeger, 1980). To be fair, I should note here, too, that many of the "classic" scholars—those who discovered "reinforcement"—urged the conduct of long-term, longitudinal studies which, they believed, would show that social change often occurs between rather than within campaigns. See Klapper, p. 25.

11. For background, see Dan D. Nimmo and Keith R. Sanders (eds.), *Handbook of Political Communication* (Beverly Hills: Sage, 1981), "Introduction: The Emergence of Political Communication as a Field," pp. 11–36; and Jack M. McLeod and Lee B. Becker, "The Uses and Gratifications Approach," pp. 67–99. Cf. Judith S. Trent and Robert V. Friedenberg, *Political Campaign Communication: Principles and Practices* (New York: Praeger, 1983), esp. 4.

12. See the studies in Paul F. Lazarsfeld and Frank N. Stanton (eds), *Radio Research, 1942–1943* (New York: Duell, Sloan, & Pearce, 1944); cf. H. Hertzog, "Professor Quiz: A Gratification Study," in *Radio Research, 1941,* ed. Paul F. Lazarsfeld and Frank N. Stanton (New York: Duell, Sloan, & Pearce, 1942).

13. See Wallace C. Fotheringham, *Perspectives on Persuasion* (Boston: Allyn & Bacon, 1966), p. 22.

14. Bruce E. Gronbeck, "The Functions of Presidential Campaigning," *Communication Monographs* 45 (November 1978); 268–80.

15. The term *reflection* is drawn from the mirroring theory of mass communication as summarized in Lee Loevinger, "The Ambiguous Mirror: The Reflective-Projective Theory of Broadcasting and Mass Communications," in *Mass Media: Forces in Our Society,* ed. Francis and Ludmila Voelker (San Francisco: Harcourt Brace Jovanovich, 1978), pp. 424–40. (Orig. pub. in *Journal of Broadcasting* 12 [Spring 1968].) The notion of "refraction" is developed in Robert O. Anderson, "The Characterization Model for Rhe-

torical Criticism of Political Image Campaigns," *Western Speech* 37 (1973): 75–96. The cognitive model in general is overviewed in Lee B. Becker, Maxwell E. McCombs, and Jack M. McLeod, "The Development of Political Cognitions," in *Political Communication: Issues and Strategies for Research,* ed. Steven H. Chaffee (Beverly Hills: Sage, 1975), pp. 21–64.

16. Louis W. Koenig, *The Chief Executive,* 3rd ed. (San Francisco: Harcourt Brace Jovanovich, 1975), p. 35.

17. Eric Berne, *Games People Play* (New York: Grove, 1964), pp. 41–47.

18. One need not use the five labels I have employed. An alternate set—"surveillance-vote guidance," "contest-excitement," "communication-utility," and "other items" (specifically, "to judge the candidates' weak points" and "to remind you of your candidate's strong points")—can be found in McLeod and Becker, pp. 88–91.

19. Habermas's works most relevant to my discussion here include *Legitimation Crisis* (Boston: Beacon, 1975) and *Communication and the Evolution of Society,* trans. Thomas McCarthy (Boston: Beacon, 1976). I expand somewhat my own understanding of the concepts in "The Rhetoric of Political Corruption: Sociolinguistic, Dialectical, and Ceremonial Processes," *Quarterly Journal of Speech* 64 (April 1978); 155–72, although in that essay, I am drawing more heavily from Peter L. Berger and Thomas Luckmann, *The Social Construction of Reality: A Treatise in the Sociology of Knowledge* (Garden City, N.Y.: Doubleday, 1966), than I am from Habermas. I should note, too, that the critical theorists' discussions of legitimation are being supplemented—and perhaps replaced among scholars interested in mass media—by discussions of hegemony. Especially in the hands of British cultural critics such as Raymond Williams (*Television: Technology and Cultural Form* [New York: Schocken, 1974]), John Fiske and John Hartley (*Reading Television* [London: Methuen, 1978]), and others (e.g. Michael Gurevitch et al. (eds.), *Culture, Society, and the Media* [London: Methuen, 1982]), the notion of hegemony becomes a powerful concept for discussing the power relationships existing between elites/institutions and a citizenry. Were I now rewriting my 1978 essay, I would discuss hegemony instead of legitimation, as the concept is much richer. The direction my discussion would take is indicated in my "Audience Engagement in *Family*," in *Rhetorical Dimensions in Media: A Critical Casebook,* ed. Martin J. Medhurst and Thomas W. Benson (Dubuque: Kendall/Hunt, 1984), pp. 4–32.

20. This charge is reviewed and documented in McLeod and Becker, esp. pp. 75–80. It is phrased generally by Maxwell E. McCombs in this manner: "To be fruitful this consolidated approach [uses and gratifications research] must be presented in theoretical terms. What has passed for mass communication theory has been, in reality, a loose collection of orientations toward data and a few empirical generalizations. While our knowledge has high empirical import, it has little theoretical import to contribute to an explanation of mass communication and its role in political behavior. The few concepts that exist should be clarified and linked with new insights. Descriptions cast in primitive terms abound about *what there is,* but explanations of *why it is* are missing." "Mass Communication in Political Campaigns: Information, Gratification, and Persuasion," in *Current Perspectives in Mass Communication Research,* ed. F. Gerald Kline and Phillip J. Tichenor, Sage

Annual Reviews of Communication Research, vol. 1 (Beverly Hills: Sage, 1972), p. 188.

21. For background, See Bruce E. Gronbeck, "Dramaturgical Theory and Criticism: The State of the Art (or Science?), "Western Journal of Speech Communication, 44(1980): 315–30; James E. Combs, *Dimensions of Political Drama* (Santa Monica, Calif.: Goodyear, 1980); Dan Nimmo and James E. Combs, *Mediated Political Realities* (New York: Longman, 1983); and Trent and Friedenberg, esp. Ch. 2 (which offers a dramaturgical phase or "act" model of presidential campaigning). Many of these themes can be traced back to some pioneering thinking appearing in Murray Edelman, *The Symbolic Uses of Politics* (Urbana, Ill.: University of Illinois Press, 1964), as well as in his later books, all of which start with the writings especially of Kenneth Burke and which explore the symbolic dimensions of political structures and behavior.

22. I have more to say about enactment in my "Narrative, Enactment, and Television Programming," *Southern Speech Communication Journal* 48(1983): 229–43.

23. For detailed analyses of two of these acts, see Judith S. Trent, "Presidential Surfacing: The Ritualistic and Crucial First Act," and Thomas B. Farrell, "Political Conventions as Legitimation Ritual," in *Communication Monographs*, 45(1978): 281–92, 293–305. Overviews of all four acts are offered in Trent and Friedenberg, ch. 2. Nimmo and Combs likewise suggest dramatic phases to presidential campaigns, tying their analysis to Oriental "seasonal" dramas; they ultimately produce a three-act melodrama (focusing on what Trent and Friedenberg term the "surfacing, primary, and general election phases") in their analysis. The idea of melodrama—in its popular, degenerate sense—certainly is useful in capturing the mood of press reports, although their analysis of particular types of campaign messages lacks the precision of Trent and Friedenberg's critiques. See Dan Nimmo and James E. Combs, pp. 49–50, 54–62.

24. The classic essay on dramatistic "image" in politics is Richard M. Merelman, "The Dramaturgy of Politics," in *Drama in Life: The Uses of Communication in Society,* ed. James E. Combs and Michael W. Mansfield, Communication Arts Books (New York: Hastings House, 1976), pp. 285–301. (Orig. publ. in *Sociological Quarterly,* 10[1969]).

25. This answer to the charge of atheoreticity is, of course, weak; it has not been especially well drawn by anyone as yet (although Nimmo and Combs, especially, are attacking in it ch. 1, pp. 1–20); Combs has taken a more general shot at it as well in his "A Process Approach," in Nimmo and Sanders, pp. 39–66. Work obviously remains to be done. The point here is that an approach emphasizing both individual motive and spectator distance seems preferable to the completely individuated theory presumably underlying traditional uses and gratifications theory (which has a disturbing post hoc quality about it), and to the more radical psychoanalytic studies of campaigns, with their heavy Freudian overtones, offered by the likes of Lloyd DeMause ("Jimmy Carter and American Fantasy") and John J. Hartman ("Carter and the Utopian Group Fantasy") in *Journal of Psychohistory* 5(1977): 151–74, 239–58.

26. See his "Political Rhetoric" in Nimmo and Sanders, pp. 225–48. Lloyd Bitzer and Theodore Rueter, *Carter vs. Ford: The Counterfeit Debates of 1976* (Madison: University of Wisconsin Press, 1980).

27. I develop this argument at considerable length in my "Qualitative Communication Theory and Rhetorical Studies in the 1980s," *Central States Speech Journal* 32(1981): 243–53, esp. pp. 252–53.

14

Elections as Ritual Drama

Dan Nimmo

The modern American presidential election campaign is many things. It is a struggle for power; a way of achieving a position of rulership without inheriting it, conspiring in secrecy to grab it, or seizing it by force of arms. It is also a competition for publicity as candidates strive for recognition of themselves and their ideas that they might not otherwise receive. The presidential campaign is a forum, providing a rostrum from which to speak and to argue positions. A presidential campaign is a conflict between diverse social groups, each attempting to impose its definition of the public good upon its allies and its rivals. The campaign offers more than a way for people to take sides in this social conflict. They may also air their aspirations and vent their frustrations and in the process assume roles in a long-running, public spectacle.

Among the many things that a presidential election campaign is or, more accurately, the many perspectives from which one may be viewed, I single out a key aspect of campaigning for emphasis. I begin with a definition. Any political campaign, and certainly a presidential election campaign, is a continuous exercise in the creation, re-creation, and transmission of significant symbols through language, both verbal and nonverbal. It is an enterprise aimed at mobilizing electoral support around a series of attractive, appealing symbols, i.e., a symbolic enterprise.

Significant Symbols

Consider first the continuous nature of the modern presidential campaign. Not so many years ago perceived wisdom was that the kickoff of a presidential election campaign did not come prior to the year of the election itself. Two decades ago V.O. Key, Jr.—one of the most widely respected of political scientists—noted in the fifth edition of his classic textbook on American politics, *Politics Parties and Pressure Groups,* a maxim of presidential politics: "a candidacy announced too soon may be blighted like an early-blooming flower; too late an announcement may give an advantage to other candidates." Key concluded that the problem of assembling an organization to fight primary battles dictate "a declaration

159

long in advance of the convention." Such, he noted, was exemplified in 1960 when both Richard Nixon and John F. Kennedy formalized their candidacies as early as January of that year.

Today presidential candidates no longer have the luxury of hiding their intentions until the election year. Formal announcements of candidacies now routinely come well in advance of the presidential election year, let alone nominating conventions. Intentions to run materialize within weeks after the preceding presidential election. Walter Mondale hinted openly at his plans soon after Ronald Reagan had taken office. Senator Howard Baker made it clear that he would not seek reelection in 1984 in order that he might devote his full time to a possible presidential bid in 1988.

In this sense the presidential campaign is continuous. No sooner has the first Tuesday after the first Monday in November of a presidential election year passed than the next campaign begins. Potential candidates organize, professional consultants make known their availability for hire—even screening likely clients—television news talk shows speculate about favorites and dark horses, and opinion polls designate front-runners for each party's nomination. Presidential politicking, like professional football or basketball, no longer knows a clear-cut season.

The American philosopher, George Herbert Mead, formulated the idea of significant symbols, an idea that comprises a second major feature of our definition of campaigning. A symbol is simply a word, action, or picture (hence is verbal or nonverbal) that designates an idea, object, event, etc. We have some sense of what the words "Walter Mondale" or "John Glenn" designate, what a military salute indicates, or what the picture of Uncle Sam signifies. We give some meaning to each such symbol. We may not all give the same meaning to a given symbol; that is, we may interpret Uncle Sam in different ways, we may each see a different Walter Mondale or John Glenn. For Mead a symbol could be regarded as significant when it produced the same response in the audience as intended by its user. For example, if a speaker and audience members interpret a simple word, say, *democracy,* in similar ways, giving it the same meaning, it is significant. Campaigners seek significant symbols, those that will elicit from voters the response sought by the candidate. In this respect, campaign appeals are efforts at manipulating symbols in order to create shared, sympathetic responses.

Such a view is scarcely new. Few of us today are unaware of propaganda, publicity, public relations, and advertising that attempts to sell products, ideas, and people using symbolic manipulation. There is another enterprise familiar to all of us that is also essentially symbolic—that of drama. Stage plays, movies, television series, even newspaper comic strips, and the news itself possess elements of drama. That is, they employ symbols to involve audiences in shared, sympathetic responses. Election campaigns and the arts of drama have some things in common. First, they both involve symbolic manipulation; second, they possess common elements.

Campaign as Drama

The actors are the essential players in any drama. Political dramas—like those in any other walk of life—are both real and fictional. They involve actors playing roles of heroes, villains, fools, victims, and assorted supporting parts be they good guys or bad, winners or losers. Think, for example, of recent elections in which certain campaigners have been publicized as heroic in stature, whereas others portray, or are portrayed as, villains. If we consider the role of fools, we can probably find a few of those in recent campaigns. If Richard Nixon was the unlabeled villain of Jimmy Carter's understated 1976 heroic appeal to give the country a "government as good as its people" (the "people" being the heroes of the drama), Earl Butz certainly was cast in the role of fool. To the degree that Gerald Ford's gaffes and pratfalls captured as much news as did his slogan that as president he "made us proud again," Ford too received billing as a fool in the 1976 presidential drama. Jimmy Carter's brother Billy provided comic relief during Carter's administration, just as James Watt seemed to be doing for Ronald Reagan. Presidential campaigns incorporate hero, villain, fool, and other actor motifs. They portray candidates as winners and/or losers, and as wearers of white and black hats. They thus meet one requirement of drama.

The task of an actor in a drama is to act. Acts in presidential campaigns are of two basic types. Certain acts are expected; they are the routines of presidential campaigning. We expect, for example, that those seriously seeking the presidency will organize to raise money. Not only do they have no other choice—since they must finance their efforts—but by doing so they qualify for public funding of their campaigns, a fact that the news media watch closely as an indicator of the viability of a candidate's early campaign for the party nomination. We expect also that candidates will travel far and wide, shake hands, "press the flesh," make countless speeches in countless high school auditoriums, make the Holiday Inn circuit, exploit photo opportunities, and display unshakable confidence. As they perform these expected, routine acts they project a distinctive characters in the public drama.

Such a persona not only derives from doing the expected; it also informs what members of the press and voters expect of a candidate as the drama unfolds. We expect the candidate to act in character; but this is not always the case. Routine and expected performances are accompanied by unexpected acts. Sometimes the unexpected renders it impossible for the candidate to stay in character. In 1976, for instance, during the presidential debates between Jimmy Carter and Gerald Ford, the unexpected developed. Ford, attempting to conform to the persona of an incumbent president made what turned out to be an out-of-character error when he revealed confusion, even ignorance, about Soviet domination of portions of Eastern Europe. Since routine news is largely no news at all, the unexpected grabs the headlines and television news leads. What might otherwise be an inconsequential act turns out to be a turning point in the drama or at least a complication that the injured candidate must waste valuable campaign time attempting to "set straight."

Whether expected and/or unexpected performances assist a candidate in acting out a consistent, credible persona depends in large measure upon another dramatic element, the scene. The scene is the stage on which the drama is played. In presidential elections the scenic background is huge; it is panoramic. It is at one and the same time a world stage, a national stage, a local stage. Just as projecting a consistent persona imposes certain expectations on a candidate, so does the scene—kissing babies when mingling in nursery settings, eating diverse foods in ethnic neighborhoods, wearing cowboy hats in Texas and protective helmets outside construction sites. For a president seeking reelection, the panoramic backdrop of the world stage yields opportunities and problems. Jimmy Carter was at a low ebb in his presidential popularity on November 4, 1979, when the United States Embassy in Iran was assaulted and hostages taken captive. The crisis setting provided Carter with the opportunity to act presidential. His "rose garden" strategy of coping with the crisis rather than hitting the campaign trail served him well in his struggle to withstand the challenge of Ted Kennedy for the 1980 Democratic nomination. As the crisis drama played itself out over the ensuing months, and in the absence of the expected resolution that the abortive rescue effort in April, 1980 might have provided, the hostage backdrop became less Carter's opportunity than his albatross.

Characters in a drama act with purpose. So too do political candidates. Such purposes are many and varied. They may include informing the electorate about positions on issues or confusing voters about stands on issues. Candidates may seek to project clear-cut images or, as an alternative, to project sufficient ambiguity in character to permit voters to see what they wish to see. Candidates for the party's nomination can seek to unify their party—winning the endorsement of a variety of special interests—or position themselves to use a particular segment of the party as a springboard for their aspirations. In any event, be they power seeking, partisan, ideological, moral, self-centered, or some combination of these and other goals, a political campaign shares with any drama the ingredient of purposeful action.

In dramas actors seek their ends by commanding selected means, that is, dramatic agents. Shakespeare gives his characters guile (as in Richard III), daggers (Julius Ceasar, Hamlet), potions (Romeo and Juliet), and so on. Presidential candidates have their own stock of dramatic agents, such as money, paid and unpaid volunteers, professional political consultants, political party ties, endorsements, and reputations. In 1984, for instance, we found Walter Mondale seeking to monopolize the agent of endorsements by organized labor, John Glenn capitalizing on his astronaut's reputation, Alan Cranston on concerns of Americans about nuclear warfare, or Gary Hart on the always attractive agent in American politics, the quality of the "new."

Actors perform acts, assuming character roles, in various seetings and with various motives, using the means at their disposal. In the process, each candidate adopts a typical stance toward the election, performing with a characteristic style. The combination of styles in a presidential campaign yields an overall stylistic configuration to any presidential contest. Historian Richard Jensen has investigated all presidential elections from the earliest days of the republic through 1980. In "Armies, Ad Men and Crusaders: Strategies to Win Elections," published in *Public Opinion* in 1980, he argues that there have been five basic styles in United States presidential elections. The first is the "army rally" which dominated campaigning in the nineteenth century. Politicians of that era, many of whom served in state militias, took their model for campaign organization from the military. They treated political parties as real armies. The party leaders endeavored to build cadres of party loyalists under precinct captains. With such an army in place it was not necessary to take to the field in order to win defectors from other units, only to drill partisan troops, rally them to the cause, and see that they delivered their assigned votes on election day. The typical campaign focus was upon monstrous rallies to reinforce feelings of duty and commitment. The chief means of communication was the official party newspaper, a document much like a military journal.

Jensen argues that after the turn of the century there was a shift from the army rally to the "advertiser" style. It derived not from the assumption that the only task of the campaigner was to deliver a loyal voting following, but from the recognition that partisan loyalties were declining. The advertising style sought to use the mass media to reach large numbers of primarily uncommitted voters. Campaigns became marketing or selling enterprises designed to project appealing images that would attract persons with no abiding loyalties and draw votes from weakly inclined opponents. The candidate—not the party—was the focus of the advertising campaign.

Although the army rally typified nineteenth-century presidential campaigns and the advertising style is typical of this century, Jensen notes a third style, the "missionary," present in both eras. A missionary style seeks to educate and to convert. The assumption is one of some voters strongly inclined toward a political party and other voters independent of party ties. The missionary campaign seeks to win lifelong adherents from both groups and, in effect, build a new army. Instead of rallies or mass advertising the missionary focus is upon grass-roots appeal—door-to-door canvasing; distribution of party literature; and face-to-face, small group caucuses. The Jeffersonian-Madisonian efforts to build the Republican party that produced electoral victory in 1800, or the Socialist party efforts in 1908 and 1912, Jensen designates as examples of such missionary zeal.

In contemporary elections, Jensen sees another style emerging. It is the "crusade" and—what it often inspires—the "countercrusade." The crusade is a campaign waged with religious fervor to overturn the status quo. The key characteristic of the crusade (and also of countercrusades) is one of moral indignation and devotion that inspires both the candidate and followers to wipe out evil from politics in the name of the goodness of the American people. Established political ways are evil; power holders are villains; the Garden of Eden is threatened. The crusade is for purification and salvation.

The crusade/countercrusade style is found by Jensen throughout American political history. He notes that in recent presidential campaigns it seems to be replacing advertising to the point of becoming the dominant mode. Ronald Reagan's 1980 campaign, Jensen speculates, was a crusade. Recall the theme of "Government is not the solution to the problem, government is the problem." Carter's Democrats responded with a countercrusade, stressing the apocalyse that would surely occur if an uncaring, trigger-happy, warmonger reached the White House. John Anderson's campaign in 1980, also had some of the flavor of a crusade, but Jensen characterizes the Anderson style as essentially missionary.

Any—campaign—like any good drama—will have its stylized performances. So too will it have one final dramatic element—a plot. The classic unfolding story of any drama involves an introduction, rising action, turning point, falling action, and conclusion. A presidential campaign has all of these essentials—an introduction in the way of speculation about candidates "available" for party nominations; rising action in the form of early organizational efforts, qualifying for public funding, formal announce-

ments, etc; turning points in the multitude of caucuses and primaries leading to party conventions and nominations; falling action (spiced with
unexpected events) in the general election campaign; and a conclusion on
election day.

Campaign Ritual

In recent presidential elections the interrelationships of the elements of
political drama—characters, acts, scenes, purposes, agents, styles, and plot
lines—have displayed a recurring pattern. So predictable has the structure
of presidential campaigning become—but not the events or the
outcomes—that it is possible to describe presidential campaigns as ritual
dramas. For this purpose I define a ritual as a series of acts that are regularly or faithfully performed or that recur in a patterned way; the acts are
repeated time and time again with minimal variations. Examples are
numerous: religious ceremonies, the playing of the national anthem and
saluting the flag, inaugurating a president, throwing out the first ball at a
World Series game, or even the football coach poor-mouthing the team's
prospects for the upcoming season.

Rituals contain the symbolism that is a key part of any developing
drama of sociopolitical action. When the elements of drama repeatedly
combine with one another in a repetitive fashion we have a ritual drama.
Such ritual dramas serve a variety of purposes. Ritual dramas permit
actors to demonstrate that they are doing something familiar, legitimate,
acceptable, valid, or socially/morally approved. How frequently do
presidential candidates, for instance, eschew "running on the issues"? Be
it Cranston, Hollings, Hart, Mondale, Askew, Glenn, McGovern, or
whomever, a ritualistic imperative dictates coming forward with an elaborate set of policy positions designed in part to position the candidate
distinctly from opponents but also to conform to politically accepted cus-
tom. The candidate "fuzzy on the issues" (Jimmy Carter in 1976) or
deemed running on "image not substance" (George Bush in 1980) receives
criticism accordingly.

Ritual drama permits actors to indicate to audiences that they are performing in a routine, acceptable, and predictable fashion in accordance
with the written and unwritten rules of ritual. Consider again the public
funding matter. Candidates routinely seek to raise the required minimum
amounts in minimum contributions in a minimum number of states to
qualify for matching federal funding. That all candidates do so would
seemingly provide an opportunity for departing from ritual to distinguish a
candidacy from the crowd. John Connolly sought to do that in seeking the
Republican nomination in 1980 by refusing matching funds. It is doubtful

that his efforts would have been any more successful with public funding (he received one delegate), but turning his back on ritual apparently did not pay off.

When actors ritualistically play out their roles in a drama they are inviting others to do the same. The candidate in the role of "front-runner" is in the enviable position of being treated as such in the news media but in the risky position of being required to maintain that performance against the challenge of those playing catch-up, the dark horses, and expected performance. (The front-runner, even in winning caucuses and primaries, may be panned by critics as not doing "as well as expected.") Ritual drama also invites voters to assume familiar roles—as partisans or independents, an issue- or image- or event-oriented, as interested or apathetic, as joining with respective candidates in the fight or ignoring their appeals.

The ritual drama in presidential campaigns performs another useful function. Through the seemingly mechanical motions of ritual many people find meaning in various aspects of life. The ritual of prayer and other religious ceremonies provides meaningful categories that help worshipers interpret and understand the meaning of the sacred. The elaborate ceremonies surrounding the crowning of an English monarch or the marriage of English royalty involve symbolic categories that join his/her majesty, subjects, and centuries of tradition in what it means to be British. Similarly, political rituals of campaigning provide voters with ways of knowing what is going on. Consider that a presidential campaign involves hundreds, even thousands, of discrete acts and events over a four-year period. If voters experience each of these as isolated and divorced from one another and from themselves, there is the risk that the electoral process will have no meaning. Experienced as the various acts and scenes in an unfolding ritual drama, a presidential campaign can be an elaborate, panoramic spectacle that catches up the audience in the action.

Here the news media have a major role to play in the ritual drama. For the news media a presidential campaign is a continuing story. A continuing story is one that runs for a long period of time, is the principal story in television, newspapers, and newsmagazines for an extended period. The continuing story has different episodes that comprise it, but the essential drama remains the same. Think of it as something like a soap opera with a story line that runs for weeks, months, or years, even through a complicated series of interlocking subplots. Television news, in particular, has a vested interest in continuing stories, for it is around them that the networks attract and build audiences. The 444-day Iranian hostage crisis was a made-to-order, continuing story for television news. It had rising action, turning points, falling action, and ultimately a happy conclusion—although not soon enough for Jimmy Carter to capitalize on the ritual drama of Iran.

For the news media, presidential campaigns receive continuing story treatment. Vast sums of money are allocated by news organizations for coverage of candidacies, caucuses, primaries, conventions, the general election campaign, and election night itself. If these sums are to be repaid—by attracting readers, viewers, and advertising dollars—they must be invested wisely. The continuing story motif offers an appealing possibility. By narrating the story of "Campaign '84" or "America Goes to the Polls," or whatever, the news media hope not only to inform audiences but to turn a profit as well. We find in news coverage certain recurring themes, story lines, and scenes that link together in a continuing way what audiences might otherwise regard as a chaotic, episodic, and senseless process.

For candidates, campaigners, the electorate, news media, and others, treating election campaigns as ritual dramas serves certain purposes. One political scientist, James David Barber, although not writing of ritual drama, suggests that the interlacing of candidate performances, news media coverage, and electorate response to presidential campaigning is so patterned as to make it possible to predict the kind of drama that will unfold in any presidential election year. In his book, *The Pulse of Politics,* Barber argues that there is a twelve-year cycle in presidential elections. The cycle begins with what he calls a "campaign of conflict" that includes a raw struggle for power, sharp social divisions among the electorate, and divisive attacks by candidates upon one another. The most recent such campaign before 1984, according to Barber, was 1972. (Tracing back the twelve-year cycles places the campaigns of 1960, 1948, etc., in the conflict category as well.) Four years later (1976, 1964, 1952, etc.) there is a campaign of conscience—principle dominates over politics, candidates appeal to the nation's moral fiber and promise to restore honesty and decency to government. After four more years (1980, 1968, 1956, etc) the campaign drama is one of conciliation—binding the nation's wounds, bringing Americans together, making us whole again, and returning to the greatness of the past.

Forms of Ritual Drama:

Whether Barber's thesis can be taken at face value is problematic. The theory calls our attention to the ritualistic and dramatic features of any presidential campaign. Instead of saying that any particular presidential election is a specific brand of ritual drama (as implied by the Barber thesis) or of style (as in Jensen's thesis), let us consider three ritual dramas that unfold and overlap in any presidential campaign.

One of the ritualistic features of any campaign is the widely held expectation that candidates will "speak to the issues." So ritualistic is such an expectation that the isolation of a few single issues by a candidate constitutes the core of what is "the speech." The speech—which may be a stock of as many as half a dozen different speeches—is a standardized address that the candidate can give in any setting and on any occasion moving from locale to locale, audience to audience. Such ritualistic standardization is a source of some concealed merriment to candidates who recognize speaking "to the issues" for what it is—an obligatory act. In the movie *The Candidate*, the character played by Robert Redford, while riding in a limousine from one campaign stop to another, becomes so aware of the absurdity of his basic speech that he begins to rehearse it using nonsense words and syllables. Real-life candidates are no less cognizant of how ritualistic their presentations are. John Anderson in 1980, in personal interviews, poked fun at the requirement that candidates should speak to the issues by obscuring them. Similarly, research has indicated that Edward Kennedy was as frequently making fun of and mocking his standard stump speeches as delivering them in earnest.

The ritualistic imperative nevertheless persists. In the introduction and rising action of a presidential campaign, candidates routinely identify issues and address them in basic speeches, press releases, and position papers. Being vague on issues or being caught by surprise and demonstrated as uniformed on an issue, may serve as one of the turning points in the electoral drama—for instance, Ford's gaffe about Eastern Europe in 1976 or Carter's reference to consulting with his daughter, Amy, about the nuclear issue in 1980.

Underlying the ritualistic addressing of issues are the unspoken, and no less ritualistic, assumptions about what the presidential election is expected to accomplish. There is in the land the routinely accepted notion that the purpose of the election is to discover the popular will and to reflect it accurately through the distribution of popular votes and the electoral winner. If all goes well and the drama plays itself out according to the script, the successful candidate can accept the party nomination as standard-bearer for a particular point of view (such as progressive, liberal, conservative, compassionate, or holding traditional values). If the presidential election provides the proper denouement to the drama, the president-elect can claim a mandate for whatever program has been represented in an endless series of issue-oriented stump speeches.

Specific issues addressed in stump and/or major speeches may get lost in the hurly-burly of daily campaigning and news media coverage. To highlight the distinctive position of a candidate in this drama the ritualistic imperative calls for a single symbol, or catch phrase, which serves in the popular mind as an index of the dimensions of the popular will that a particular candidate claims to represent. Jimmy Carter's indexical phrase in 1976 was "trust me." "Change" too has served as a successful indexing term in many presidential contests. Note, for example, television ads of the National Republican Campaign Committee in 1980 urging "This time vote Republican—for a change." As rhetoric critic Ernest Bormann points out, one of the most frequently used symbols is the simple word "new." It is a symbol with particular dramatic reference in a nation that still views itself as a new nation on a new continent doing new things. In recent years its political applications have included the "New Deal" of Franklin Roosevelt, the "New Left" of a later generation, the "New Politics" of George McGovern, and the "New South" of Jimmy Carter. In 1984 the candidacy of Gary Hart promised another application as he spoke of "New Ideas."

Such symbols not only provide ways of condensing under a single appealing label a whole series of complementary and contradictory positions on issues. They also give a candidate room to maneuver if successful in winning the party nomination or the presidential election. The ritual drama of speaking to the issues then claiming a mandate if victorious, would be entirely too confining if there were no maneuvering permitted by the use of vague symbols. The specific issues of a general election may differ substantially from those of the nomination campaign. The problems a party's candidate must address are not always the same as those the candidate faced when seeking the nomination. Nor is the popular will that the candidate purports to represent all that stable. In short, things change over the course of a four-year presidential campaign drama, both in the campaign for the presidency and in the exercise of the office if victorious. The exploitation of appropriate condensation symbols such as "new," "trust," "experience," and "tested" (all of which are staples of dramas of consumer-oriented product advertising) is vital to a candidate who wishes to perform with critical acclaim a role in what we may call the ritual drama of the quest for the popular will.

As this drama unfolds during any presidential campaign so too does another. It has become commonplace in recent years for many scholarly and journalistic analyses to note, and sometimes decry, the decline of the influence of political parties in presidential elections. For example, opinion surveys reveal a lessened commitment of voters to either of the two major parties. Those who were once weakhearted Democrats or Republicans have become independents. Those who were once strong willed Republicans or Democrats have become weakly identified partisans of one stripe or another. Party organizations, according to conventional wisdom, have been on the decline. Grass-roots organizations are not what they used to be. The national organization of each party takes a back seat in the management of presidential campaigns, and party pols have little or no influence over selecting party nominees.

I need not detail the efforts that the two major parties have taken to counter these alleged tendencies in the American electorate and among party organizations. Even if parties are on the decline, there is no indication in the ritual drama of presidential elections that "the party's over." Each presidential campaign involves not only a rhetoric of the "popular will" but also one of "popular control" in the ritualistic drama indicated by that rhetoric, political parties continue to play a key role.

One way to think of popular elections is to accept the definition of democracy offered decades ago by the economist Joseph Schumpeter in his *Capitalism, Socialism and Democracy*: "The democratic method is that institutional arrangement for arriving at political decisions in which individuals acquire the power to decide by means of a competitive struggle for the people's vote." That struggle, be the parties weakened or not, is still a struggle in which the parties themselves constitute dramatic agencies on the electoral stage. Consequently candidates must take them into account in seeking nomination and election. The result is not only a rhetoric that speaks to the issues but a partisan rhetoric as well. Ronald Reagan, George Bush, and John Anderson at the height of the contest for the 1980 presidential nomination all claimed to best represent the vision of the Republican party. Reagan's vision was one of a party too long out of office whose conservative values had too long been ignored. George Bush's vision was of a party of moderation. John Anderson was the candidate of new ideas and a renewed Republican party in 1980. In the end, it was the Reagan vision that triumphed, a vision that Reagan did not turn his back on once nominated but continued to emphasize as the Republican vision during the general election.

The partisan ritual drama acted out by candidates in both major parties has clear-cut goals. In the heat of the presidential campaign it aims at activating the interest of party followers, a return to the army rally depicted by Jensen. It seeks to secure and enforce partisan loyalties, to make Republicans proud of being Republicans and Democrats proud of being Democrats. This is not a drama of conversion but rather one of exhorting the faithful to fulfill their destiny.

In the past decade particularly, the ritual of partisan drama which has always been with us seems to be returning to center stage. Consider as one example the televised campaign of the Republicans building toward the election year of 1980. In a series of televised five-minute spot commercials designed to revamp the image of the party, entitled "America Today," a public service advertising format addressed such problems as housing construction, aid to the disabled, and crime in the schools. It explained precisely the Republican concern and provided an address to which viewers could write for free booklets on the problem. The success in renewing a sense of Republican unity of outlook was such that in 1982, looking toward the 1984 presidential election, the Democratic party undertook a parallel series.

The key scene for the playing out of the partisan ritual drama is the nominating convention. Keynote addresses, speeches by party notables, acceptance speeches, and so on, all hearken back to party traditions, values, and goals. The clear implication is that the future of America lies with the part presently in convention, disaster awaits if the opposition party triumphs. Given that studies of when voters make up their minds regarding their choice for president indicate that from one-fifth to one-third do so during the period of the nominating conventions, we can at least speculate that a good portion of the electorate is moved to accept its role in the presidential drama in keeping with the imperative of the partisan ritual.

In the theater of politics that is the presidential election there is a third ritual drama playing alongside those of the quest for the popular will and for partisan popular control. It is a ritual quest for popular support. In his seminal work, *The Symbolic Uses of Politics,* Murray Edelman argued that among the functions served by political forms, such as popular elections, there is that of providing a "powerful means of expression for mass publics." Elections, in particular, he urged, give people the opportunity to participate in policy formulation only to a minor degree. Employing the kinds of ritual I've noted results in relatively little tangible effect from the ritual dramas of the popular will or of popular control. The principal function of elections, wrote Edelman, is that "they give people a chance to express discontents and enthusiasms, to enjoy a sense of involvement." Election rituals serve a psychological purpose, providing a spectacular drama in which voters play more of a passive spectator role as audience members than an active one, providing the opportunities for sublimating potential resorts to mass action, even organized violence.

Viewed from this perspective the ritual of a presidential campaign is the appearance of popular support for the victor of the election. V.O. Key,

Jr., argued that voters by and large do not go to the polls and choose between presidential contenders on the basis of specific issues (i.e., the underlying myth of the ritual of the quest for the popular will). Nor do they blindly decide on the basis of party loyalties which major party shall control government in the name of the populace—a vital scenic, or background, assumption of the ritual drama of popular control. Instead they engage in "retrospective" voting. Members of the electorate, wrote Key in *The Responsible Electorate,* "have in their minds recollections of their experience of the past four years." On the basis of their evaluations of those recollections, voters, often transcending party loyalties, decide to stand pat or switch, that is, grant or withdraw popular support from the incumbent administration. No clear-cut definition of the popular will, no mandate, emerges from election results. Nor, since party loyalties are not deterministic, is it clear that voters seek popular control through their choices. Instead they have a sense of being involved precisely because, as Edelman suggests, they can air their discontent and satisfaction with what they recall has happened in the preceding four-year period.

From the standpoint of campaign ritual certain imperatives follow from the quest for popular support. Presidents seeking reelection routinely trumpet the successes of their administrations and minimize failures. "Experience" becomes an important symbol in their campaigns. In 1972, for example, Richard Nixon stressed competence and managerial experiences in his campaign to "Re-Elect the President" over the untried, untested George McGovern. Similarly, Jimmy Carter in 1980 bowed to ritualistic expectations and emphasized a string of accomplishments in television ads including "a pioneering energy program, an economy now heading in the right direction, a peaceful nation now searching for a wider peace." Although there had been mistakes in his first term, asserted Carter in one ad, "Today I'm an established and experienced President."

For challengers the imperative of the popular support ritual dictates other tactics. Even if no incumbent president seeks reelection the retrospective record of the administration is a target for challenge, as John Kennedy campaigned against Richard Nixon in 1960 holding the vice president responsible for the sins of commission and omission of the Eisenhower administration. Nixon returned the favor against Hubert Humphrey in 1968, holding Lyndon Johnson's vice president culpable for the Johnson years. An incumbent president may be especially vulnerable for attack if voter's "recollections of their experiences of the past four years" are not positive. At the conclusion of the Carter-Reagan debate in 1980, Reagan asked the viewing audience to reflect on whether they were better off than they had been four years earlier. The Reagan query was a skillful rhetorical device, but it was also a dramatic performance shaped in part by the nature of the ritual of the search for popular support that was being enacted in the presidential campaign.

Rituals of 1984

It is my contention that in any presidential campaign contenders and the news media stage all three of the ritual dramas described—popular will, control, and support. In the 1984 campaign the Reagan camp ran on a record of achievements, seeking a mandate to continue a quest to serve the popular will and return control of government to the people. The Democratic nominee—emerging from a series of the same three parallel and overlapping ritual dramas in caucuses, primaries, and the nominating convention—challenged the incumbent to debate the issues so that the popular will could truly be served, addressed Republican failures so that popular control could be wrested from the fat cats, and endeavored to appear more presidential than the encumbent president in order to enlist popular support. Each ritual drama was introduced early in the campaign. Action rose through the nomination drama played out among Democrats. Turning points were reached in July and August in San Francisco and Dallas. Action fell in the general election campaign. Some members of the audience might decree that each drama was one act too long. In any case, the curtain fell on November 6 only to rise again on November 7 as the ritualistic theater of presidential politics opened a new dramatic season. Agatha Christie's *Mousetrap* is the longest running theatrical production in history. Like that mystery, the ritual dramas of the American presidential campaign never close either.

15

Voters' Control of Information

Thomas E. Patterson

Consider the degree to which voters shape their information environ-ment and the degree to which it is shaped for them by the mass media. There is a lot of scientific literature on this subject, much of it technical. It is usually ambiguous and sometimes contradictory. My perspective cov-ers a period of forty years in campaigns and tries to suggest how selec-tivity has changed in that period of time.

The first election studies to systematically address the subject of selec-tivity and the degree to which voters control their information environ-ment were done by Paul Lazarsfeld and Bernard Berelson. They studied the 1940 and 1948 presidential election campaigns. Their studies were in part a response to the notion that the mass media had a powerful influence on the audience. This idea had come out of the experiences of Nazi Ger-many, where by marshaling propaganda and using it effectively, a regime had seemed able to control in many ways the behavior of its citizens. The studies in the United States responded to the assumption growing at that time that many had very little control over his information environment, that skilled propagandists could tailor that environment and influence how people view the world.

The assumption of the Lazarsfeld and Berelson studies was quite dif-ferent. They assumed that individuals had extraordinary control over their environment. Their data seemed to prove that point. They pointed out that there is a lot of selective exposure occurring during communication, that people selectively take from their information environment materials that are favorable to or support their predispositions or their political outlooks. The data indicated that Democrats were more likely to be exposed to information that touched on Democratic themes. Republicans were more likely to be exposed to information that was strong on Republican candi-dates and strong on Republican issues and ideas. This suggests selectivity on the part of the audience members, that people select material to sup-port their preorientations.

This work also demonstrated that there is a lot of selective perception occurring during communication. People are able to see what they want to see when they are exposed to information through the mass media. They project their own predispositions, their own attitudes, on much of the information coming their way. Exposed to the same information, a Democrat or a Republican might draw different kinds of conclusions, ones that would be supportive of their earlier partisan predispositions. According to this view, people have a psychological need for supportive information, a need to develop an information environment around oneself that is supportive of one's own political attitudes. People not only have that need, but they are able to tailor a supportive environment for themselves. This is called the *limited effects model* of communication because media messages are filtered through attitudes and structured by predispositions toward politics.

The impact of such messages is quite limited. People take messages out of their environment and use them primarily for their own purposes. A quotation from Lazarsfeld, Berelson, and Gaudet's *The People's Choice* indicates just how strong a statement they make on this particular tendency in the electorate:

> As interest increases and the voter begins to be aware of what it is all about, his predispositions come into play. Out of the wide array of available propaganda, he begins to select. He is more likely to tune in some programs than others; to understand one point in a speech than another. His selective attention thus reinforces the predispositions with which he comes to the campaign. At this stage the initiative is almost wholly with the prospective voter rather than with the propagandists. Whatever the publicity that is put out, it is the selective attention of the citizen which determines what is responded to.

This finding and this conclusion had a substantial effect on scholars. One of the first effects, and an unfortunate one, was that it directed scholarly attention away from the study of the mass media of communication. It emphasized that the important factor in the equation was the individual citizen and his or her predispositions. Thus, it was important to study the citizen rather than the media. During the 1950s and most of the 1960s there were very few systematic studies of the mass media and their impact on the electorate. Most of the studies were simply of the electorate and their attitudes and predispositions.

A second effect, and a more positive contribution, was to inspire related theory such as Leon Festinger's theory of cognitive dissonance which argued that people have a psychological need to reduce dissonance. People handle incoming dissonant information in ways to make it conform with their predispositions, which could mean denial of information that conflicts with their prior beliefs. This could be reflected in selective recall, i.e., when exposed to communication, people would remember those things that tend to be supportive of their views and forget more easily what would conflict. Thus, a perceptual distortion takes place. This theory led to a number of other studies that arrived at similar conclusions. A study published in the late 1940s was called "Why Information Campaigns Fail," in which Herbert Hyman and Paul Sheatsley tried to point out why some information campaigns do not succeed in persuading people to accept a particular premise or argument. It pointed out that people bring to an information campaign their own ideas about public affairs and public matters. They will overlay those ideas onto the communication. They will select out of their communication environment those things that support their prior views and reject what is not consistent with their views.

There were some dissenters from this particular view of the media and its audience. David Sears and Jonathan Freedman, for instance, suggested that the evidence was much weaker than Lazarsfeld and Berelson and their advocates suggested. They particularly questioned that there was a psychological need for a supportive information environment. Sears and Freedman pointed out that what may be perceived to be selective exposure was de facto exposure, not something reflecting a psychological need. They pointed out, for instance, that Republicans tend to be better educated on average than Democrats. Better educated people are more likely to read the newspapers than less well-educated people. Newspaper content, particularly at that time, tended to be Republican in content. Democrats, being somewhat lower on the socioeconomic scale than Republicans, are more likely to rely on broadcasting communication which is more neutral and in some ways more Democratic in its orientation. They suggested that there may be selectivity going on, but it was factual selectivity. It did not reflect a psychological need on the part of individuals for supportive information. Most scholars accepted the limited effects theory, and the behavior of voters seemed to conform to that particular outlook. Campaigns at the time mostly activated the latent predispositions of the voters. In surveys done in the 1940s, 1950s, and early 1960s, by the time of the party conventions about 80 percent of the American electorate had decided which candidate they would vote for. A large proportion of those people had decided to support the nominee of the party that they had previously favored. Voting was primarily an extension of partisanship; most of the decisions people made about candidates were made early in the campaign.

Studies of voters' perceptions and attitudes seemed to support this view: the parties were consistent with people's attitudes about the parties; the information that voters received in the campaigns seemed to be structured around these attitudes and party loyalties and to be supportive of them. What people brought to the campaign was more important than the campaign itself in determining their orientation to the candidates.

In my judgment, the limited effects model is much less accurate and much less precise a description of the situation today. In its place I suggest a model, using a term that has been used in another context. *Learning without involvements* describes a type of media effect and relationship between media and audience. The learning without involvement model fits the situation much better than the limited effects model. The latter implies strong political attitudes, particularly an emphasis on strong party loyalties and party identification. The selectivity documented occurred primarily around partisan predispositions as to whether one was a Republican or a Democrat. The activation in the campaigns was primarily the activation of party loyalties. Thus, Republican and Democratic candidates tried to bring their party members around to a partisan point of view during the campaign.

We live in a much less partisan age now than twenty or thirty years ago. In polls conducted in 1960, about 80 percent of the American electorate indicated their loyalty, their partisan identification to one of the two major parties. They considered themselves psychologically to be either Republicans or Democrats. Of this 80 percent about half considered themselves to be strongly committed to the party of their choice. Twenty years later we find a different situation. Only about 65 percent of the electorate calls itself Democratic or Republican, and most of these people call themselves weakly committed to their party. They do not consider themselves to be strong partisans. Their behavior conforms to that view. There is much more ticket splitting among the electorate today than previously. Some people think the electorate may be even less partisan than suggested by the poll results. There have been recent polls in which nearly 70 percent of the American people say that it is much better to vote for the person, regardless of his or her party. Nearly half the American people—who may call themselves Republicans or Democrats—think there are no appreciable differences between the two major American political parties.

Americans are generally less political now than they were twenty or thirty years ago. This is evident in a number of ways, such as the lower voter turnout in election campaigns or the diminished sense of efficacy, the feeling that they can do something in the political arena or a sense of trust in government, a feeling in the population that the government and they have less in common or that they have a less clear stake in the political process. If politics is less important, there is less ego involvement now than earlier.

A second feature of the limited effects model applies less fully: the idea that information that is out there is easily controlled by the audience. Newspapers permit people substantial control over the content to which they expose themselves. We can choose to buy or not to buy a newspaper. We can choose to read or not to read the political sections. Even within the political sections, the headlines are a good cue as to the content of the news stories. It is easy to pick and choose our way through the newspaper. Television is different. To some extent, and I think it has been exaggerated, television news exposure is inadvertent. Some of what we see on television about politics we see not because we seek it out but because it is there, and we happen to be near the set at the time. That is also true for single stories about politics. Television news flows in series, one story after another. If we are going to sit and watch television news we have to watch, at least to some extent, all of the stories; we cannot pick and choose.

More important than this, television is a medium requiring low involvement. Marshall McLuhan argued otherwise. He argued that television was a high-involvement medium. He was right for the time that he was writing about. I recall when television first came along, and I watched with my parents and friends. Eyes were almost glued to the set. Three or four people would be in the room and all their attention would be directed toward the television. It was at that time a high-involvement medium. It no longer is. For many people television is something that is on many, many hours of the day. It is background communication almost in the way that radio is background. Television, because it has visual component, requires more attention than does radio, but we use it as background. It may be on, and we may be doing other things much of the time that it is on, picking up bits and pieces of information without carefully attending to it. Television advertising exposure, and exposure to political advertising, result in inadvertent and relatively low levels of involvement. We are there to watch television entertainment programs. Advertisements simply happen to come in the middle of those programs. Rather than turn off our television, we sit through the commercials and wait for the entertainment programming to resume.

These two changes, the decline of party and the emergence of television, have created the basis for a learning without involvement model. There is still a lot of selectivity occurring among individuals relating to their media environment. Political interest still plays an important part in the decision to expose ourselves to communication. Media exposure in the United States is highly stratified. People with a lot of interest in politics are much more likely to pay regular attention to the news than those without much interest in politics. That holds not only for the newspaper, where the relationship is stronger, but also for television. Some social scientists, looking superficially at the data, have argued that television has really changed the formula: that television has reached the unwashed as well as the washed; that virtually everybody watches television news with about the same frequency; that it is as appealing to the uneducated as to the educated, to the politically interested as well as the politically disinterested. That is not the case. There still is some stratification. For the most part, television news is something, at least ordinarily, that people seek out.

There is a relationship between interest, selectivity, and exposure. Importantly, this relationship is largely habitual. Evidence suggests there is no surge in exposure that accompanies election campaigns. It is not as if election campaigns suddenly awaken people to their citizen's duty, and they start paying more attention to the newspaper or start following television news more regularly than otherwise. It is a habit related to their political interest.

There is still some selective exposure in political communication. It is most evident in partisan broadcasts. If the Republican or Democratic national conventions are on, or if one or the other of the parties has a telethon, or if one candidate from one party or the other stages a documentary on television, selectivity is clear. Those kinds of communications draw principally partisans from the sponsoring party of the candidate. Those people are also more likely to have favorable responses to that programming.

Selective perception is still a very strong influence on people's responses to communication in election campaigns. Debate studies provide good evidence of the importance of selective perception. How people feel about the candidates going into the debate is going to affect their judgments about how the candidate performed in the debate. There is a very strong tendency for people already committed to a candidate to feel that he or she did a better job in that communication setting. The debate studies are interesting since they show that this is a much less substantial effect today than in the past. If we compare the 1980 and 1976 debates with the 1960 debates, those predispositions are less important now than before.

Recall the second debate of 1976 between Ford and Carter in which Ford made the blunder about Eastern Europe being free from Soviet domination. The many polls conducted immediately after, in the twelve-hour period following the debate, showed that most Americans thought Ford had won the second presidential debate and by a fairly substantial margin. On their own, people failed to see the significance that the media would later attach to that blunder. The media came into play when most of their news coverage, including the follow-up news coverage of the debate, dealt with Ford's mistake. The polling conducted twelve to forty-eight hours after the second debate showed that there had been a dramatic change in the public perception of who had won and lost the debate. The public began to accept the media's definition of winners and losers, and by a very significant proportion. That would have been impossible in the 1960 campaign. The data for those debates show a strong structuring of people's perception of who won and who lost, of who had presented himself effectively or not effectively.

Most of what goes on in the communication process in campaigns today relates to our perception, our images of reality, and what we believe the facts to be. Some of these are fairly simple, for example, they relate to the viability of the candidates. At an early point in the 1984 campaign, we thought there was only one viable Democratic candidate—Walter Mondale. Then Gary Hart became an even more viable candidate for a while than Mondale. This was a perception, not an attitude. For most of us it was the reality of what that particular election contest happened to be; it was related to our perception of the issues of the campaign. We were told that Walter Mondale was the candidate of special interests. Most of us took that as a statement of fact based on Walter Mondale's promise to various groups in the early stages of his campaign. In 1976, the media told us about the *Playboy* interview with Jimmy Carter. That was an important issue, an issue that dominated news coverage for a period during the campaign. Polls showed that people thought it an important issue, even though it had nothing to do with the governing process. The information available suggests to us the nature of candidates—Reagan as a relatively genial, if not too intelligent, guy; the claims of Hart that he somehow reflects the Kennedy generation and is the alternative for youth. In 1976 throughout the primaries there was the notion of Jimmy Carter being trustworthy and very different from the politicians of the previous four years who had been tarnished by Watergate. These are images based on more than our direct experience. We do not know whether Carter was trustworthy or not. We do not know what is meant by Hart as an alternative for youth. More to the point, these images do not threaten our predispositions or stereotypes to any substantial degree. They do not conflict with our basic attitudes and political values.

Earlier studies suggested that uncertainty reduced selectivity and that if people were unsure about politics they were more susceptible to communication influence. Uncertainty is one of the major characteristics of today's campaigns. It makes them fundamentally different from campaigns of thirty to forty years ago. Partisanship lent predictability then. In 1984, eight candidates were in the Democratic race. In an earlier period that kind of uncertainty for the most part would not exist. Then people entrusted the party leadership to make judgments about key leaders. They would respond to the nominee chosen.

Earlier studies also suggested the indifference to politics reduced selectivity. The less we care about politics, the less selective we are in our use of information. I suggest that the general decline in political interest and political commitment has created an electorate that as a whole is more indifferent than it was earlier. As a result, it is less selective. It is less protective of itself. It has fewer psychological defenses. It has less ego involvement in any kind of political commitment. We can argue that the flow of news is not likely to activate political values. Sometimes it activates them but I suggest that it is not well designed to draw out our basic feelings about politics. I argue in *Mass Media Election* that there are a number of reasons more and more election news reflects the preferences of journalists. The media still feel some responsibility to act as common carrier and provide candidates with an outlet for reaching the electorate.

We now have very long campaigns. What the candidates have to say about the key issues and key leadership questions take up only a small portion of media reports on the campaigns. The media, as a consequence, have a much more substantial influence on the general flow of information in the election than it did twenty, thirty, or forty years ago. Not surprisingly, the news reflects news values, not political values. There is a substantial emphasis on the game rather than on the issues at stake in political conflict. The principle focus of election news is on winning and losing, strategy and tactics—not on basic questions of policy and national leadership. Before the primary there, New Hampshire was not talked about in terms of the nature of political leadership in the Democratic party or what it might signify to the country if Hart, rather than Mondale, were to be the nominee. It was treated as a game that Hart's candidacy and strong showing in New Hampshire opened up the Democratic race for the nomination for a while.

Even when issues are covered in the news, there are certain types of issues that journalists like to play on. These are issues that reflect news values. The most heavily covered issue in the general election in 1976 was not détente, inflation, or unemployment; it was the *Playboy* interview. That interview received more space in the news than any other issue in the campaign. In 1980, the most heavily covered issue again was not one of the substantive issues. It was the debate about the debate. It was the continuing argument between the Anderson, Reagan, and Carter people about whether there would be a debate among the candidates and, if so, what the conditions of that debate would be. Those issues received heavy coverage because they were of interest to the news people. They made good stories. They had conflict, were controversial and colorful. They were a little different. Everybody talks about peace, unemployment, inflation; not everyone gives interviews to *Playboy* magazine. People do not pay very close attention to these stories. What we learn about politics from this kind of communication is superficial.

The electorate has very low recognition levels of our candidates for public office. There was a poll published in which interviewers asked,

"I'm going to read you a list of names. Could you tell me if you've heard of this person or heard nothing about him?" Sixty percent of the American public said they had never heard of Caspar Weinberger. Nearly 50 percent said they had never heard of Speaker of the House Tip O'Neil. This suggest that even though the information environment is out there, and something is being communicated, it does not settle in. We learn things from what we gain in our exposure, but we do not learn a lot of detail and we learn very slowly. In campaigns, partly because of the flow of news and partly because of the way we attend to the news, there is a relatively low level of information on most issues. Most people do not know where the two major candidates stand on most of the issues of an election. Not even 50 percent in almost every instance can say where the two major party nominees stand on the most significant issues.

At the same time, we are becoming more vulnerable to communication. The media have more of an influence on our reality in some ways than we do. Hart rose in the national public opinion polls because he was the alternative to Mondale. When George Bush won the Iowa caucuses, Bush came from nowhere in the national polls within a ten-day period to tie Ronald Reagan for first choice among rank-and-file Republicans. Before the Iowa caucus in 1980, Bush was the choice of fewer than 7 percent of Republicans nationwide. A week after the Iowa caucuses, he was the choice of almost 30 percent of Republicans; that was also Reagan's level at the time. Looking at 1976 and Jimmy Carter, we see a similarly phenomenal rise in the polls as a result of a strong showing in an early contest. Carter was at about 5 percent in the national polls before the New Hampshire primaries. Within a week of the New Hampshire primary, Carter had risen roughly to 30 percent in a national poll as the choice of rank-and-file Democrats. He was virtually tied with Hubert Humphrey who, going into the primary, had been the first choice for the nomination.

These tremendous surges that candidates have in the polls are not associated with anything else. People know almost nothing about the candidates as they rise in the polls. People did not know very much about George Bush in 1980 at the time that they said he was their preference for president of the United States. In 1976 they knew almost nothing about Jimmy Carter when they made him their preference for the Democratic nomination.

The model that I am suggesting conforms with William Stephenson's play theory of communication, that communication for us is mostly pleasure. It is not a duty; it is not pain. We derive some pleasure out of it. We follow the news in a relaxed, casual manner. We do not study it. We are largely uninvolved in this communication. We are selective mainly in the amounts that we receive. Some of us take in a lot of information. Others take in very little of that information. We are mostly spectators. If we were conducting political polls different from the networks' polls, we might ask people, "What do you make of this?" A lot of people would say, "It's surprising." A lot would say, "It's interesting." I do not think many people would say, "It's important." Who knows if it is important or not? In part that is because people know so little about the individuals involved and so little about politics. In this respect, I think Americans are much more vulnerable now to information campaigns than in earlier periods. Elections no longer simply activate or mostly activate as they did in an earlier time. Note a statistic from the 1980 campaign that reveals clearly how far we have come or gone, depending upon your perspective. In 1980, in the campaign of Jimmy Carter and Ronald Reagan, a real choice was offered. Ten percent of the people who voted did not make up their minds until the day of the election. One out of ten Americans did not decide if they were going to elect Jimmy Carter or Ronald Reagan until election day. Thirty-five percent did not make up their minds until the last week of the campaign. I suggest that only indifference and lack of political commitment can produce these findings. Once we have an uncommitted and uninvolved electorate, we also have an electorate that is vulnerable to the media's image of politics.

16
Magical Words and Plain Campaigns

Doris A. Graber

In "Words and Their Meaning," Aldous Huxley remarked that words do have magical effects, but not in the way that magicians suppose. To Huxley: "Words are magical in the way they affect the minds of those who use them. 'A mere matter of words,' we say contemptuously, forgetting that words have power to mold men's thinking, to canalize their feeling, to direct their willing and acting."

Words are like Pavlovian cues—just as animals can be taught to associate the sound of a bell with food—so people are continually conditioned to associate verbal cues with past direct and vicarious experiences. Verbal conditioning can be done most effectively through what political linguists call *condensation symbols*. These are more popularly called *code words*. Examples are: "the American way," "racism," "special interests," "rainbow coalition," and yes, "where's the beef?" which hints at disappointed expectations and a lack of substance. Condensation symbols create meanings economically—one phrase or word does all. The symbol conveys facts, visual images, feelings, evaluations. Condensation symbols are very important but they are not the only tools in the kit of the politician. Meanings can be conveyed in other ways: through the selective use of ordinary statements, through pictures, and through contrasts developed in interactive settings such as debates between candidates. For instance, in the late-March, 1984, debate just prior to the New York primary, Gary Hart and Fritz Mondale squabbled and called each other names. Jesse Jackson looked presidential as an eloquent and inspiring commentator. In the New Hampshire debate, the candidates, like schoolboys, had to raise their hands to get the attention of moderators Ted Koppel and Phil Donahue. It conveyed the impression that they were children permitted to speak only at the request of an authority figure. John Glenn and Fritz Mondale accused each other of "gobbledegook" and "baloney" and of working with "voodoo numbers." These kinds of performances carry powerful messages, quite aside from what is being said. What is actually said is often totally drowned out by the symbolic meanings.

My focus is on the magical effect that words and word surrogates have in molding our thinking and our actions and their impact on the political process. The setting is the 1984 election campaign. I examine five ways in which candidates use language to create meanings that go far beyond the literal meanings of the words used. The meanings that are conveyed through condensation symbols and other well-chosen words and pictures are a major factor in structuring the political scene and the course of politics. Unfortunately, these meanings often harm the political process. The 1984 campaign set the stage for destroying the good images of basically worthy contenders. It provided grounds for cynicism about the political process. It served to confuse the public through faulty linkages. It managed to enhance racial polarization in politics. And it tempted the candidates to make untenable political commitments that were apt to haunt them in their presidency. This list of problems is merely illustrative, not exhaustive.

The use of words and symbols may be magical, but it is not a surefire magic wand for being master of the political scene. For several reasons, what politicians do with words does not always work perfectly, as planned. Politicians often work at cross-purposes; their goals do not coincide or they may deliberately attempt to block each other's goals. Sometimes, when we look at particular politicians and wonder why their appeals fail, we have forgotten about the interactive aspects of language. Politicians compete for attention and support. Their efforts may cancel each other out. Also, language very often misfires when politicians fail to assess audience thinking correctly and to tap into it successfully. They do not know how to connect very well with the audience. Symbols may also evoke clashing meanings. The favorable feeling conveyed to some listeners by support of "affirmative action" may be balanced by the hostility engendered in those who view it as "reverse discrimination."

Language strategies are geared to an anticipation of the course that political events will take and to an anticipation of how the mass media will respond to the strategies. Misjudgments are easy; events happen in unexpected ways, and the media can blunt strategies and turn them against the user. Even considering all these problems, language nonetheless remains the politician's most potent tool.

Creating Reality

Candidates use language to create current political reality: not just any reality—*their* reality. They choose what they wish to tell us so that it supports their claims and enhances their image. They try to ignore the rest or deflect attention from it. A good example is the way Democrats handled economic issues during the 1984 presidential campaign. They did not talk much about inflation or interest rates or even unemployment—all issues on which the Reagan administration was doing better than its predecessor. They focused on failures in foreign policy. When Mondale was asked by a listener how he could claim that Reagan policies were an economic disaster, he had a ready answer. Instead of jobs and inflation, he called attention to large federal deficits and decline in United States foreign trade. He also referred to long-range economic declines that were presumably inevitable in the future. The power to define the current situation is crucial. As has been said, "he who can define is master."

The power to define is not exercised in a vacuum. Political rivals and opponents will battle for control of definitions and battle to undermine the definitions propagated by others. In the process, reputations of good candidates are often sullied, and the role of the politician is debased, party unity is damaged, and sound policies are undermined or precluded.

It did not help the image of the Democratic party when Mondale called Hart inconsistent, a candidate of flip-flop, an opportunist lacking in leadership qualities, a hamburger sandwich without the beef. It did not help the image of the Democratic party when Hart returned the favor by calling Mondale a captive of special interests, a throwback to old and failed ideas, a man who could not bridge the every-widening generation gap, a spendthrift who would bankrupt the nation. It did not help when the media pictured Jackson as the "black" candidate, seeking "black" support, and thereby created a reality of polarization contrary to what Jackson sought with his rainbow coalition imagery. Jackson and his supporters played this game as well, insisting that blacks must support Jackson merely because of shared racial identity. Such racial appeals made Jackson's "rainbow" largely an illusion.

To make their points, battling politicians often play with deep human emotions—fear and hatred as well as love and compassion. They paint the world of the opponent as a world of war, poverty, and lack of opportunity. If their cause wins, they promise deliverance into a world of peace, prosperity, and opportunity for all. Thus Gary Hart claimed to be a bringer of peace and blamed President Reagan for needlessly spilling the blood of Americans in Lebanon. Reagan, in turn, claimed he was working for peace and blamed Congress for the massacre of Americans in Lebanon. These are two different worlds. How can we tell which is real? Different people accept different realities; the reality ultimately accepted by those in power is the reality that shapes political action.

Plays on the public's emotions tend to raise undue fears. Reality becomes clouded and politics may take irrational turns. It was hardly an invitation to rational decision making when Ronald Reagan, during a foreign policy address at Georgetown University on April 7, 1984, posited an emotionally unacceptable choice against an emotionally acceptable one.

He told his audience, "We have a choice: Either we help America's friends defend themselves and give democracy a chance or we abandon our responsibilities and let the Soviet Union and Cuba shape the destiny of our hemisphere." Who would choose abandoning responsibilities, betraying democracy, and delivering the world to communism? Such code words and phrases inspire us to fight wars, shed our blood, and risk our lives to make the world safe for democracy. They are very powerful. Social and political movements that lack rousing symbols and code words generally fail.

In a less consequential example from the Democratic side of the political fence, Roy Spence, Jr., who handled Mondale's media campaign, played on the public's belief in the importance of public opinion and careful deliberations in order to turn back an attack on Mondale for being too cautious. Notice the play on words: Spence announced that "Mondale has strength: he dares to be cautious." Then he added: "I don't think the American people want a quick fix, quick action, without a great deal of thought." So slow and cautious Mondale was the answer; he represented what the American people wanted. Spence sought to create a different reality—one where great caution was a virtue, not a vice.

When politicians define reality, the definitions are usually vague. They leave room for the audience to fill in its own meanings. Vagueness also allows the candidate to define ultimately what was meant. Nobody knows what is meant by "a fair share," or "reform," or Gary Hart's "new politics." Hart promised to "bring new thinking to crucial issues." That sounded great, but he did not specify the nature of the thinking or the issues. He talked about "new ideals, new leadership, and a new sense of purpose." He said, "We cannot go back to special-interest politics, a narrow agenda of old arrangements, old deals." What did he mean?

What did Mondale mean when he promised to use power "for peace in a way that is feasible, internationally defensible, mindful of history and supported by the American people." What precise policy was he advocating when he told members of the Foreign Policy Association on March 31, 1984, that in dealing with China, he would pursue more trade, improved diplomatic relations, and "defensive-oriented military assistance" which had "to be carefully handled"? These are vague statements that evoke positive feelings. They also suggest, indirectly, that something is wrong with current policy and must be changed. The change agent is the candidate making the speech. Even if this is not said outright, it is clear to nearly everyone. Such suggestions, which are not clearly identifiable as propaganda, are likely to be effective because people are caught offguard. Overt propaganda, like a red flag for a bull, may make people angry.

Pinning down the meaning of code words is made even more difficult by the fact that the meanings often vary. This depends on the subcultural setting in which they are used. Currently, the word *reform,* for instance, means "more power to blacks," to black politicians while still carrying more traditional connotations for others. Jesse Jackson turned around the meaning of the code words that picture blacks and Hispanics as the bottom of the economic heap—the lowest level of society. He urged black and Hispanic voters to unite, telling them "we are not the bottom of this society, where everything ends." Instead, he said, "we are the foundation where everything begins."

Meanings also shift over time. In the past, a reference to "special interests" rarely encompassed organized labor. The 22 million Americans who belong to unions represent such a wide array of trades and crafts that it has seemed inappropriate to call them a "special interest" group. That has now changed. The New Deals, Fair Deals, and Great Society of Democratic presidents no longer stand primarily for the politics of social consciousness and compassion. They stand for the politics of excessive welfare, excessive spending, and huge deficits. The rich and big business have become the devils of the eighties replacing communism and Nazism, the devils of earlier decades. Politicians who toy with code words or try to interpret them must carefully assess the historical and situational context.

Past and Future Realities

Much of reality creation is not concerned with constructing current reality. It involves reconstructing the past and predicting the future. This is the second major use of campaign language. Reconstruction of the past and future is, in many ways, easier than constructing the current scene. There is some limited opportunity, for most people, to test current reality. Ronald Reagan played on that in 1980 with his famous invitation to the public to judge whether they were better off and felt safer in 1980 than at the beginning of the Carter presidency. Democrats used the same tactic against Ronald Reagan. They asked: "Do you feel safer in 1984 than you did in 1980?" "Is peace any closer at hand?"

The past lends itself to verbal reconstruction because it leaves too few well-known, readily available tracks to allow extensive reality testing. George Orwell satirized this idea when he advocated establishing a Ministry of Truth in his mythical dictatorship in *1984.* The ministry would be charged with day-to-day falsification of the past. It is even easier to predict the future, which has no tracks at all for reality testing. Political campaigns, including party platforms, are veritable marathons of political pledges of future performance. Each candidate and party tries to outdo the opponents. Success in painting believable political futures often becomes an admission ticket to political office. It is a purely mental construction, but it is the only way in which promised futures can become a base for political decisions. Word mirages must take the place of reality.

A full-page advertisement by Gary Hart advocated moving "from the policies of the past to our possibilities for the future. From the campaign promises of 1980 to our prospects for 1984 and beyond." The ad painted the Reagan past as full of failures; fattening the federal deficit; gutting social security programs for women and children; allowing marines to die unnecessarily in Lebanon; and failing to halt the arms race, which may lead to nuclear war. Hart then suggested that he would change all that and Americans could participate in making this bright new future happen. In his words: "The Hart experience is inspiring voters to step forward with new hope for our future, for our commitment to social justice, for our demand to end the nuclear arms race, for our call to compete in the world marketplace." It was a bright picture, full of wonderful hope; but who is clairvoyant enough to judge its accuracy? Voters must buy the future on the basis of promises. What are promises? They are mere words.

Another important aspect of future projection is its use to manipulate important expectations. This occurs most commonly when candidates predict how they will be doing in forthcoming primary elections or caucuses. If they do better than predicted, their status is enhanced. If they do worse than predicted, their status is diminished. This would indicate that low predictions are a good idea; but if the prediction is so low that winning seems impossible, the voters may desert the candidate who appears to be a sure loser. The trick is to maintain the image that the candidate can win in the future—that he is not a sure loser—without escalating expectations to the point that the happenings about to occur may become disappointing.

There are many examples of how this game is played. In the New York primary, Gary Hart described himself as a long-shot underdog, suggesting that he need not win—just coming close, in his words, "will be a political miracle." He set up expectations in the Pennsylvania primary, by entering under the protective label of "underdog," which suggests a likely loss but does not exclude a win. Mondale, who began the campaign under the "front-runner" label, believed that it made his early losses all the more damaging. After his losses in New England he said, "Don't call me front-runner any more." He resumed the title later when his victory in the Democratic nominating contest seemed assured.

Mondale adopted a label initially because it was deemed highly beneficial. When people expect a candidate to be a sure winner, they flock to that candidate with support—votes, volunteers, and money. Everybody loves a winner. The image becomes a self-fulfilling prophecy. Fortunately or unfortunately, the "winner" image can sustain only a limited amount of contradiction from reality. It does have to be confirmed periodically. Since this is one of the few areas in which reality testing is possible, the public's perceptions can change rapidly.

When candidates cannot claim the winner label in the ordinary ways, they may resort to alternatives. In the presidential game, winning means getting the prescribed number of delegates. Gary Hart claimed that winning must be defined by the number of primaries and caucuses won, rather than by the number of delegates won. He pictured himself as the popular choice who just happened to be trailing in delegates. This ignored the fact that the nomination goes to the candidate who wins the largest number of delegates. By redefining what winning meant, Hart could be the winner, even though he was the loser.

Jesse Jackson, who early on suffered from being stigmatized as the candidate who could not possibly win, used a different tactic. He created his own definition of what winning meant to his candidacy. Gaining delegates was last on the list. He kept his following by insisting, as he put it, that "We must measure the success of our campaign by our own value system." Said he: "For us, success is our effort leading to increased voter registration; it's more people running for office; it's a coalition of white, Hispanic, black, Asian, peace activities, environmentalists coming together. For us, success is getting the burning issues of the day on the national agenda of the country." He added that success also was changing some of the Democratic party rules that he believed discriminate against poor and minority candidates. Jackson showed that even when candidates cannot win in the way the word is usually defined, they can be winners of sorts. In the process, they might be able to keep their followers, as long as followers are willing to accept the candidates' definitions.

Interpretation and Linkage

In the process of creating past, present, and future realities, candidates interpret the political scene. This is the third major function of campaign language. Politicians explain the significance of events, indicate their causes and interrelations with other events, and pass judgments about the merits of particular situations. Most political situations are complex, lending themselves to many different interpretations. These interpretations are mental constructions—hard to prove or disprove. Audiences are eager to get such interpretations to help them make sense out of the confusing march of events.

Interpretations and evaluations are often done through the use of condensation symbols which draw parallels between the present and known persons, between known events and known situations in the past. A number of examples of different types of interpretations and linkages can be drawn from the 1984 presidential campaign. Person linkages were very common. Gary Hart linked himself with John F. Kennedy because of the Kennedy legend and myth and with Harry Truman to show that, like Truman, he too was a tough fighter in an uphill struggle. One of Hart's ads linked him to Einstein, claiming that the two shared ideas. Hart also linked himself to the younger generation, suggesting that Mondale and Reagan represented an age group whose time had passed.

Mondale, too, linked himself to Kennedy and the Camelot legend. He tried to uncouple himself from the Carter administration, even though this produced a rift between Mondale and Carter. Mondale's rivals linked him to Hubert Humphrey and to Lyndon Johnson, hoping that this linkage would convey a taint of failure. Humphrey and Johnson would evoke image of spend-thrift administrations, going overboard and bankrupting the country. Robert Teeter, a Reagan pollster, said that he preferred to see Mondale as Reagan's opponent, because "If you run Ronald Reagan against the New Deal or the Great Society, you can win." Jesse Jackson linked himself to Martin Luther King, Jr., claiming the civil rights leader died in his arms and that he had a bloodstained shirt to prove it. Others deny that this really happened; but the symbolism is interesting, and it created a powerful image.

Besides person linkages, there are group linkages. Some of them come about through endorsements such as Mondale being considered, for good or ill, as labor's candidate. Others are pinned on candidates, often to discredit them. Reagan was called the candidate of the rich. Rich is a dirty word these days; it suggested that he had no concern for ordinary people. Hart was called a supporter of "Big Oil" because he voted for some tax legislation that benefited oil companies; Jackson was the candidate of "blacks."

Linkages may also be activities of the candidates and the meanings that can be inferred from them. Thus Glenn's qualifications as space hero and military ace, and Jackson's success in winning the release of Lieutenant Robert Goodman from captivity in Syria, presumably indicated that these candidates would succeed in the presidency. This is sometimes called *stimulus generalization:* if the candidate is good in one activity, he must be good in another, even if it is only remotely related. Hence candidates try to picture themselves in activities that carry favorable connotations. In Jesse Jackson's case a number of activities involving him have been interpreted as evidence of anti-Semitism. His friendly relations with Yasser

Arafat and Andrew Young, his views on the Middle East, his reference to New York as "Hymietown" are examples. Jackson denied anti-Semitism—but his linkage to these activities canceled the denial in the eyes of most observers.

The process of inferring meanings from linkage to activities becomes particularly delicate and damaging when disadvantaged groups are involved. Any action that is disliked or resented by groups such as women, blacks, Jews, or Hispanics, can readily be labeled as proof of hostility to the group. If carried out, the action increases dangerous cleavages in the population. If not carried out, policy decisions may have been made for the wrong reason—the desire to avoid faulty linkages. It has become very hazardous politically to criticize the conduct of minorities in today's political climate. No white candidate would have escaped an avalanche of criticisms, had he refused to dissociate himself from a supporter with the anti-Semitic views expressed by Louis Farrakahn, a prominent Black Muslim leader. Jackson was able to do so. Justifiable criticism was stifled lest it be condemned as a racial slur.

Linkage may also be used to link current politics to past ones, to demonstrate success or failure, approval or disapproval. Thus Mondale's Central American policy proposals were condemned as leading to "another Vietnam." Jackson called Reagan's Central American policy his "Watergate." John Glenn was linked to "Reaganomics" when Mondale wished to diminish his stature. Jackson used a neat figure of speech to tie his rivals to the policies of the Reagan administration. After reciting the evils of that administration, he concluded by saying: "We have not made progress if we just get off a Republican elephant and on to a Democratic donkey to go in the same direction just a little slower." That statement painted his rivals as quasi-Republicans.

Interpretations also suggest linkages. When candidates assign causes to problems, the realm of solutions becomes focused. For example, when Gary Hart claimed that the problems of Central America are rooted in poverty, and not in communism, this indicated that a policy change was in order. While communism may have to be fought with guns, as Ronald Reagan contended, poverty requires other solutions. Similarly, when candidates link the deficit primarily to the defense budget, cutting of defense expenditures becomes a high priority. When they blame the social services budget for the deficit, a different policy becomes appropriate.

Candidates and the media can specify all sorts of benchmarks by which the importance of events should be judged. For instance, observers proclaimed, rightly or wrongly, that the New York primary would be a touchstone to indicate whether Mondale could succeed in industrial states. His success was interpreted accordingly—a sign that he would be victorious in other industrial states. Similarly, observers passed the word that Mondale could not retain political respectability unless he carried Illinois. It would take that victory to smash the giant-killer image that Hart had earned by his string of New England victories. Again, the outcome of the Illinois primary was interpreted in line with the verbally declared marker. Many of these markers have become part of political folklore—the importance of a New Hampshire win or the Iowa caucus win are examples. These events became crucial because media and politicians declared them to be crucial. The myth persists, even though the reality is often different. Hart lost Iowa and then earned a string of victories. Mondale lost New Hampshire but won the nomination.

Agenda Setting

A fourth major function performed by political language during campaigns is agenda setting. When candidates, or the media which cover their campaigns, select certain topics for discussion, these topics have a chance to move to the center of public attention. Once they become matters of public attention, they are likely to become matters of public action as well. For example, the major Democratic candidates discussed extensively the policy of a nuclear freeze and committed themselves to definite nuclear weapons policies. Gary Hart promised to take remedial action on the very first day of his presidency, suggesting that a nuclear freeze was his first priority. Mondale raised the issue as well. Jesse Jackson vowed to shut down all nuclear plants and reduce the defense budget by 25 percent. Ronald Reagan tried to show that he, too, was concerned about nuclear war. In a major foreign policy address in February, 1984, he called for "constructive cooperation" between the United States and the Soviet Union. His mission to China was billed as a "Crusade for Peace."

In part, extensive attention to the nuclear issues may be credited to the activities of members of the nuclear freeze movement. They worked hard to get the candidates to address the issue. They even planted questioners during political meetings to ask the candidates what they were planning to do about nuclear war. Proponents of a nuclear freeze were found to remind winning candidates about the commitments made during the campaign. The same holds true for some of the issues that Jesse Jackson placed on the public agenda in his efforts to redirect national attention to the civil rights and antipoverty goals of the sixties. To quote *Washington Post* columnist David Broder, "At the verbal level, he [Jackson] has proved himself quick in debate and has shown he can translate a variety of issues into his preferred idiom—a rhetoric of 'empowering the poor' that has been absent from American politics for almost 20 years." Jackson moved these issues into the limelight again, increasing the chances that they would receive a lot of attention from a Democratic administration.

Hart influenced the agenda for foreign policy when he stated that "We will not, we must not, send our sons to die in Lebanon without cause or to serve as bodyguards for dictators in Central America." Such remarks suggested that President Reagan's Middle Eastern and Central American policies must be reconsidered. Even more specifically, in an address to the Conference of Presidents of Major Jewish Organizations on March 23, 1984, Hart pledged that "the Hart administration will not cater to the changing whims of King Hussein. . . . Giving and selling and doing whatever the so-called 'moderate' Arab states demand of us will end with the Hart Administration. If King Hussein wants us to provide stability to his regime, let him recognize the State of Israel." Hart also pledged that "As President, I will move the United States Embassy from Tel Aviv to Jerusalem." Ironically, these pledges, which could hamper the freedom of negotiation of a Hart administration, also did him political harm because they were viewed as a cynical pitch to Jewish voters. As commentator David Axelrod put it, "A man who is preaching the new politics of the national interest over special interests cannot afford to get caught in such a blatant special interest appeal."

Often the subjects politicians omit from discussion are as important as those they include. Topics that are omitted may be neglected when they ought to receive attention because they are important for public policy or because they might illuminate significant candidate characteristics. Little was said during the 1984 campaign about the plight of public education, or the problem of illegal immigration. These were deemed politically too controversial to put on the agenda for political action. Such issues are likely to be shunned because politicians fear that discussion will alienate many of their supporters.

As part of the political contest, opponents often expose topics that their counterparts have tried to ignore or even to conceal. The campaign waged by Mondale against Glenn and, to a lesser degree, by Glenn against Mondale, contained many examples. Usually these take the form of referring to past votes or actions of the candidate which may be embarrassing and hard to explain satisfactorily. Mondale's charges that Glenn supported a number of Reagan economic policies, and Glenn's claim that Mondale backed Carter's foreign policies are examples.

Stimulation for Action

A fifth major function of political language is action stimulation or making words a surrogate for action. Insofar as the agenda-setting function results in policy in line with the issues placed on the agenda, it is stimulation for action. During the course of a campaign, the chief actions that are desired from the audience are voting for the candidate and supporting the candidate with money, work, and various types of endorsements. Jesse Jackson put it fervently and eloquently in a church in Montgomery, Alabama, when he reminded his largely black audience of his civil rights activism. He said that he had "paid his dues" and now he expected "a return on my investment." Then he pleaded: "Who marched with you in 1965 from Selma to Montgomery?" and answered himself: "Here am I. Send me. Who risked their lives that your right to vote might live? Here am I. Send me. Who spent the most nights in jail that you might be free? Here am I. Send me."

The Jackson campaign also provided a good example of the use of words as a surrogate for action. Jackson publicly threatened to deny support to the Democratic nominee unless the nominee guaranteed to oppose runoff primaries in the South, as currently provided for by Democratic party rules. Most likely, the threat would produce the desired action and thus serve as a surrogate for the deed—withdrawal of Jackson's support. Threats, promises, praise, blame, endorsements—are all are widely used verbal maneuvers to accomplish purposes that might otherwise require nonverbal action.

If we take an overall look at the impact of language on political campaigns, it is encouraging that so much can be accomplished with words as long as expression is free and unhampered. Battles fought with words can leave a lot of wounds, but they are usually preferable to battles fought with other weapons. The chance to compete for the support of various publics through verbal interchange provides an opportunity to air disputed ideas and to disseminate at least a modest amount of information and some slivers of truth. Abuses of the right to engage in verbal contests are tolerable and must be tolerated.

Nonetheless, verbal contests in campaigns involve serious dangers. First, campaigns, as currently conducted, often lead to verbal demolition of good candidates and good policies for the sake of temporary partisan advantage. This, in turn, leads to cynicism about politics and difficulty in attracting good people to political office. Second, verbal sparring often leads to untenable commitments which then haunt future policymaking. If commitments are broken, credibility gaps result. Finally, the creation of false linkages obscures the perception of reality for the public as well as for the political leadership. Bad policies may result from the uses of political language. As Harry Truman once said, elections are no parlor game. There is more to an election than winning.

17

PACs, Parties and Presidents

Larry Sabato

It is important to know what a political action committee, or PAC, is. The term is bandied about but we do not often define it. A PAC is a segregated campaign fund of a labor union, business corporation, trade association, or an independent group that is created solely for political purposes. It is a fund of campaign money that is kept separate from all other expenditures of the organization or the union or the corporation. PAC is actually a colloquial expression; it is not found anywhere in the federal statutes. Party committees are not PACs and are completely separate from PACs. PACs use nonparty campaign funds; they are not formed by nor are they connected to political parties. While PACs have existed since the 1940s, most PACs have been formed since the 1970s. They were a product of the reforms spawned by Watergate. The federal election campaign act of 1971, amended in 1974, amended again in 1976, amended again in 1979—a decade of campaign reforms spurred the growth of political action committees, by making it possible for corporations and trade associations as well as labor unions to form them.

The numbers of PACs has grown tremendously; there are more than 3,500. In 1974 only about $12.5 million was contributed by political action committees to presidential and congressional candidates. By 1982 PACs were contributing close to $84 million to political candidates. How does that compare with political expenditures before all these PACs were formed? We have no way of knowing. the one positive reform that came out of the 1970s was reporting and disclosure. For the first time ever, we are able to find out what groups spent their money and how they spent it. It is all reported to the Federal Election Commission. We can trace the expenditures, although the reporting process is slow. Since we are about one election cycle behind, we are just now analyzing what happened in the 1982 congressional elections. We are always behind the times because the reports are so thorough.

We will never know what was spent before the 1970s because no reporting or disclosure was required. Reports were filed, but they generally contained an estimate—only 3 or 4 or 5 percent of what the expenditures actually were in many cases—by labor unions and businesses. Old campaign laws were filled with loopholes, and it was easy to hide what was actually spent. Most groups did that. PACs were a product of reform. As all good reformers know, reforms always conform to the law of unintended consequences. That is, reforms always produce unintended effects—effects that were not even considered to be possible when the reform was proposed and enacted.

There is great diversity in the PAC world. There are PACs on the Right and on the Left. There are labor PACs and there are business PACs. There are Democratic-oriented PACs and there are Republican-oriented PACs. There are PACs that are violently opposed to the party system, that actively try to upset the current party balance. When we generalize, we have to keep in mind that there are many kinds of PACs.

The diversity among PACs extends to their organization and to their fund raising as well. Some PACs are democratically organized; they have representatives of all the individuals who are contributing to the group on their candidate selection committee so that there is some form of representation in choosing which candidates receive the PAC's money. There are many other PACs that are autocratically governed; the chief executive officer of the corporation makes all of the decisions on how the PAC money is dispensed. They never report to their constituents—to the contributors—about how the money was actually spent.

Many PACs raise their money through direct mail. They get money in ten or twenty-five dollar contributions from tens of thousands of people. Because they are getting small amounts from many people, there is little accountability. People contributing money through the mail have no say about how their money is actually spent. There is no democratic process involved in many of the PACs that raise their money through direct mail. Similarly, there is no democratic process in labor PACs because millions of people contribute only a dollar or two to the labor union; generally the chief executive officers of the union make all of the decisions about candidates. The members have little to say about who gets the PAC contribution. Disbursement is separate from the solicitation process.

The most visible element of PACs is contributions to candidates; that is what we associate with political action committees. The presidential race in 1984 serves as an example. Both Walter Mondale and Gary Hart made early headlines by declaring very forthrightly, very virtuously, that they would accept no contributions from political action committees despite what it was going to cost the campaigns and their candidacies. They were standing up against special-interest politics. By this self-sacrificing action, they implied that once in office they were going to do something about the scandal of political action committees. They may have been sincere in their beliefs about PACs, but in truth they made almost no sacrifice at all.

On average, presidential candidates receive less than 2 percent of their total financing from political action committees.

PACs do not generally contribute to presidential candidates because most PACs are congressionally oriented. It is in Congress and with congressional candidates that they believe they achieve their greatest influence. They believe that too many people and too many interests contribute too much to presidential candidates. Their maximum contribution of $5,000 is a drop in the presidential bucket; they would be gaining very little from a maximum contribution. Whereas with a congressman a maximum contribution counts for more. More can be achieved with less; they do not even have to give a maximum contribution to a congressman.

Presidential candidates do have a connection with the PAC process. Their connection is through candidate PACs. It is now an accepted part of the campaign process for serious presidential candidates to establish their own political action committees. They do it because they can form a PAC prior to declaring their candidacy for president, at which point they come under all the rules and regulations of the Federal Election Commission (FEC). Prior to this, they can operate without the strictures candidacy places upon them, as long as they are not a candidate while traveling from state to state. For example, there is an overall campaign spending ceiling established by the FEC for each state. When a declared candidate goes to a state, all or most of the expenses of that trip have to be allocated to that state's spending ceiling. For example, if candidates travel in New Hampshire up to four years prior to the campaign, they could approach the spending ceiling two years prior to the presidential election if they were not careful. It is preferable not to declare their candidacy and to have a political action committee raise money to support their travels. They also use PACs to contribute to other candidates, to establish obligations to draw upon during the presidential election year. They give $5,000 to a congressional race, hoping that candidate will return the favor with support in a presidential race. PACs are a vehicle for raising money, developing contacts around the country, supporting candidates' travels and a number of other activities. Presidential candidate PACs raise money mainly through direct mail. They send out millions of fund raising letters which identify potential contributors to the candidate. These contributors become a golden campaign list once candidacy is declared. Thus, PACs do almost all the hard, preliminary work for the candidate's presidential election campaign.

Presidential candidates do have a connection with PACs. Mondale, for example, had his Committee for the Future of America operating for three years prior to his declaration of candidacy. In 1980, Ronald Reagan had his Committee for the Republic operating for four full years prior to his announcement of candidacy, raising millions of dollars to support his activities. John Glenn, in order to be taken seriously as a presidential candidate, felt that he had to create a political action committee. Gary Hart was one of the only candidates who did not—not because he opposed PACs, but because he did not have the organization and the financing to be able to start one. Prior to 1984 Hart was not considered a major candidate.

There is one other presidential connection to PACs. Even though Walter Mondale said that he would accept no PAC money, he directly benefited from PAC contributions. His strategy was to spend early and eliminate all of his challengers. He planned to be the nominee by Super Tuesday. Things did not work out that way. Instead, he spent more than half of the total amount allowed under the public financing rules before Super Tuesday. He had a severe financial crunch. Whereas Gary Hart, because he raised so little prior to New Hampshire, could spend almost three times what Walter Mondale could, assuming he could raise the money by the end of the primary season. If Walter Mondale was in danger of being dramatically outspent by Gary Hart, what could he do? The financing rules have a lot of loopholes; one loophole in the financing rules is that PACs can not only give to a presidential candidate, they can separately and independently support delegate slates or individual delegates running for positions available at the national convention. In New York, in that crucial primary, Hart outspent Mondale; but, most of Walter Mondale's delegates, both as slates and as individuals, were raising money from PACs. They were spending separately—supporting their own election as Mondale delegates. Mondale benefited from PAC contributions even though he could properly say he was not accepting any and had no direct connection to PACs.

PACs are formed for the sole purpose of supporting candidates in political races. Before 1982, they were heavily Republican. They were groups such as NCPAC, the National Conservative Political Action Committee, and about 70 percent of all nonconnected PAC funds went to Republicans. Because of that Republican bias, Democratic nonconnected groups have begun to form. By 1982 there were so many Democratic nonconnected groups that the Democrats actually gained a majority of the funds contributed by nonconnected PACs. There is a balance in the PAC system. When there is an imbalance in the system over time, a balance is developed because groups that are out of the system see PACs as a way to get involved and to have influence on political campaigns.

There are also a couple of current trends in PAC giving. One is not giving money to presidential or congressional candidates, but giving what are called "in-kind" gifts. These are services rather than money, such as a phone bank instead of a $5,000 contribution. This is done for a number of reasons. If a contribution is given, a check is sent from the PAC treasurer to the campaign treasurer. The candidate never sees it and probably never even knows it is there. He pays no attention to it. Instead a PAC decides to give an in-kind service. If they decide to take a poll for the candidate, they spend the same $5,000 that they would give in a contribution. In deciding on a poll they get to meet with the campaign manager and the staff, and they probably request a meeting with the candidate to show the results of the poll. They establish personal contact with the candidate and his key staffers, and they get noticed. They are known for giving $5,000, even though it was given in-kind.

Another trend is independent spending. NCPAC is our best example of this. With independent spending a political group does not give money directly to a candidate or campaign. Instead, without the knowledge of the campaign leadership, and without the candidate's approval, it spends money on behalf of the candidate or the campaign. NCPAC usually supports Republican candidates and opposes Democratic candidates. They will spend more than $100,000 on media opposing a Democratic candidate and supporting a Republican candidate. How can they do that if the limit is $5,000? The contribution limit is supposed to be $5,000 per election. They can do it because they spend the money independently. Without contacting the Republican candidate, and without calling any of the key staffers, they simply hire consultants, design their own media ads, place them with the television stations, and let the chips fall where they may. Independent spending is being done more and more by PACs because it allows them to spend more than the $5,000 limitation, and to have more influence on the racers that they consider to be important.

The biggest controversy about PACs is about vote buying. Do PACs buy influence in a presidential administration? Do they buy votes on the floor of Congress? The evidence is very mixed. The pro-PAC people— business people—say, "Oh no, PACs are merely a means for average independent citizens to join together in carrying the flag in the election campaign, to contribute to the candidates of their choice as Americans have done since the Revolutionary War."

Common Cause says that PACs are buying votes and buying influence in a presidential administration. There is no other reason for contributing, and they are very blatant about it. Common Cause attempts to prove it by showing in vote after vote on the floor of Congress that a congressman who received thousands of dollars from a particular special interest group voted for that group's bill. They have many examples of that and also examples of presidents supporting a PAC interest. Ronald Reagan has long been a favorite of the American Medical Association's PAC; a person close to that PAC, and for many years an official of it, is now the chairman of the Federal Election Commission. Reagan appointed a number of

PAC managers to political positions.

Is there truth to the charges of vote buying on the part of PACs and influence peddling in presidential administrations? The answer is a quali- fied yes, sometimes. Truth is often in between the extreme possibilities, and I think this is so with PACs. It is clear that PACs buy access. When they contribute money to a presidential or congressional candidate, they are probably buying access to that candidate or his key staffers, in the event that the candidate is elected. If the PAC has given money its representatives can probably call and say, "We gave you $5,000, we'd like five minutes to present our case on the upcoming bill, or we'd like five minutes to back this particular nominee or suggest to the president that he nominate this particular individual." If they have made a large enough contribution and have enough key supporters, who have backed that par- ticular candidate, they can probably get in to see the officeholder. They do therefore buy access, but that is very different from buying a vote or buy- ing the eventual judgment. Having one's case heard displays influence, but it is not the whole ball game. It is not the decision. While Common Cause frequently points out the correlations between PAC contributions received during an election campaign and votes cast on the floor of Congress, the whole truth is much more complicated. For example, congressmen who receive contributions from the dairy PACs usually vote for price supports for dairy farmers, but it is also true that many congressmen who receive money from the dairy PACs have large numbers of dairy farmers as their constituents. Are they voting for the price sup- ports because they received dairy PAC contributions or are they voting for the price supports because a large number of their voters are dairy farm- ers? When political scientists look at correlations such as those offered by Common Cause, we use more sophisticated forms of regression analysis. We find that most congressmen's votes are not explained solely or even mainly by PAC contributions. They are explained more by party affilia- tion. Whether the congressman is a Democrat or Republican determines more of their votes on special interest legislation than do PAC contribu- tions. Their personal ideology determines more of their votes than do PAC contributions. Their constituency, whether dairy farmers or others, deter- mines more of their votes than do PAC contributions. All of these ele- ments are better predictors of votes on the floor of Congress than are PAC contributions. While there are no studies of presidential decision making comparable to the congressional studies, the same pattern may prevail.

PAC contributions do make a difference in some votes on the floor of Congress. What kind of votes are they? They tend to be low visibility issues, out of the public spotlight. They tend to be committee votes that the press is not covering and that the public never hears about. When the press focus is absent, when the only people following the process are officers of the special interest group, congressmen probably are going to vote for the special interest in return for the PAC contributions. It is important to remember that normally there are competing interests in any individual vote. A business interest and a labor interest follow a particular bill, each pressuring the congressman to vote its way. The congressman is the recipient of countervailing pressures. Ordinarily a major issue will receive press coverage, so that most votes simply are not directly influenced—or not overwhelmingly influenced—by PAC contributions. It is ludicrously naive to think that PAC money never influences a congressman's vote or a president's decision. It is also irredeemably cynical to believe that PACs always or even usually push the voting buttons on the floor of Congress.

What then could be the overall evaluation of political action committees? We have to go back to Madison's concept of America and special interest. James Madison felt that special interest, which he called factions, were essential to the operation of American democracy. In a free society in which liberty is the value we cherish most, he thought we should actively encourage the formation of special interest factions—the more factions the better. The more factions we can encourage to form, the less chance there will be that one or a small group of factions will dominate the political process. That is what we are seeing in the PAC system. More and more PACs form on all sides of the political spectrum. At first the PAC system was labor dominated; then it became too heavily weighted on the business side and the independent group Republican-leaning side; then more PACs started developing on the Left and independent groups on the liberal, or Democratic, side. We are achieving a new kind of balance in the PAC system, which is all to the good.

PACs are also limited in other ways. First, by general suffrage—voters in the home district matter more than money to most politicians. If a politician is faced with a vote, say, on the floor of Congress, by voting affirmatively he might secure a maximum $5,000 contribution from a special interest group. If that special interest group is a particularly unpopular one with a large segment of his constituency, by voting affirmatively on that particular issue he can lose 5,000 votes. What do you think the congressman is going to do? Is he going to vote "yes" to get $5,000 or is he going to vote "no" to avoid losing 5,000 votes? In nine out of ten cases he is going to vote "no."

Maybe in a perfect world PACs would not exist and would not be necessary. Unfortunately, there is no heaven on earth; and just as governments and are here to stay, PACs are here to say.

18

Campaign Commercials

L. Patrick Devlin

Ronald Reagan received almost $30 million in federal funds during the 1980 campaign. He spent $18 million, or 60 percent of it, on advertising. He spent approximately $13 million of that on television advertisements, so that 70 percent of the money that Ronald Reagan spent on advertising in the 1980 campaign was spent on television advertising. In 1976 Jimmy Carter spent 74 precent of his advertising money on television. In 1984 Reagan and Mondale spent approximately $25 million each on advertising. Candidates are spending more on television advertising. Or are they?

An analysis of the money spent on television advertising in the 1952 Eisenhower campaign uncovers some interesting comparisons. In a paper on the 1952 Eisenhower television campaign, Stephen C. Wood estimated that Eisenhower's television spending ranged from $2 million to $6 million when all television time buying—national, state, and local—was factored in. Eisenhower's campaign spent approximately $1.5 million on network television spots. In 1980, Reagan's network spending approximated $6.5 million. If these two network spending figures are analyzed in terms of the 1967 base year for constant dollars, Eisenhower spent $1.9 million on network spots, Reagan spent $2.5 million. If Eisenhower spent a possible total of $6 million while Reagan spent a total of $13 million on television ads, Eisenhower actually outspent Reagan $7.5 million to $5.9 million in terms of 1967 constant dollars.

Well financed presidential candidates always have and always will spend vast sums and a major portion of their budgets on television advertising. Few corporations, aside from Proctor and Gamble, McDonalds, or Miller beer, advertise year-round at the volume reached by political advertising during the months of September and October and the first week of November. During a presidential campaign commercials flood the airwaves.

Political commercials come in various time frames. They come in half-hour speeches or biographies. They come in mini programs, or four-minute-and-twenty-second segments that are sandwiched in before Johnny Carson or the evening news. More commonly they come in sixty-second or especially thirty-second segments. Political commercials can also be categorized as to type or format—documentary, talking head, man-in-the-street, cinema verité, and production idea spots.

The advantage of political advertising is that it can be controlled. Candidates may not be able to control what the opposition says or does, or control what the media televises or prints. But candidates, if they are properly financed, can control the message and image conveyed through paid television advertising. There are other advantages of political advertising.

One purpose of political advertising is to make an unknown candidate a better known candidate. Examples of unknowns using television in presidential races to become known is less frequent than in gubernatorial or senatorial campaigns. McGovern in 1972, Carter in 1976, Bush in 1980, and Hart in 1984 used television extensively to become better known during their primary campaigns. Ads are also often aimed at late-deciding or disinterested voters. Ads are unobtrusive and unavoidable invaders into peoples' living rooms. They reach thousands, even millions in large media markets. Many of these uninvolved voters see little else of the campaign except what they may possibly see on the evening news. Lynda Lee Kaid has concluded that "political advertising is more effective when the level of voter involvement is low." Late-deciding or uninvolved voters are the crucial 10 to 20 percent of the electorate. Normally they are reached only through television in the last stages of the campaign.

In 1972, Patterson and McClure researched the effectiveness of political ads and found that only 18 of 100 voters were late deciders. In 1972 many people had made up their minds. The ads of the campaign were found to have influenced about 3 percent of the total electorate, but there was a 23 percent spread between Nixon and McGovern in the final tally. A 3 percent impact along with a 23 percent spread is not much of an impact. In the 1976 campaign there was only a 2 percent disparity between Ford and Carter in the final tally. If the 1976 ads had affected 3 percent of the electorate, there being only a two percent spread, the effectiveness or ineffectiveness of ads might be crucial.

Ads are also used to reinforce supporters and partisans. When partisans saw pictures of Ronald Reagan on the cliffs of Normandy or of Jimmy Carter standing in front of a gigantic American flag at town meetings, these reinforced partisan feelings. For example, partisans watch half-hour programs but few others do. Only one in twenty people—primarily partisans—watch half-hour programs. Their partisan feelings are reinforced, and they may give more money to the campaign because of these commercials.

Ads can also be used to attack the opposition. As Reagan's 1980 pollster, Vincent Breglio, maintained, "It has become vital in campaigns today that you not only present all of the reasons why people ought to vote for you but you also have an obligation to present the reasons why they should not vote for the opponent. Hence, the negative campaign, or the attack strategy becomes an essential part of any campaign operation." A mix of positive and negative ads is increasingly used to convince voters why they should vote for one candidate and not vote for the opposition.

Ads can develop and explain issues. Research, by McClure and Patterson has demonstrated that there is more substance and more information on issues in presidential ads than in television news. A sixty-second ad has, on average, five times as much information about the candidate's position on issues than a sixty-second snippet on the evening news. Ads also have a cumulative effect. In presidential campaigns a multiplicity of ads are used and often repeated. Using thirty-second time frames voters see ten or twenty ads during the course of a campaign, with five or six of them repeated. The idea comes across not simply in thirty seconds, but in thirty seconds multiplied by the number of times voters see that thirty-second ad and are attentive to it.

Ads can soften or redefine an image. If a candidate has a reputation for not caring about unemployment or is weak on defense issues, ads can be created to emphasize these positions and the candidate's commitment to these areas. In 1968 candidate Nixon was redefined through television. In 1976, Jimmy Carter had been accused of not taking strong stands on issues. His advertising man created strong issue-oriented spots to redefine this hazy image through a series of ads in which Carter took strong stands.

Ads are used to target particular demographic groups. In this manner, they go hand in hand with polling. Polling tells where the potential voters are and ad demographics tell how to reach them. For example, women, blacks, males, single mothers, or union members might be targeted voters. Careful buying of airtime is used—for example, the buying of time before, during, or after key programs such as a hockey game to reach more male voters or the Phil Donahue show to reach more female voters. Polling and time buying help to maximize the potential to reach a particular category of voter.

Ads cost money but they can also be used to raise money. Appeals for money often are used at the end of half-hour or five-mintue ads. McGovern in 1972 and Anderson in 1980 paid for their television commercials mainly through such appeals. In 1984 Mondale used a special five-minute commercial beamed into house parties to raise money. People did send in money so that future ads went on the air.

Ads are adaptable. They can be made. They can be revised. They can be discarded as the necessities of the campaign change. Multiple generations of spot commercials are extremely common during the presidential campaign. Often several hours of ads, including six or seven distinct generations, are made. Ultimately, ads are used because the competition uses them. Few candidates, aside from Jesse Jackson in 1984, can afford the luxury of foregoing commercials. There is an adage in campaigns stating that half of all advertising money is wasted. Since nobody in a campaign knows which half, all advertising continues.

Primitive Ads

The first advertisements I examine are labeled "primitive ads." These were created in 1952 and 1956. The first Eisenhower campaign used three sixty-second spots and over twenty twenty-second spots with an "ask General Eisenhower" theme. A "Man from Abilene" spot was primitive because it had the announcer's voice screaming at the viewer—"Vote for peace! Vote for Eisenhower!"—in a manner similar to the loud announcers' techniques used in movie theaters during the "March of Time" or "Movietone News." In his spots Eisenhower was ill at ease in front of the camera, and his voice and eyes gave him away as an uneasy communicator. In the twenty-second spots Eisenhower was asked a question by a voter and then answered. Both the unspontaneous and contrived questions and the answers by Eisenhower reading from cue cards demonstrate the primitive nature of these ads.

The Stevenson campaign in 1952 concentrated on half-hour speeches rather than spot commercials. In 1956 "A Man from Libertyville" was created to counteract the "Man from Abilene" approach. Stevenson discussed the high cost of living while holding a bag of groceries. The lesson learned from this spot was, if you want to be elected president don't carry a grocery bag. Eisenhower had been wise enough not to carry grocery bags. Both the Eisenhower and Stevenson ads represent a primitive form of television advertising no longer used in campaigns today.

Talking Heads

The year of the "talking head" spot was 1960. Both John Kennedy and Richard Nixon emphasized ads that had them speaking directly to the viewer in a communicative way. The "talking head" format was as much in use in 1984 as it was in 1960. Within the general format, there are differences. For example, a Nixon spot was formal. Nixon was serious; he had a presidential image. The visual background was blank, while concentrated and complimentary lighting was used on Nixon's face—he was almost angelic. This brightness contrasted with the photogenic darkness that Nixon displayed in the debates. In the debate footage he came across with a five o'clock shadow. The ads—in which he had a dark suit and a light face—were made to compensate for the light suit and dark face of the debates.

A Kennedy "talking head" spot was much more informal. His gestures and his voice were more conversational and he had family pictures in the background. Pictures and plaques were used just as flags or family pictures are used today to give the viewer additional information. Some ad makers want the background to be blank; others want some kind of additional information to be communicated visually. Research by Patterson and McClure found that a candidate can develop a more favorable image through issue-oriented spots like these which seek to convince the voter that the candidate has positions on civil rights or medicare and that he can thus handle the difficult problems of a presidency. These spots convey a better image than "image" spots which try to create directly a favorable feeling about the candidate's personal qualities. Research indicates that the best way to make a positive impression on the voter is to use issues— in this case medicare or civil rights—as a vehicle or a tool to effect a positive image. The purpose of most "talking head" spots is to focus on an issue and use the candidate to convey an impression that he can handle the issue. Most importantly, he should convey the impression that he can handle the job of president.

Negative Ads

The year of the negative ad was 1964. Both Goldwater and Johnson emphasized ads that tried to tear down their opponent rather than build up themselves. Two 1964 commercials are representative of negative commercials made to provoke or bring out negative feelings already within voters. In the "Daisy Girl" spot a little girl is shown in a field of flowers. An atomic bomb explodes with a flash. President Johnson's voice elaborates, "These are the stakes: to make a world in which all God's children can live, or go into the dark." "Daisy Girl" was shown once and then taken off the air because of the outcry and protest it caused. The ad had an after-life through newspaper articles and radio and television news commentaries about it. The creator of this spot, Tony Schwartz, had a philosophy about making good political ads: commercials attempting to bring something to voters, that is, convey some information and bring something new to them, are inherently not as effective as those that try to appeal to an idea that is already within voters. The goal is not to get something across to people as much as it is to get something out of people. Nowhere in the "Daisy Girl" spot is Goldwater mentioned, but the ad evoked a feeling that Goldwater may indeed use nuclear weapons. The mistrust was not in the spot—the mistrust was in the viewer. Similarly, many voters already had feelings that we were not a very loved people, and that other countries were using us and burning our flag. A Goldwater ad used familiar riot footage with a "Yankee go home" motif to reinforce the feeling that was already within many Goldwater-prone voters.

The first year in which color was used in presidential commercials was 1968, and color enhances the visual nature of television ads. A Humphrey ad had visual simplicity but little visual variety and excitement. Humphrey simply started small and grew visually as his accomplishments grew and were enumerated by the announcer. Nixon's advertising people took advantage of the first year of color by creating a series of spots giving life and vitality to well chosen still photography to give the effect of visual variety. Photography is important because research has shown that people remember the visuals in spots more than the specifics of the narration. One study found that 80 to 85 percent of the information retained about television commercials is visual. Good presidential commercials have to be visual.

Memorable Ideas

Television is an excellent tool for conveying a memorable idea. In 1972, production spots were created to convey important ideas about candidates. Production spots also allow the use of graphics to make the information more memorable.

In 1972 as other candidates were pictured on the evening news trudging through the snow in the New Hampshire primary, President Nixon was shown in his trip to the Soviet Union. Five-minute travelogues were created to emphasize that Nixon was the first president to visit our former enemies, China and the Soviet Union. These spots stressed that with Nixon we would have a greater chance of having peace with our former enemies. As McGovern became more the issue in 1972, three anti-McGovern spots were shown more frequently. These negative spots were found by Thomas Patterson to reach low- and moderate-interest voters for several reasons. First, they were perceived as entertaining or funny. If people perceive an ad as entertaining or funny that helps them to look at it. Second, committed vote switchers—Democrats who were going to vote for Nixon—had their attitudes reinforced. The idea spots provided reasons for their decision and gave them comfort in knowing that there were many others like them. Similarly, McGovern voters wanted to reduce military spending. When they watched an anti-McGovern commercial about that, it was consistent with and reinforced their perception of the candidate.

In political advertising, selective perception is constantly working. If pro-Nixon voters viewed the defense spot they might say, "I knew that about McGovern. That is terrible. That is why Nixon needs to be reelected to save this country." Undecided voters might look at that defense spot and say, "I didn't know that about McGovern. Is he really going to do that to the air force? Is he really going to do that to the navy?" McGovern voters might look at that defense spot and say, "Right-on George! We need to reduce the military." Selective perception allowed different people to take away different ideas from that single commercial.

Nixon's "turn around" spot is also visually important. It is another idea spot, but with additional visual simplicity. McGovern is shown repeatedly rotating—physically and intellectually—from one position in one year to an opposite position in the following year. The announcer ends with, "What about next year?" Voters did not have to remember one specific instance of a McGovern change—not one issue, not one statement from the spot. The impression given was that McGovern had frequently switched his stance. The expectation of future switches was the important idea to get across. That was achieved through a rotating picture.

When the polls showed that literally millions of Democrats were defecting to Nixon, Tony Schwartz, the creator of the Lyndon Johnson "Daisy Girl" commercial, was hired by McGovern. Schwartz created five spots of which "Voting Booth" is representative. This ad was only shown twice—too infrequently to do much good—but the spot represents the best of what Schwartz classified as an "idea" spot. The real problem for McGovern was millions of defecting Democrats. Schwartz tried to reach them in a catchy, stream of consciousness way. He showed an indecisive man in a voting both thinking out loud, pondering the choices. The speed of the ad made it captivating, yet at times statements could be missed because they were not heard the first time around. Crucial statements were: "This hand voted for Kennedy;" "Me vote for Nixon? My father would roll over in his grave;" "My gut feeling, my gut feeling, McGovern." These statements represent the kind of emotional idea that the ad tried to evoke.

Cinema Verité

Filming a candidate in real life settings interacting with people is a technique called "cinema verité." In 1972, McGovern's principal ad creator, Charles Guggenheim, did not believe in the ethics or effectiveness of negative advertising. Guggenheim was an award-winning documentary filmmaker who preferred to film McGovern in real settings interacting with real voters. Guggenheim used the cinema verité technique to show

McGovern as a concerned and compassionate candidate. This format allows the ad maker to take footage of a candidate speaking with voters during the course of a day or several days. The footage is then edited down to thirty- and sixty-second snippets in which the candidate concentrates on one issue—in McGovern's case, medicare. The technique can also be used to show the candidate shaking hands, listening, and simply being open and communicative with potential voters in group settings.

Changing Spots

Clearly, 1976 was the year for changing ad campaigns. President Ford used three ad makers and three different advertising campaign techniques. Candidate Carter evolved in his ads from a farmer in a plaid shirt to someone who looked presidential. Therefore 1976 is a good year to examine the changes in presidential campaign advertising.

At first, Ford was portrayed as an effective president who had restored faith in the presidency. Following Watergate and Nixon's resignation, these ads really had Ford running against Nixon and reinforced Ford as an effective president. When Ronald Reagan started doing better in the primaries, pressure for changes in Ford's advertising occurred. In California, Ford agreed to air for the first time in presidential politics "slice-of-life" advertisements. These used paid actors in little theater situations—the tried and true techniques of selling detergents or Preparation H. In one, two women discuss how food prices are no longer going up the way they used to because, "President Ford has cut inflation in half." He is "leading us back to prosperity." When I show the "Two Ladies" ad to an audience, laughter indicates that presidential candidates cannot be sold like soap or Preparation H. The "slice-of-life" technique is too blatantly obvious and has too many product advertising associations.

In Ford's "Feeling Good" ad, featuring happy Americans going about their business, music was used to create an upbeat mood about the country and its people. Music is often an integral part of the mood setting devices of political ads. If a viewer's toe was tapping to the tempo of this ad, the music accomplished what the ad maker wanted.

In 1976, Carter started campaigning by running as a personable outsider. He was the first candidate to run for president wearing a plaid, open collared shirt in his ads. Carter finished the campaign in a suit making a series of "talking head" spots which made him appear to be presidential. In 1976 campaign advertising, the personable candidate became more presidential and the president became more personable. Ford started out using his office as his trump card and finished by using ads that highlighted his personal qualities. Carter started out by using ads that focused on his casual personableness and finished by using ads that made him appear more presidential.

Most candidates in a long campaign use a multiplicity of ads and their ad makers create multiple generations of many different types of ads—often too many different types of ads. Ford's media people created almost two hours of varied television advertising. By making and playing so many different spots, they negated the impact of their more effective spots.

No candidate emphasized documentary ads more than Ronald Reagan in 1980. During the 1980 general election campaign, Reagan's ad makers wanted to play down the perception of Reagan as an actor and play up the perception of Reagan as an effective governor. A one minute ad, "The Reagan Record," and a longer four-minute-and-twenty-second version, were the most heavily played ads of the entire campaign. The ad talked about the accomplishments of Reagan as governor and how as a good governor he would make an effective and good president. Partisans did not like the ad because it emphasized things they already knew, but this ad was played over and over again. It was effective in swinging votes of late-deciding voters because its format gave out crucial information.

Man-in-the-street ads have real people saying nice things about one campaign and/or nasty things about the opponent. In 1976, Jerry Rafshoon, Carter's ad creator was on the receiving end of Ford's man-in-the-street ads which characterized Carter as "wishy-washy." Man-in-the-street ads are used to reinforce perceptions of candidates that are revealed in polling. In 1980 Rafshoon wanted to reinforce the perception of Reagan as a scary guy who shot before he thought. Man-in-the-street ads are excellent reinforcing tools but they are seldom persuasive tools. Too often the impression of undecided voters upon seeing these ads is "you can get somebody to say anything about anybody." Because these ads do use real people saying real things, many ad makers use them. They think they have a quality of believability.

Testimonial ads have prominent politicians, movie stars, or television personalities saying things on behalf of candidates. A Ted Kennedy testimonial ad in 1980 used a popular star, Carroll O'Connor, to attack Carter's economic policy and to hopefully convey trust for Kennedy. Testimonials by other personalities or politicians and trust were two things Kennedy did not have in abundance during his campaign. Thus, "Archie Bunker" endorsed Kennedy and said "I trust and believe in him folks."

Independent ads are those financed by individuals or organizations that are separate from the presidential candidates. The real story of the 1980 campaign might be not in the candidates' ads but in those that were independently financed. The ads from the Republican Congressional Committee (RCC) and the National Conservative Political Action Committee (NCPAC) were representative of ads aired by a host of independent organizations. The RCC spent $7 million on television advertising while all of the political action committees spent about an additional $13 million on television advertising. Most of these ads were pro-Reagan and anti-Carter. When added to the Reagan ads, Carter's ad maker concluded that he was actually outspent by 2:1 or 3:1.

Most independent ads are hard-hitting, negative ads. The Republican ads were humorous but the NCPAC ads were deliberately provocative. Terry Dolan, the national director of NCPAC, wanted ads that created reaction, and he was unconcerned about negative reaction. As he said in an interview, "I don't care what Ronald Reagan, Jimmy Carter, or CBS says about our ads. The people we serve are 300,000 throughout the U.S. who could care less about respectability." Independent ads were a potent factor in 1980 and they will continue to be a factor in future presidential campaigns.

In the early years of presidential spots, 1952 through 1968, there was an emphasis on short spots of twenty or sixty seconds. In 1972 and 1976, the four-minute-and-twenty-second spot predominated. In 1980 and 1984, the thirty-second spot did. We have seen an evolution of length preferences dependent on the campaign.

A mix of lengths and types of spots are used in presidential campaigns. An analysis of the 1980 Reagan spots will illustrate this. Between Labor Day and Election Day in 1980, Reagan's "Campaign '80" ran 255 network television commercials. Seventy-four or 29 percent were five-mintue spots, 41 or 16 percent were one-minute spots and 140 or 55 percent were thirty-second spots. Of the 74 five-minute spots, 60 were versions of the documentary "The Reagan Record." Of the 41 one-minute spots, 35 were shortened versions of "The Reagan Record." Of the thirty-second spots 10 percent were documentary "Reagan Record" spots, 45 percent were "talking head" spots, and 45 percent were "anti-Carter" spots. Of the total commercial allocation by "Campaign '80," 41 percent were documentary spots, 33 percent were "talking head" spots, and 26 percent were "anti-Carter" spots.

The thirty-second spot has become the dominant time frame for political ads. Research on product commercials has demonstrated that thirty-second spots are just as effective as sixty-second spots in getting the message across. Research has found that five-minute spots are not significantly more successful than sixty-second spots in terms of the quantity of items that can be recalled after seeing a political spot.

Political advertisers have increasingly emphasized the use of the thirty-second spot in relation to the sixty- or four-minute-and-twenty-second spot. For example, in 1972 Patterson and McClure found that only 2 percent of all presidential ads were thirty-second spots while 41 percent of all commercials in 1972 were five minutes in length. In 1980, 55 percent of all Reagan spots were thirty-second spots. From 2 to 55 percent in eight years is a shift reflecting that stations are set up to sell time and viewers are prepared to view commercials in thirty-second units.

Five-minute spots work best as mood pieces, developing feelings through music and emotional appeal, or as spots that give biographical or personal information about the candidate. In 1976, Jerry Rafshoon, creator of the Carter spots, became a champion of longer spots. He later proclaimed, "I'd be very happy if the networks and stations said, 'From now on we'll sell candidates nothing but five minutes.'" In 1976, when Carter was an unknown, five-minute spots were used in abundance by Rafshoon. In 1980 Rafshoon used fewer of them. This happened because as a candidate moves from being unknown to being known there is less need for five-minute spots; however, they are still good as money raisers. In 1984 Walter Mondale raised $1.4 million for his campaign by beaming in a five-minute network commercial to fund raising house parties held around the United States.

In 1984 candidates Mondale, Hart, and Glenn emphasized television commercials in their campaigns. Although Hart's ads were more graphically innovative—using infinity grids, smaller inserted picture frames, and peel-back frames—all candidates used variations of the talking head, cinema verité, documentary, and production idea spots. These types, along with testimonial, man-in-the-street, and negative spots are generic ads that will be seen over and over again in future campaigns. One ad maker may not like or think his candidate could benefit from testimonial or man-in-the-street spots, but four years later another ad maker returns to these basic forms.

More sophisticated cinematography is in use today that was used in the fifties, sixties, or seventies. Carter's ads in 1980 set a standard for beautifully photographed and produced commercials that Reagan surpassed in 1984. In Reagan's initial ads of 1984 the president is neither seen nor heard. Instead we see beautiful pictures of weddings, hugs, churches, boats, flags, and homes. These ads reinforce the traditional values of love, family, church, and community, and renew faith in America. Good feelings have been emphasized in ads since the "I'm Feeling Good About America" series for Gerald Ford in 1976. Pictures of America and its people are really attempts at getting the electorate to vote for an idyllic view of themselves. Reagan is not unique in his attempts at ads that use this strategy; however, the fine quality of his ads indicate that he has raised the technique to a new art form.

It is difficult to determine the effectiveness of political commercials. Douglass Bailey, who handled the 1976 Ford media stated, "It is extraordinarily difficult to look at a political commercial and judge it. Because any reputable agency . . . can produce pretty commercials . . . but to judge their political effectiveness is very hard to do." Aside from trying to separate a commercial's creative merit from its political impact, there is another reason it is difficult to uncover the effectiveness of political commercials. There is so much happening simultaneously in a campaign that it is difficult to isolate the impact of only the political advertising.

Political ads are but one of the many influences on the outcome of a presidential campaign. Certainly there are other communicative events—debates, speeches, evening news broadcasts—that affect a campaign; yet campaigns have and will continue to spend a massive amount of their available money on political advertising.

About the Contributors

Vincent Breglio is president of Research, Strategy and Management. He was a senior vice president of Decision Making Information, the firm that did the polling and strategy for the Ronald Reagan Campaign of 1980.

David Broder is a national political correspondent and columnist for the *Washington Post*. He has written several books on politics and is among the most respected journalists covering politics today.

L. Patrick Devlin is a professor of speech communication at The University of Rhode Island. He is an archivist and analyst of presidential campaign commercials, the author of *Contemporary Political Speaking* and many articles on political communication.

Doris Graber is professor of political science at the University of Illinois, Chicago Circle. She has written several books on political communication among which are *Mass Media and American Politics* and *Political Language.*

Bruce Gronbeck is professor of speech communication at the University of Iowa. He has written numerous articles on political communication.

Randy Huwa is vice president of membership and media communications for Common Cause. As a former director of the Campaign Finance Monitoring Project for Common Cause he became an expert on fund raising, campaign spending and campaign reform.

John Mashek is a national political reporter *U.S. News and World Report*. He has covered numerous campaigns for his news magazine.

Roger Mudd is the senior political correspondent based in Washington for *NBC News*. He has been an anchorman for CBS and NBC. He won a Peabody Award for excellence for his probing interview with Edward Kennedy during the 1980 campaign.

Dan Nimmo is professor of communication at the University of Oklahoma. He is the author of numerous books on political communication among which are *Political Communication Handbook, The Political Persuaders,* and *Mediated Political Realities.*

David Nyhan is a political reporter for the *Boston Globe*. He has covered presidential campaigns since 1968 and has been a White House reporter.

Richard O'Reilly, a New York advertising consultant, was president of Campaign '80, the advertising agency for the Reagan campaign. The agency was responsible for the creation, production and placement of all broadcast and print advertising.

Thomas Patterson is a professor of political science at Syracuse University and is the author of *The Mass Media Election* and *The Unseeing Eye*—both books about political campaign communication.

Kirby Perkins is a political correspondent for WCVB-TV in Boston, Massachusetts. He has covered numerous primary campaigns in New Hampshire and Massachusetts.

Larry Sabato is a professor of political science at the University of Virginia. He is the author of several books on politics among which are *The Rise of Political Consultants* and *PAC Power: Inside the World of Political Action Committees.*

Tony Schwartz is a media producer of radio and television ads for hundreds of campaigns. He created the historic "Daisy Girl/Atom Bomb" ad for Johnson in 1964. His most recent presidential campaign was the 1976 Carter campaign.

Robert Smith is president of Targeted Communications. His firm coordinated the mass mail fund raising appeals for Walter Mondale during the 1984 campaign. Smith also coordinated the mass mail appeals of John Anderson and Edward Kennedy in their 1980 campaigns.

Jerry terHorst is director of public affairs for Ford Motor Company in Washington, D.C. He was a national correspondent and a syndicated columnist for the *Detroit News*. He was press secretary to President Gerald Ford and resigned that position to protest Ford's pardon of Nixon.

Laureen White was an assignment editor for *WLNE-TV* in Providence, Rhode Island. She is currently press secretary for a congressional candidate.